CULTIVATING JUSTICE IN THE GARDEN STATE

Dedicated to the love of my life
Salena Carroll Lesniak 1976–2019

Wedding picture with Salena Lesniak, Benito's restaurant, Union, New Jersey. Photograph by Joshua Cultillo.

CULTIVATING JUSTICE IN THE GARDEN STATE

My Life in the Colorful World of New Jersey Politics

FORMER STATE SENATOR
RAYMOND LESNIAK

With a Foreword by Bill Clinton

RUTGERS UNIVERSITY PRESS
New Brunswick, Camden, and Newark, New Jersey, and London

Library of Congress Cataloging-in-Publication Data

Names: Lesniak, Raymond, author.
Title: Cultivating justice in the Garden State : my life in the colorful world
    of New Jersey politics / Raymond Lesniak.
Other titles: My life in the colorful world of New Jersey politics
Description: New Brunswick : Rutgers University Press, [2022]
Identifiers: LCCN 2021035477 | ISBN 9781978824973 (cloth) |
    ISBN 9781978824980 (epub) | ISBN 9781978824997 (mobi) | ISBN 9781978825000 (pdf)
Subjects: LCSH: Lesniak, Raymond. | Legislators—New Jersey—Biography. |
    Politicians—New Jersey—Biography. | Lawyers—New Jersey—Elizabeth—
    Biography. | New Jersey—Politics and government—1951– | Elizabeth (N.J.)—
    Biography.
Classification: LCC F140.22.L47 A3 2022 | DDC 974.9/043092 [B]—
    dc23/eng/20211110
LC record available at https://lccn.loc.gov/2021035477

A British Cataloging-in-Publication record for this book is available from the
British Library.

References to internet websites (URLs) were accurate at the time of writing.
Neither the author nor Rutgers University Press is responsible for URLs that may
have expired or changed since the manuscript was prepared.

∞ The paper used in this publication meets the requirements of the American
National Standard for Information Sciences—Permanence of Paper for Printed
Library Materials, ANSI Z39.48-1992.

www.rutgersuniversitypress.org

Manufactured in the United States of America

CONTENTS

FOREWORD

I first came to know Ray Lesniak when I was running for president in 1992. We had never spoken before when Ray came out in support for me early in the campaign and started working hard on my behalf. At that point my mother was perhaps the only other person in America who thought I could win—so it was a welcome surprise to have the strong backing of New Jersey's state Democratic chairman, who had a long track record of getting things done in the legislature and winning elections against long odds.

Throughout the primaries, Ray stood by me when I was up and when I was down. And on June 2, New Jersey was one of the states that helped me clinch the nomination. But Ray wasn't done. As hard as it might be to imagine today, New Jersey hadn't voted for a Democrat in a presidential election since 1964, and we were determined to change that. Ray played a big role in our campaign, and we carried the state by two points. Four years later New Jersey had the biggest increase in our margin of victory of any state, also thanks in part to Ray's continued work.

The campaigning that Ray and I did together in 1992 was the start of not only a productive political partnership but a genuine friendship. I liked Ray immediately. Though we may have seemed from the outside like the odd couple—he a Polish American Catholic from Elizabeth and me a Southern Baptist from Arkansas—we had, and still do have, a lot in common. Most important, we share a belief that politics and policy are fundamentally about creating opportunities for other people to make the most of their own lives and rise as far as their intelligence, talent, and determination will take them.

Ray is good at both politics and policy because he likes and is interested in people, cares about their lives and their stories, and believes we shouldn't give up on anyone. He has never been shy about the purpose of political power: use it or lose it. Building up seniority and credibility is not a worthy end in itself, but something you put to use on behalf of your constituents—or your conscience, when it comes to that.

There's no better proof of the strength of that belief than the record he compiled in his four decades in office. Throughout his career, Ray was a friend to working people, a staunch defender of the environment, and a passionate advocate for the most vulnerable among us. As an unapologetic progressive, he had the ability to connect with allies and adversaries alike, with a keen sense of when to compromise and what lines he couldn't cross. He passed groundbreaking legislation signed by both Democratic and Republican governors. And he knew that even with his strongest opponents across the aisle, if he kept showing up and scratching at the surface, he just might find underneath a real person with whom he could forge common ground and get things done for the good of the state.

I've shared a lot of good times with Ray over the past thirty years, from the White House to his house in Elizabeth, from Air Force One to the golf course. You'll read about some of them in the pages that follow. More important, you'll get a lifetime's worth of hard-won wisdom and insight. Like Ray Lesniak himself, this book is candid and colorful, humorous and human. I hope you'll enjoy reading it as much as I did.

Bill Clinton

PROLOGUE

There is no escaping history in the bustling small city of Caen, France. It was here that William the Conqueror constructed an imposing fortress in 1060, six years before he led the last successful invasion of England. And it was here where the Allies arrived in 1944 to liberate the city from the death grip of the Nazis, more than a month after landing on the beaches of Normandy on D-Day. And it was here where I saw the flag of Poland, land of my ancestors, flying alongside the flags of the United Kingdom, Canada, and the United States—the nations that stormed the beaches of Normandy all those years ago.

Much of the city was destroyed during World War II, although William's fortress remains, standing watch on a gentle hill near the city center. Even though it has been rebuilt since 1945, there's no mistaking Caen for my native city of Elizabeth, New Jersey. Its narrow streets, ancient abbeys, and colorful cafes offer an Old World feel, even when a modern streetcar rumbles past or traffic backs up near the magnificent Hotel de Ville.

With the painful lessons of history in mind, Caen plays host to an annual human rights event that brings together international activists, dignitaries, and advocates to call attention to injustice wherever it exists. The event consists of a competition among lawyers from around the world, each of whom has to submit a five-hundred-word essay on a human rights violation. The contestants are narrowed down to semifinalists who have to submit a ten-minute speech. I entered the competition in 2009 and was selected to submit a speech. When I finished writing it, I declared to my friends that I would win. Ten finalists are chosen to speak before an international panel of judges who weigh the final arguments and then select the one they find most deserving of the Memorial de Caen Human Rights prize, named for the museum that hosts the event. And that's where I found myself in February 2009, one of only two Americans who made it to the final round.

My topic would have sounded familiar to colleagues in New Jersey's state legislature: the abolition of the death penalty around the world. It's a cause I had been pushing for years, and overcame opposition from those who believe that the government has both a right and a duty to put people to death if a jury found them guilty of murder. As I prepared for my presentation, to be delivered in a museum dedicated to the memory of the brave soldiers who landed on D-Day, I couldn't help but reflect on the unlikely journey that brought me from the streets of postwar Elizabeth to the lanes of early twenty-first-century Caen, sharing a stage with some of the world's best and brightest minds. Unlikely it certainly was, for there was nothing about my childhood and upbringing in Elizabeth that even hinted that one day I would be invited to speak anywhere, never mind in a museum thirty miles from Omaha Beach.

I was born in the Elizabethport section of Elizabeth, a block away from the waterfront and across from the Bethlehem Steel Plant. Later, we moved to the city's Bayway section, near where Bruce Springsteen would meet "neath that giant Exxon sign" and the petrochemical plants that employed people like my father, the hardest-working and smartest person I ever met. My mother was a housewife raising my sister, Mary Margaret—Marge to everyone—and me. I was not a particularly motivated student, in part because I saw myself wearing a Major League Baseball uniform someday, maybe for my favorite team, the New York Giants. I dropped out of college twice and served a stint in the Army before finally earning a degree. People who knew me back then, including my first love, Patty Rogers, later told me that they never imagined I'd turn out to be a successful politician and lawyer. I didn't see it coming back then, either. But there I was, in the city of Caen in 2009, about to speak to a prestigious panel of judges and in the company of some of the world's most passionate advocates for human rights. I had shed my lack of ambition and was determined to win.

I had one very important decision to make before I spoke. Should I give my speech in French or English? I'm fluent in French, and my competitors, other than one American, were from France, Belgium, and Senegal, with one Israeli woman who grew up in Paris. They spoke beautiful French. I had begun to learn French during my first trip to Paris. I was forty-five years old and sitting in a cafe in Montmartre at the foot of the grand cathedral Sacré-Cœur and students were conversing in English, Spanish, Italian, and German in addition to French, and I didn't even speak Polish, the language of my grandparents. I felt I was missing something. I began to listen to French-language tapes (tapes existed at that time) and would spend two weeks every summer in a little village, Giens, in the South of France where there was very little, if any, English spoken. I had a room on the third floor of a small hotel overlooking the Mediterranean. In the evenings I would go out on my tiny balcony with a Cuban cigar and a bottle of Bordeaux. In the mornings I would wake up to the smell of freshly brewed coffee and baked croissants. During the day I would hang out with the villagers, speaking only French. It was two weeks of heaven on earth. So I knew I could make my argument in French. But I decided against it.

Why? Well, most of the judges themselves were native French speakers, and despite my proficiency in the language, I still spoke with a definite New Jersey accent. I imagined it would grate on the judges' ears—and bear in mind that while everybody in the room was devoted to making the world a better and more just place, it also was, after all, a competition. And I've always been a competitor, back to my days on the sandlots and basketball courts of Elizabeth. I wanted to win. And I figured that speaking in English, rather than in my New Jersey–accented French, would give me a better shot at winning. My speech, titled "The Road to Justice and Peace," was then simultaneously translated into French. "I come here today not to plead a case for a victim whose fundamental human rights have been violated," I began. "But, rather, to plead the case that the death penalty violates the fundamental rights of mankind. In my country, the United States of America, over three thousand human beings are awaiting execution, some for a crime they did not commit. I plead the case that the death penalty in the United States, Iraq, Pakistan, Japan, wherever, exposes the innocent to execution, causes more suffering to the family members of murder victims, serves no penal purpose and commits society to the belief that revenge is preferable to redemption."

I spoke with the passion of a convert to the cause, because that's exactly what I was. In 1982, when I was in the Assembly, I voted in favor of a bill that reinstated the death penalty. In 1972, the Supreme Court had declared that "the imposition and carrying out of the death penalty . . . constitutes cruel and unusual punishment in violation of the Eighth Amendment." However, only four years later, the Court reversed its ruling and held that the death penalty was constitutional after all. Shortly thereafter, thirty-four states, including New Jersey, enacted new death penalty statutes. Crime was surging in several of the state's largest cities, and public opinion in the region and throughout the country clearly favored capital punishment. Just a few years before I cast my vote, New York City had elected Ed Koch as mayor in part because he favored capital punishment—even though the mayor had no say in whether or not New York State reinstated its death penalty.

In the years after that vote, I reflected on what it means for the state to take a life, and how the thirst for revenge can and does make us less civil, less humane, less than what we aspire to be. By the time of the new millennium, I had a spiritual conversion brought on by the loss of a girlfriend who broke my heart, but which led me to change my approach to life and my political attitudes. I became more thoughtful about life and the immorality of the death penalty and not the politics behind it. I became New Jersey's most vocal opponent of capital punishment.

"The death penalty," I said in Caen, "is a random act of brutality. Its application throughout the United States is random, depending on where the murder occurred, the race and economic status of who committed the murder, the race and economic status of the person murdered, and, of course, the quality of the legal defense."

I spoke about the case of Byron Halsey, a resident of Plainfield, New Jersey, who was convicted of a most heinous crime, the murders of a seven- and eight-year-old boy and girl after sexually abusing them. One juror held out against imposing the death penalty, and Halsey was sentenced to life imprisonment. Nineteen years later, as a result of the work of Barry Scheck and the Innocence Project, which, through the use of DNA evidence, proved Brian could not have been the murderer, Halsey was released from prison. The evidence led to the conviction of the real murderer. But for one juror, the death penalty would have killed an innocent person and the murderer never would have been brought to justice.

I wrapped up my ten-minute argument—and was glad I decided to speak in English, knowing I had made the correct choice after hearing the other contestants' beautiful French—and took a seat with my friend, Dawood Farahi, president of Kean University in Union Township. "You nailed it," Dawood said. "I know," I replied. And I had. Not long thereafter, the judges announced they had selected my speech as the winning entry. I was presented with a check from the Caen city council for 7,600 euros, just under 10,000 dollars, which I donated to a nonprofit group I had created to lobby against the death penalty nationwide. Some of my opposing lawyers protested, saying I broke the rules because I didn't advocate for an individual deprived of human rights but for a human rights cause. The mayor of Caen, Philippe Duron, who was chairman of the contest, in a typically French manner said to me, "Don't worry about those idiots. I'll take care of them."

I've been lucky enough to be on the winning side of many political battles and policy debates. But one of my proudest moments was that day in Caen. And if you had told me thirty years earlier that I'd be on that stage in France, I'd have said you were crazy. I didn't see it coming. And neither did anyone else, not my first girlfriend Patty, not my dad and mom or my sister, not any of my friends. But I did, when I eventually turned my life around.

CULTIVATING JUSTICE IN
THE GARDEN STATE

1 · MY HOMETOWN

I was born in Elizabeth. I was raised in Elizabeth. I still live in Elizabeth. I'll probably die in Elizabeth. The city of my later years is, in some ways, very different from the city of my childhood. Once-familiar landmarks, like the Regents Theater on Broad Street, are gone. Many of the industries that defined this proud working-class city have disappeared. But in other ways, things haven't changed all that much. It's still a city that attracts immigrants looking to make a better life, although now those newcomers tend to come from Central and South America rather than eastern and southern Europe. And it's still a city of small business owners who bring life and culture to Elizabeth's vibrant and distinct neighborhoods. The city was not immune to the hard times that fell on America's urban areas beginning in the 1960s, but these people—my neighbors—were persistent and resilient. I'm proud to have been their voice in Trenton for four decades.

My parents, John and Stephanie, were born in Elizabeth, the children of immigrants from Poland who left their native land in the early twentieth century, before Europe was enmeshed in two world wars. They grew up in heavily Polish neighborhoods, my father in Bayway, which was three-quarters Polish in the 1920s, and my mother in Elizabethport, where she attended a Polish school, St. Adalbert's. They were blue-collar communities that revolved around Catholic churches, company recreation halls, and the home. Both neighborhoods were growing throughout my parents' childhood and young adulthood as the city neared maturity. New housing was going up, Polish immigrants and their children were building their churches and schools, like St. Hedwig's in Bayway, where my dad and I graduated grammar school, and modern corporations began to dominate the waterfront along the Arthur Kill. Standard Oil's refineries were an enormous local presence, especially in our neighborhoods. DuPont bought the old Grasselli Chemical Co. in the late 1920s, further establishing the city and that portion of New Jersey as a center of the petrochemical industry. These companies, along with Singer Sewing Co., with its massive plant in Elizabethport, employed thousands of Elizabetheans and others from nearby areas like Linden. People didn't think of the damage some of these industries were doing to the environment—even when dark slicks developed on the Elizabeth River, which flowed from Essex County into the city near its border with Union Township, or when the smell while driving past Elizabeth on the New Jersey Turnpike was obnoxious. It wasn't until a toxic dump site on Front Street, near where I was born, exploded in the late 1970s that I became fully aware of the extent of the damage to our environment and health caused by nonexistent environmental regulations. After that explosion, I became a persistent champion of environmental protection, sponsored the most significant environmental protection laws in the country, and personally sued the petrochemical industry in federal court to force its compliance with my legislation.

I was born on May 7, 1946—one day less than a year after VE Day—just as times were about to change. Elizabeth and the nation were on the verge of the postwar boom that would make America more prosperous than anyone living in Depression-era Bayway or Elizabethport could have ever imagined. My parents met in the late 1930s and were married on April 14, 1940. We were living on Franklin Street in Elizabethport when I arrived. Our home was a block away from the docks that would soon be humming with postwar commerce. And across from our home was a shipyard owned by the Bethlehem Steel Company, a colossus of industrial-era America that now means nothing to the children of the twenty-first century.

We soon moved to the Bayway neighborhood, which is where I spent most of my childhood. And it was in that home that I learned something about the way immigrant families in America, then and now, manage to hold onto their culture and identities even as they embrace their new country and modern life. My maternal grandmother lived with us in Bayway—my grandfathers had passed away before I was born—and my dad's mother lived across the street from us. Both my grandmothers spoke only Polish. My parents insisted that we speak only English, even though that meant we really couldn't communicate with my grandmothers. My parents were proud of their Polish heritage, but they were raising my sister, Marge, and me to be good, English-speaking Americans. I was named after my dad's father, Roman, but my parents Americanized it to be Raymond. That notwithstanding, we were very much a Polish American household. We attended Polish cultural events in the neighborhood, we danced polkas, and all of our christenings and weddings were Polish affairs. But even then you could see the cultural exchanges. On the tables at family weddings were bottles of Scotch whiskey and American rye, which you poured yourself, and, of course, Polish vodka.

Although I didn't realize it at the time, I was learning valuable lessons about what really makes America great. It's about the way we adapt to each other, the way we borrow from each other, and the way we tolerate each other. I saw America not as a melting pot but as a casserole wherein the individual flavors are maintained while enhancing the overall dish. There are plenty of non-English-speakers on the streets of Elizabeth at this very moment, and to be just as sure, there are people who resent hearing Spanish or Portuguese or Creole while doing business on Broad Street or waiting to be called for jury duty in the city's courthouse. Well, my grandmothers never spoke a word of English, even though they lived in America for more than sixty years. And my mother raised a couple of very American kids who turned out pretty well. I wish people who get upset over hearing a Spanish speaker in a bank or on a train or in a restaurant would take a moment and think about their own family's journey. We all have one.

My dad taught me a lesson in tolerance and acceptance when I was twelve years old. A family from Columbia bought the local convenience store. Our neighbors organized a boycott, but my dad continued to go to the store. One day when walking out of the store with my dad, we were confronted by a handful of angry neighbors. "Why are you going to that Hispanic store?" someone asked impolitely. "We're boycotting it. If we don't stop it now they're going to take over our neighborhood." My dad responded, "I needed cigarettes and that's where they sell cigarettes. That's why I went there." My dad was quiet, but had a powerful presence. The neighbors shook their heads and went away. The boycott ended, the store thrived for many years, and I learned a lifelong lesson of acceptance of others who don't talk or look like me or worship in the same church.

I dreamed of playing baseball in the old Polo Grounds, home of baseball's New York Giants, someday. My mother and some of the nuns at St. Hedwig's elementary school had another dream for me—they thought I'd be a priest. Needless to say, neither dream came anywhere close to fruition. I graduated first in my class from St. Hedwig's, and my parents wanted me to go to Don Bosco High School, a prestigious Catholic school in Bergen County where I would not have been happy, not even for a minute. To the surprise of everyone (except myself), I failed the school's entrance exam. I tanked it so I could go to the local public schools, Roosevelt Junior High School and Thomas Jefferson High School, with my friends.

My mother was the dominant presence in our home and in my life. In addition to raising Marge and me, she helped clean the home of one of our neighbors whom she befriended, Tom and Bridget Vaughn. Tom, a labor union leader, treated me as an adopted son, filling in the gap left by my dad, who worked hard all day, came home, argued with my mom, drank beer, and went to sleep. Tom would take me to the Polo Grounds in Upper Manhattan to see the Giants play. My hero was the great Willie Mays, who made the basket catch famous and somehow lost his cap every time he broke into a sprint. When Tom and Bridget were in their late nineties and living in Runnells Hospital in Berkeley Heights, we were frequent visitors and spent a lot of time talking about the old days. Bridget, a devout Roman Catholic, would often ask, "When is the good Lord going to take us away?" Tom, a great Irish wit, would respond, "Speak for yourself, honey."

My mom was involved in local politics, eventually becoming a Democratic Party committeewoman in Elizabeth. I don't think she ever envisioned that one day her son would serve in the legislature for forty years, sponsor and pass legislation of national significance, and run for governor. But there's no doubt she had a hand in steering me in that direction.

My father was the smartest person I ever knew and a hard worker. Bruce Springsteen's "Jack of All Trades" could have been written about him:

I'll hammer the nails and I'll set the stone . . .
I'll pull that engine apart and patch her up
'Til she's running right.

My dad dropped out of school after graduating from St. Hedwig's grammar school to work on the docks to help support his family, but with his brains and his work ethic, he rose to become manager of a building owned by the chemical manufacturer General Aniline and Film, better known as GAF. He resented having to report to company managers with advanced college degrees who didn't have the know-how about chemical production that he had, based on hands-on, real-life experience. But he put his head down and did his job. It was tough work. The company, which was German owned until the government seized control of it during World War II, specialized in dyes and chemicals. I worked there one summer while attending Rutgers University, and one summer was all I needed to see the dangers associated with these materials. Workers at the dye plant said that even though they show-ered at the plant after their shift was over, their bedsheets were stained with dye the following morning. That thought, along with years later seeing toxic drums exploding into the skyline along the Arthur Kill, shaped me into a champion of environmental protection.

My father was a good provider and, as I said, smarter than anyone I've ever known. Sadly, he also was an alcoholic. He never missed a day of work because of his drinking, but it certainly had an impact on our lives. My father kept me at a distance, never allowing me to get close to him. One day he was tearing apart the engine of his car—just like the jack of all trades in my favor-ite Springsteen song—and I offered to help. He shooed me away, coldly. I can picture the scene even today, all these years later. He was in a place of his own, and I wasn't allowed in. I've finally understood how that feeling of rejection has led to my own fear of intimacy. And I suppose that's why I took on the challenges I've faced in life as a one-man gang, determined to do whatever needed to get done by myself. In later years, I participated in Al-Anon twelve-step programs for adult children of alcoholics suffering from the effects of substance-abuse problems in their families. I heard their stories and related them for the first time to my life. That led to my advocacy for recovery pro-grams for those suffering from substance use disorders. So because of my father's distance and his drinking, it was not the warmest of homes, certainly not like the perfect postwar suburban settings that were popular on 1950s television shows. One night we found my dad peeing off the roof of our first-floor porch. We thought it was funny at the time. It wasn't funny.

My dad's alcoholism notwithstanding, my sister and I knew, even as children, that we were part of something larger than ourselves. We were part of a proud neighborhood of hardworking people, we were part of a vibrant Polish community that kept old traditions alive even as we embraced our Americanism, and, most of all, we were a family. We looked out for each other, especially when times were difficult. We gathered coal that fell off trains from the nearby railroad tracks to help keep the house warm. I remem-ber getting up first on cold, dark mornings to stoke the furnace so that the house was warm when my parents and sister awoke. These were the days before people in our neighborhood had refrigerators, so I remember deliver-ies from the iceman and the milkman, who made his rounds in the predawn darkness, and the beer delivery man, of course. A knife sharpener made the rounds to keep our kitchen utensils in good working order. It was a different world in so many ways. We were active parishioners at St. Hedwig's, and I served as an altar boy while in grammar school. We were all raised in deeply religious Catholic families, but that didn't mean we were always impeccably reverent. The altar boys had a nickname for one of the priests, Father Joe, whom we called "Slow Joe" because his Mass was a lot longer than the other priests. Needless to say, we winced when we checked the assignment sheets and saw that we were paired with Father Joe.

I had ideas of playing football at Jefferson High School because I was a pretty good athlete and a ferocious competitor. But my mother would have none of it—decades before doctors began to warn about the dangers of brain injuries from playing football and other contact sports, my mother was worried about my getting injured on the gridiron, which ultimately did happen at Rutgers University. Not only did my mother forbid football, she also insisted that I learn to play the accordion, a staple instrument at any Polish gathering. I wasn't particularly musical, but as usual, mother knew best. Not only did I learn to play the accordion but I even got paid for playing (which is more than I can say about baseball) and eventually hooked up with a polka band, Jolly Rich and the Polka Stars. I was a part of several of the band's albums, including Billboard chart-maker *Polkas With a Kick* and *In Heaven There Is No Beer?*, which featured my original song, "Good Cheer Polka." I eventually hung up the accordion when politics and elected office got in the way of playing. But I came out of retirement to play for my parents when they celebrated their fiftieth wedding anniversary on April 14, 1990. Academically, I wasn't any more motivated in high school than I was in grammar school, but I managed to graduate twenty-sixth in my class of about two thousand despite being bored through most of my classes. Expectations about college were not the same as they are now: not many of my friends continued their education because there was plenty of work to be had in Elizabeth and the surrounding area back then. Higher education was not seen as a way to advance yourself.

The immediate postwar years were good to Elizabeth, as they were for most of the country. By the early 1950s, the city clerk's office was inundated with permit requests for commercial construction. Warehouses, terminals, and petrochemical facilities were popping up in Elizabethport, Bayway, and other areas near the Arthur Kill. The Port Authority of New York and New Jersey made the key decision to move the region's port facilities from New York to Newark and Elizabeth, bringing thousands of good-paying, unionized jobs to our waterfront. Lots of high school graduates in the early 1960s took advantage of the opportunities that postwar New Jersey had to offer. I decided to continue my education and play football and baseball in college rather than getting a job. I applied to only one university, Rutgers, the State University of

New Jersey. I knew that Rutgers was a terrific school, but its main appeal was the bottom line. I had a baseball scholarship to New York University but wanted to stay in New Jersey, and Rutgers was the least-expensive option.

I started in the College of Arts and Sciences with a liberal arts curriculum. Within two weeks I was bored to tears and asked to be transferred to engineering. It was quite a dramatic change, but I had always been good at math, so I took a shot. My confidence seemed well placed when the head of the department, the renowned physicist Dr. Richard Plano, gave me a math test before I could be admitted to the program. It was a tad more difficult than remembering "person, man, woman, camera, TV." The test was supposed to take an hour; I finished it in half the time and aced it. I was allowed to attend Dr. Plano's famous, or infamous, physics course, where I heard of his introductory remarks to freshmen, "Look to your right and look to your left. One or two of you won't be here for next semester."

All the while I was playing freshman football for Rutgers. (My mother couldn't stand in the way now that I was in college.) Freshmen weren't allowed to play varsity in those days, not that I would have made the varsity team even though Rutgers wasn't the football giant, or sleeping giant as is its reputation, that it is these days. We played the likes of Princeton and Lafayette, not Ohio State or Michigan State, as we do now in the Big Ten Conference.

Not long into the season, I tore my left lateral meniscus in the freakiest way, taking a step back from my fullback position to pass block, and without being hit, my knee collapsed, putting an end to not only my season but my fledgling football career. I thought it was just a bad sprain, but it was much worse. Ultimately I had to have surgery, which was hard enough in the days before arthroscopic surgery, but then during my recovery my knee became infected and swelled up like a softball. It was a nightmare. I couldn't play football but was able to make the freshman baseball team even with a nagging knee.

At the same time I was troubled by the breakup with my first love, Patty Rogers, whom I met in my senior year in high school. Adding insult to injury, she left me for my high school athletic rival, Bill Simo, who signed with a Major League Baseball team after high school. I was heartbroken and devastated. I would write to Patty, telling her how much I missed seeing her, and then I'd go to my student mailbox every day to check for a response that never came. Years later, when I was a lawyer and state assemblyman, Patty came back to Elizabeth to visit her parents after marrying someone other than Simo and moving out West. She had read about me in the newspaper and

called to say hello and say she was surprised to see I was a lawyer and a legislator, that my life wasn't going in that direction when she knew me. And it certainly wasn't.

After my first year at Rutgers, I dropped out to get my knee repaired.
Because I was no longer a college student, I was now eligible to be drafted,
and that's exactly what happened. The Vietnam War was raging in 1965 as
President Lyndon Johnson escalated our presence there from about twenty-
three thousand troops in 1964—when he was campaigning for a full term in
his own right—to nearly four hundred thousand two years later. I showed up
at the draft office with a bandage around my left knee. The draft officer was
skeptical, which was no surprise. "Take that off!" he commanded, pointing to
my knee. I did. The infected wound was still oozing. "Put it back on," he said.
I was classified as 1-Y, physically unable to serve while I was still recovering
from surgery.

I returned to the College of Engineering at Rutgers, but while I did fine in
the math and science classes, I struggled mightily with engineering graphics.
I couldn't draw a straight line even with the help of a ruler and had trouble
visualizing in three dimensions. I barely made it through, "passing" with a D.
What's more, I barely knew how to use a screwdriver. Engineering was not
meant for me. And so, uncertain again about what I wanted to do, and still
pining from the loss of my first love, I dropped out again.

Leaving college meant that once again I lost my student deferment from
the draft, and this at a time when the buildup in Vietnam continued, month
after month, eventually reaching more than a half million in the fateful year of
1968. I figured my knee injury would keep me out of the service, but I was
mistaken. A bum knee didn't make me 4-F. If only I had a case of bone spurs.
I got my draft notice in the summer of 1967 and passed the physical. I was
declared fit to serve. Although concerned for my safety, my parents did what
all first-generation immigrant parents did—they gave me a pat on the shoulder as I left, while quietly worrying about me getting sent to Vietnam.

I didn't have to travel very far for basic training—I was sent to New Jersey's legendary Army base, Fort Dix in Burlington County, about sixty-five
miles from Elizabeth. After basic training, I was ordered to Fort Polk, Louisi-
ana, for advanced infantry training in jungle warfare, obviously to prepare for
deployment to Vietnam. But my company commander at Fort Dix had other
ideas. He noticed I played baseball at Rutgers, so he stepped in and transferred me to the Army's Special Services Division. That's not to be confused
with Special Forces, the home of the Army's elite troops. Special Services was
where the Army placed, among other things, its organized sports teams on

military bases. I was picked to play for the Fort Dix baseball, football, and wrestling teams. I even made it to the semifinals of the Fort Dix Wrestling Tournament, where I faced Paul Seiler, who had been an offensive tackle at Notre Dame and a first round draft choice of the New York Jets (who play in New Jersey by the way). He crushed me in the first period, but it gave me an opportunity to tell that story here and to my friends, as New Jersey's great storyteller, Bruce Springsteen, sang in "Glory Days": "We went back inside, sat down, had a few drinks, but all he kept talking about was glory days."

Being placed in Special Services was an enormous moment in my young life. First of all, I was spared deployment to Vietnam at a time when the war was becoming deadlier for everyone involved and more unpopular at home. I had friends with whom I went through basic training who were killed in Vietnam. I was prepared—as much as anybody can be prepared—to serve my country in that conflict, but fate thankfully stepped in and kept me home even though "I wasn't a Senator's son" (Creedence Clearwater Revival). But I was a lucky one.

My assignment to Special Services led me to sharing a barracks with lawyers who were going through basic training before heading off to officer training school. I found myself listening in on their conversations and even joining in on their discussions. That's when my life truly changed. I noticed that these lawyers were no smarter than I was. In fact, I considered myself— a two-time college dropout—smarter than the hotshot lawyers. I said to myself, "You're smarter than these guys and they're lawyers and you're a two-time college dropout. What's wrong with you?" I came away from those conversations with a new sense of purpose and with a lot more confidence. As a kid from Elizabeth, I didn't know any lawyers growing up. And kids like me tended to look at lawyers, doctors, and other professionals with awe, as if they were somehow better and smarter than we were. I found out that wasn't true. Not at all. Now I had something to think about for life after the Army.

I was discharged in June 1969 and went back to Rutgers with a new sense of direction. I changed my major again, this time to economics, finally graduating in January 1971 after a long and circuitous journey on the banks of the Raritan River. Next step: law school. It's a step I would not have considered without those discussions in the barracks at Fort Dix. I scored in the top one percent of the country on the law school admission test and decided to attend St. John's Law School in Queens.

Once again, like with my decision to go to Rutgers, I was driven by practical realities. St. John's was close enough that I could commute there while living with my parents in Elizabeth. And I could afford the tuition, thanks to the GI Bill and accordion gigs on weekends at weddings. My mother said I went to law school to avoid getting a job. That wasn't far from the truth. In any case, I graduated fourth in my class even though I reverted to my old ways and often skipped classes to spend the day at Aqueduct Racetrack, which was off the Belt Parkway on the way to the school, as I did while I was at Rutgers going to Monmouth Racetrack with my friends Ray Molski and Jefferson Walker McCullough. Years later, Ray and I would play 2 on 2 pickup games against local high school players and just about always won. Glory days!

In addition to playing accordion gigs on weekends, I worked the night shift as a security guard at a local factory, which helped pay for tuition, books, gas and tolls. My father bought me a Buick from winnings at Monmouth Racetrack.

I made the honor roll and was invited to compete to join the prestigious law review staff. The first assignment was completing pages of citations, tedious work that's often assigned to judicial law clerks and young lawyers in law firms. I began the work but quit after an hour of drudgery. I still wasn't determined to work hard enough to excel. I was satisfied with being at the top of my class and nothing more. That changed when I was introduced to politics and discovered that this two-time college dropout could be somebody and could shape public policy.

As graduation approached, it was time to figure out how I was going to put that law degree to use. Like other top law school graduates, I was recruited for jobs on Wall Street. I went on exactly one interview to see what the firm had to offer. After the interview, I was brought to see the shower stalls where I was told the junior lawyers freshened up after putting in days of twelve hours or more. That was it for me—I was not going to turn my life over to a Wall Street law firm. Luckily, somebody else—an extraordinary political leader from Union County—did have a plan for me. And among other great qualities, this leader had the most interesting nickname in all of New Jersey politics.

They called her "Ma."

2 · MA GREEN'S BOY

In the mid-1970s, when I got my start in politics, women like Bella Abzug and Shirley Chisholm were blazing trails for future female politicians. Yet given the times, they were exceptions to the rule. But in my political career, it was the women who wrote the rules.

This was years before New Jersey elected its first (and thus far only) woman governor, years before women like my Senate partner in fighting for marriage equality, Loretta Weinberg, rose to power in the legislature and Christie Todd Whitman was elected governor. It's difficult enough for women in politics today. Imagine how hard it was in the 1970s. But I had the good fortune of being mentored in politics by women. I was a protégé of an extraordinary woman who rose to political power in Union County during my young adult years. Katherine Green was a legend in her time, though she is not nearly as well remembered today as she should be. Everyone called her "Ma," which reflected her concern and involvement in their lives.

Ma Green was a successful realtor throughout Union County. That role alone would have kept her in touch with grassroots voters. But she also was a vibrant presence in the Polish American communities of Elizabeth and adjacent Linden, and through those connections, as well as her work in real estate and in her family's insurance business, she became influential in local Democratic politics in the middle of the twentieth century. She held no formal leadership title, but with her support for candidates and her deep connections to voters, she became one of the most powerful women in the state and arguably its first female "boss." She was, in several ways, like South Jersey's George Norcross, who doesn't have an official title or public office but has become one of the state's most powerful political leaders. Ma Green was never as powerful as Norcross, who makes and breaks governors, but within Union

County, and especially in places with large Polish communities, she was the boss.

In tribute to her fame throughout the Polish American community, in 1971, when she was seventy-six years old, Ma Green was named the first female grand marshal of the annual Pulaski Day parade up Fifth Avenue in New York. Years later, in 2004, I was honored to be the grand marshal. As I marched past the viewing stand, my old band, Jolly Rich and the Polka Stars, played. Marching with me was New York mayor Michael Bloomberg, New Jersey governor Dick Codey, former governor Jim McGreevey, and U.S. senator Chuck Schumer. You can imagine what was going through my mind. From picking up coal as it fell off trains, twice dropping out of college, to getting the highest honor of my heritage accompanied by the political elite. I said to myself, "Mom, Dad, and Ma Green, this one's for you." My mother got to know Ma through her church, St. Adalbert's in Elizabethport, and eventually Ma recruited her to work on the campaign of Steven Bercik, who served as mayor of Elizabeth from 1956 through 1964. Bercik ran Elizabeth during the height of the city's postwar prosperity and later became a judge in Union County. My mom liked what she saw in politics. She later decided to run for Democratic committeewoman from her election district in Elizabeth. She was gregarious and well liked, definitely a natural at retail politics, although anybody who tried to get too familiar with her by calling her "Stella," which sometimes happened, soon found out she wasn't fond of that nickname. She was Stephanie.

At the time, the city had 156 Democratic committee members, and elections to the committee posts were truly grassroots affairs. Neighbors spoke to neighbors. It was all about getting people interested, getting them talking, and then getting them out to vote. That remains true today, of course, but nowadays conversations between neighbors just don't happen as they did a couple of generations ago. They happen on Facebook, Twitter, and other social media platforms, where you lose some of the personal connections we had way back when. My mother won that election the old-fashioned way, by getting her friends, their friends, and the friends of friends to the polls. She would go on to serve on the committee for years, long enough to see me elected to the legislature several times over.

As for Ma Green, well, she was a shrewd political operator—she had to be, given how few women there were in politics at the time. She was a true-blue Democrat who supported the party through thick and thin in Union County, but she also had a personal goal in mind. She used her influence to help get more Polish Americans involved in politics and on the ballot. To advance in politics in New Jersey everyone needs a godfather. In my case, I had a god-mother. The importance of ethnic politics in communities like Elizabeth can't be underestimated. Back in the day, the Irish were supporting, and elect-ing, Irish candidates in places like New York City and Boston. "Elite" reform-ers complained that this was all about "tribalism." But that's a very shallow, unproductive, and outdated way to describe the voting patterns of people who simply want to ensure their interests and values are represented in poli-tics. Ma Green was delighted when a fellow Polish American won an elec-tion; the higher the office, the greater the pride. She also understood that the people she met at church and in community meetings saw ethnic politics as a path to power and influence, especially for underrepresented groups.

After I graduated law school, I was not motivated to turn my degree into a career even though I finished fourth in my class. My mother persuaded me to go to a local Democratic club meeting, although I was more interested in meeting young women there than in local politics. But that meeting led to another moment of revelation: the speaker was Adam Levin, who was running for Congress from the area after just having graduated from the Uni-versity of Michigan Law School. Adam's father was a successful developer, Philip Levin, who built Madison Square Garden.

The year was 1974, Richard Nixon had left the presidency in disgrace, and young Democrats were poised to change the direction of the country. Adam Levin represented a real sense of hope in the aftermath of Watergate's corrup-tions and Nixon's lies. While I don't remember the exact words he spoke at that meeting, I know I was captivated by Levin's message of social justice. I signed up as a volunteer for his campaign and spent the next few months working for his election with all the young energy I had. In the end, though, Levin lost in a landslide against incumbent Republican Matthew Rinaldo (they had a rematch eight years later, in 1982, with similar results). I was dis-appointed for sure, but exhilarated as well. I had definitely caught the bug. And pretty soon it became clear Ma Green had plans for me.

I landed my first job out of law school in 1974 through Ma's influence with the Union County Democratic organization. The county chairman, Chris Dietz, contacted me and said he had arranged an interview for me with the State Office of Legal Services, which administered legal services to the poor. I jumped at the opportunity, seeing it as a way to act on my developing sense of social justice, which was inspired by the hard times my dad had going with the flow of life and my mom's involvement in local politics. I wasn't going to go with the flow. I wanted to stand up to "the Man" regardless of whomever "the Man" was. In other words, it was a far cry from that Wall Street job I interviewed for, and that's exactly why it was so appealing. By now I was certain I would eventually follow my mom's involvement in politics. Indeed at one of the local Democratic meetings, my mom was asked if I was going to be her committeeman in the district. My mom replied, "Committeeman? My son's going to be a councilman." I was thinking, councilman? I'm going to be an assemblyman. But before I ran for political office, I needed to develop my legal skills, and I needed a job.

I went down to Trenton for a formal interview with Legal Services director Bruce LaCarubba, a graduate of Rutgers Law School. I was pretty excited about the opportunity to fight for justice for poor folks and had the impression the job was mine. At least I was told by Chris Dietz the job was mine. Not that I felt entitled, but I thought it was exactly the right job for me at that point in my life, and I felt I had the makings of a very good lawyer, plus I was Ma's boy. That had to count for something. Or not. I quickly discovered that the interview was not just a formality, or at least not the way I imagined it. After a few pleasantries, Bruce looked me in the eye and told me that he was interviewing me only because someone "from above" told him he should. He had no intention of hiring me, he said, because I had no legal services experience. So the interview really was a formality. Just not the formality I expected.

I suppose lots of people might have been upset at the waste of time—driving to Trenton to be told I had no opportunity to get the position. Others might have angrily walked out of the interview or, at a minimum, politely excused themselves. And understandably so. Bruce made it clear I wasn't getting the job. Nevertheless, I stuck around and continued to chat. After discussing our mutual interests, including basketball, for a while, I was able to demonstrate my passion and commitment to helping the poor and my legal knowledge. I was a natural in the law and it showed. I also showed I was no political flunky. Bruce perked up and told me he had changed his mind, that he would take a chance on me after all. I quickly proved it was a good chance to take, so much so that when he left his director's position for private practice, he named me interim director.

My accession in politics was fueled by strong-willed women, Ma Green and my mom, who gained power at a time when politics was dominated by males. But there were other women I dealt with in politics and government through the years who succeeded in previously male-dominated positions. Indeed, the Union County Democratic Party selected the first female county chair in the state, Charlotte Defilippo, who ruled Union County politics with an iron

fist from 1995 to 2013 and presided over a turnaround in its Board of Freeholders from 9–0 Republicans to its current 9–0 Democratic composition—with
a majority of female members.

I helped strike a symbolic blow for equality in sports about a decade after
the passage of Title IX, which ensured that girls and women would have
equal access to participation in sports. Title IX was a cultural revolution that
led to the boom in women's sports today, but it wasn't necessarily embraced
by many males at the time. At that time I had moved up to the state Senate.
The Senate president, Carmen Orechio, put together a fast-pitch softball team,
with Orechio himself starring as pitcher. They were pretty good, and they
regularly beat a rag-tag team I put together. I was sick of losing to Orechio and
one year recruited the star pitcher from the old Trenton State (now College
of New Jersey) women's softball team. She had a nasty fastball, a curve, and a
pitch that dropped like it fell out of a window. She tied Orechio's team in
knots, and I loved every minute of it. Yes, it was a win for my team. But it also
opened the eyes of more than a few men who couldn't catch up with a young
woman's fastball. That was a win as well.

But getting back to my interview with Legal Services, I quickly proved I was
the right person for the job. Not long after I started there, Governor Brendan
Byrne was facing budget problems just as our neighbors across the Hudson
River were coming to terms with their own—and much larger—financial
struggles. The nation was heading into the doldrums of the late 1970s, putting
an end to the historic prosperity of the post–World War II era. New Jersey had
gotten used to double-digit increases in state spending as the government
expanded to meet the needs and demands of our growing, more diverse, and
older population. In the summer of 1975, the aftershocks of the first oil embargo
took hold in the Garden State, as they did elsewhere. The mood was summed
up by New York governor Hugh Carey, who famously declared in his inaugural address in 1975 that "the days of wine and roses are over." What was true in
New York was true in New Jersey. The state had to tighten its belt for the first
time in many years. Byrne's proposed budget for fiscal year 1976 actually cut
spending—not slowing the growth of spending but actually reducing spending, this after increasing it by more than 10 percent the previous year. Included
on Byrne's hit list was Medicaid, the joint federal-state program that provides
health care to the poor. Not only did Byrne propose to cut Medicaid coverage
for dental appliances and eyeglasses, he also was looking to implement a
copayment from Medicaid recipients who could little afford to pay it.

I seized the opportunity to come to the defense of my clients, the poor
of New Jersey, and challenged Byrne's Medicaid cuts in court. I crafted a

well-founded argument that Byrne didn't follow the procedures required under law to make the changes. I was well aware that ultimately Byrne could follow the correct process, but in the meantime my legal arguments would hopefully buy time to put political pressure on the uncharacteristically unkind cuts Byrne proposed. And they did.

My arguments won the day. I persuaded state Supreme Court justice Morris Pashman to issue a temporary restraining order against the cuts after being twice denied in lower courts. I caught up with Justice Pashman at his home in West Paterson on a Saturday afternoon and explained I wanted a temporary restraining order against the Medicaid cuts. Justice Pashman said, "I don't know the legal arguments you're presenting, but I know people are going to be hurt. I'll sign the temporary restraints. We'll figure out the law later." Once the temporary restraints were ordered and a date set for oral argument in court, Byrne decided to back down rather than continue to litigate the issue. It was a victory for poor people who were in no position to absorb the cuts to the state budget.

Later in 1975, when I was still just a year removed from law school, I took another highly charged case that became a landmark for women's rights. My fellow Legal Services attorney Phyliss Warren and I represented a client named Judith Ponter, who wanted to be sterilized after she gave birth to her fourth child. But doctors refused to do so without her husband's consent, even though the recent *Roe v. Wade* decision had given women power over their own bodies. Judith Ponter hadn't lived with her husband, John Ponter, since 1969, and the father of the child she was carrying was not her husband's, who obstinately refused to give his permission, leading to our legal action. We needed a court ruling to send a message to the medical community that *Roe v. Wade* went beyond abortion—that the right to choose extended to any medical procedure on a woman's body. The court agreed. "Women have emerged in our law from the status of their husband's chattels to the position of 'frail vessels' and now finally to the recognition that women are individual persons with certain and absolute constitutional rights," wrote Judge Philip Gruccio. "Included within those rights is the right to procure an abortion or other operation without her husband's consent. A natural and logical corollary of those rights is a right to be sterilized without her husband's consent."

My fights against cutting health care for the poor and on behalf of a woman's reproductive rights were a manifestation of my developing need to challenge injustice when I saw it. All these years later, I think that desire came from seeing the hard life my father had and the way it affected him, and his relationship with me. He never fully had the chance to develop his talents and intelligence. It wasn't fair, and it left me with a desire to fight for fairness when and where I could.

I worked hard at Legal Services and validated the support of LaCarubba, its executive director, and my county chairman, Chris Dietz. If Ma Green was my political godmother, Dietz was my godfather. He soon became chair of the state's Parole Board and chose as his executive director an ambitious, energetic young man from Middlesex County named Jim McGreevey. The future governor's star was just beginning to ascend. After several years with Legal Services and then, for a short time, as Planning Board attorney with the city of Elizabeth, I thought it was time to take my commitment to justice and equality to the next level. In 1977, I decided to run for state Assembly, knowing that I would have the formidable help of two shrewd politicians—Ma Green, and my mother.

In Ma Green's eyes, I was the great Polish hope in local politics. I say that not as a brag but because ethnic politics, as I've noted, were important to her. Having a Polish American in the legislature and in other public offices was more than just a point of pride. It was a sign of acceptance and arrival. And it meant that the young generation of Poles saw that somebody like them could aspire to leadership. Of course there's nothing uniquely Polish about that attitude. That's how ethnic and racial politics play out in neighborhoods across the country to this day—and add to that list gender and sexual orientation, as Kamala Harris and Pete Buttigieg and many others are demonstrating.

With Ma's support, I won the backing of the Union County Democratic organization for the Assembly seat. In New Jersey, unlike other states, candidates supported by the county political parties have a huge advantage. I will be referencing it often during my journey through and around the New Jersey political system, where county political parties have the power to award candidates with a favored ballot position—the party line—by bracketing them with other endorsed candidates up and down the ticket. Reformers have tried for years to change the system, but, not surprisingly, to no avail. And New Jersey does not allow initiatives and referendums, which enable citizens to petition to change laws by putting referendums on the ballot. I've had the advantage of getting the "line" often but upset it once (more about that later), and I was waylaid by it in my gubernatorial campaign (more about that later also).

But I digress. Back to Ma Green. Even as powerful as Ma was, she couldn't simply dictate to the organization. There was more than a little Jersey-style intrigue behind the scenes. No surprise. After all, it's New Jersey.

Timing can be everything in politics, as in life, and I chose to run for Assembly the same year that an unpopular Brendan Byrne was up for reelection as governor. Confronted with a desperate need for new revenue to fund state government, Byrne just a year earlier managed to get a state income tax bill through the legislature. Needless to say, it was highly unpopular, leading commentators to dub him OTB—one-term Byrne. Early on in 1977 Byrne seemed to be on the verge of dropping out of the race. That's how bad his prospects seemed. Ten—yes, ten—other Democrats were preparing to challenge him in a Democratic primary, including two members of the state's congressional delegation, Bob Roe and Jim Florio, and a member of his own cabinet, Labor Secretary Joe Hoffman. It was an extraordinary rebuke of a sitting governor from people in his own party. But the Union County Democratic chairman, Don Lan, gave some new life to Byrne's prospects by promising him the organization's support—if, that is, Byrne would support him for the post of New Jersey secretary of state. Lan already had served Byrne as his executive secretary—today's chief of staff—early on in his first term, so it was not entirely surprising that Lan wanted Union County in Byrne's column. It turned out, though, that Lan had a big problem right in his backyard. John Zaleski, the Democratic chair of Linden, was a vocal leader of those who wanted Byrne out of the race and replaced with another Democrat. But Zaleski also was an ally of Ma Green and shared her passion about the Polish community. So he offered to stand down against Byrne as long as Lan delivered the organization line for the great Polish hope, Ray Lesniak. And so the deal was done.

Sealing the deal, however, was not that easy. The seat I was seeking had been held by Linden's mayor John Gregorio. But Lan, the county chair, was battling with Elizabeth mayor Tom Dunn, who also served in the state Senate. Lan stripped Dunn of the party's support for reelection to the Senate, giving the nod instead to Gregorio and giving me a shot at his Assembly seat. The other Assembly spot was held by two-time incumbent Tom Deverin. But Lan had to maneuver out of a political and personal dilemma in order to get Byrne and me the Democratic organization support. For political junkies, Lan's maneuvering was the equivalent of a Picasso masterpiece. Lan needed to deliver the organization's support for me to secure his position as secretary of state, but my competitor for the organization's support, advanced by Dunn, was Elizabeth councilman Abe Rosensweig. Dunn's strategy was well thought out, but Lan's was better. Assemblyman Deverin was everyone's choice. Rosensweig was vice chair of the county Democratic organization and was a social friend with Lan—they worshiped at the same temple—so Lan promised Rosensweig he would break a tie vote in his favor, leaving me out in the cold in the event Rosensweig got two votes, or so he thought. Rosensweig already had secured commitments from the municipal chairs of Elizabeth and Winfield Park, so he figured he had the organization's support locked up with Lan being the tiebreaker. Not so fast. The entire district was made up of Elizabeth, Linden, Carteret, and Winfield Park. The chair of Winfield Park was on the payroll of the incumbent, Tom Deverin, a salient fact in the upcoming intrigue. So the vote began, in the order determined by Chairman Lan. Elizabeth voted Rosensweig and Deverin. Linden voted Deverin and Lesniak. Carteret voted Deverin and Lesniak. Rosensweig needed only his commitment from Winfield Park fulfilled to get his two votes for a tie with my votes from Linden and Carteret, to get to the tiebreaker, except he didn't count on the Winfield Park chair not supporting his employer, Deverin, who had a majority of three votes and had already secured one of the nominations. The Winfield Park chair voted for Rosensweig, fulfilling his commitment, and then voted for Lesniak, leaving his boss Deverin off his ballot so I could have three votes for the organization support without needing to go to a tiebreaker. Rosensweig didn't know what hit him, and yet everyone kept their commitments. It was a political masterpiece—cunning, yes, but a masterpiece nevertheless.

So my name was on the primary ballot as the organization's choice along with my running mate, Deverin. Putting your name on the ballot is always anxiety ridden, especially the first time. Despite having the support of the county's Democratic organization, I didn't know what to expect. My mother had some advice for me, and it was the counsel not of a mother but of a good political strategist. "All you need is five women to run your campaign," she said. I thought that was a pretty interesting—and very progressive—idea, and I asked her why. "Men will sit around and tell you what needs to get done," she said. "Women will actually get things done." My mom's connections to the Polish community and her fellow Democratic committee members in Elizabeth would prove to be crucial as the campaign unfolded. Yes, the women got things done all right. My campaign was unlike any you'd see today. We held spaghetti dinner fundraisers (six bucks a head) and handed out potholders and sponges that expanded when wet with a "Lesniak for Assembly" message. Nice touch. We also reached out to our neighbors and friends, who then in turn reached out to their neighbors and friends. I had an army of women volunteers recruited by my mom and Ma Green going door-to-door on my behalf. On the Sunday before the general election, I played accordion for the last time professionally at Hank's Starlight Lounge in

Linden. I had continued to play at weddings and polka parties during the campaign because it was an effective way to connect with voters and make a little money on the side. But I was ready to put aside the old squeezebox. I was hoping other things were about to get in the way of practicing and playing the accordion.

On Election Night, I monitored the returns at our campaign headquarters on Elizabeth Avenue in Elizabeth. The first results to come in were from four election districts in Peterstown, the Italian section of Elizabeth. I was losing by a six-to-one margin to James LaCorte, the son of Elizabeth's former mayor who was running "off the line." I was devastated. My mother and Ma Green were at my side. Ma Green saw how I was feeling. Using her nickname for me, she said, "Raymush, don't worry. Wait until our vote comes in."

Sure enough, shortly thereafter results from my home district—where my mother handled the get-out-the-vote campaign—came in and I won by a ten-to-one margin. Likewise the tallies from heavily Polish areas of Linden and Carteret. I was off to the races, coming in as the leading vote getter. My running mate, Deverin, finished second and clinched the nomination for the district's other Assembly seat.

At my victory speech I thanked everyone who helped get me there, especially John Gregorio who, because of Ma Green, embraced my candidacy from the start. But I paid special tribute to my mom and dad and Ma Green. My dad, to be honest, didn't quite grasp the significance of the achievement, but my mom certainly did, and of course so did Ma Green.

As I look back at that moment and recall the tribute I paid to my parents, I actually wonder if my mom and dad ever understood me. My mom, because I didn't marry a good Polish girl and raise a family, and my dad because I didn't work for a living—I was a lawyer and a politician. In any case, I wasn't the only winner that night. Brendan Byrne managed to snag the party's nomination after all, although it certainly helped that the field was so divided. He won only 30 percent of the vote, but that was more than enough in a field of eleven candidates. Congressman Roe finished second with 23 percent. In the subsequent general election, even more shocking news for those who had written off Byrne: he beat Republican Ray Bateman in a landslide, winning 55 percent of the vote to Bateman's 41, with the rest split among minor candidates. Byrne's resurrection from the political dead in 1977 remains one of the more remarkable comebacks in recent state political history and one that few know was engineered primarily by Ma Green.

I won the general election as well. The district was so heavily Democratic that the real election was the primary. In a more interesting contest, my friend and supporter John Gregorio knocked off Tom Dunn for the district's Senate seat—Dunn had tried to win reelection by running as an independent. Dunn lost, but he wasn't finished. After all, he was still mayor of Elizabeth, and he had a powerful organization of loyalists. Our paths were destined to cross again.

On the day of my swearing in, my proud mom and dad were seated behind me in the Assembly chambers along with Ma Green and her son, Michael Green, who also was a political force in the community. It was an unusual occasion for my dad, who wasn't used to public gatherings. But my mom reveled in it. As I familiarized myself with committee work and constituent service, my mother again sprang into action. Or, should I say, even more action. She and several of her friends, all of them can-do women, formed a new organization called Friends of Raymond J. Lesniak, which held monthly meetings in the Bayway Polish Home, which was located on—where else?—Pulaski Street. The organization sponsored visits to senior homes to conduct bingo games, polka dances at local nursing homes where I played accordion, spaghetti dinners for local Democratic committee members, and a Christmas party, complete with gifts from Santa, for more than a hundred local foster families, a tradition that exists to this very day. The organization did wonderful work for some very worthy causes. And, of course, it was a great help to me, especially when the mayor of Elizabeth decided to put me on his hit list.

The State House in Trenton is the third oldest of its kind in the country, dating back to 1792—only Virginia and Maryland have older capitols. The building's golden dome, rising over a rotunda, is a literal and figurative landmark, a familiar sight not just for lawmakers and lobbyists, but for thousands of motorists and rail passengers who catch a glimpse of it every day. And it was my home away from home for four decades. I certainly didn't expect that when I showed up for work for the first day of the 1978 legislative session. My first few weeks in the Assembly were not unlike your first days in high school—they were all about making new friends (and identifying unfriendly foes), trying to fit in, and figuring out how things get done, but I was no shrinking violet during those early weeks and months—I was all in from the policy side as well as the political side. Befitting my status as a lowly freshman, I took a seat in the back of the chamber. But even as I gained seniority, both in the Assembly and later in the Senate, I stayed in the back row because it gave me the freedom to move around the chamber and pay visits to colleagues whom I had to cajole to get them to see my point of view. It was easier to get to reporters from the back row as well. In other words, the back row was where the real action was, not up front by the speaker's podium. It was also where some of the characters were. Sitting two chairs from me was Assemblyman Mike Mathews, who was also mayor of Atlantic City. Little did I know he was close with a mobster from Philadelphia named "Little Nicky" Scarfo. That relationship led to a federal investigation, an indictment, and a prison term—the fate, unfortunately, of all too many mayors of Atlantic City. At another point, I was joined in the back row by Michael Adubato, brother of legendary Newark power broker Steve Adubato, who would come to be the most significant figure in Jim McGreevey's first gubernatorial campaign. More about that later. Michael had a very specific goal in mind when I arrived in Trenton: he was determined to change the hallowed name of Rutgers University to the State University of New Jersey. He was not the only one who pointed out through the years that the flagship schools in other state university systems bear the name of their state. Rutgers, because it was a private school before the state took it over after World War II, is not known as "the University of New Jersey" or "New Jersey State." That bothered Adubato, who attended Seton Hall University and the old Jersey City State College, now called New Jersey City University. Adubato introduced a resolution to mandate the name change. As a Rutgers alum, I was appalled. On the day of the vote, I planted our school colors, a scarlet red Rutgers banner, on my desk so Adubato could see it in all its glory. He must have been moved by my passion for the school because he decided to withdraw the measure. (Or more likely he just didn't have the votes!)

The most flamboyant member of the Assembly during my years there was Kenny Gewertz, who would come to sessions with a cowboy hat and fur-lined cowboy boots. He had long sideburns and drove an orange—yes orange—Corvette. In 1980, he was robbed of eight thousand dollars in jewelry, including an expensive watch and ring, by four prostitutes he invited to his Atlantic City hotel room. He reported the robbery, and the press picked it up off the police blotter. Needless to say, the story made headlines in all New Jersey newspapers. When asked why he went public with the incident, Gewertz responded true to form: "I asked myself, 'What would John Wayne do?'" He really said that.

The Assembly speaker at the time was Chris Jackman, a legendary Hudson County politician who was elected to the Assembly in 1968, when he was fifty-two years old. Suffice it to say he was from a different generation than some of the Young Turks in the chamber who were elected in the post-Watergate votes of the 1970s. He kept bottles of booze in the speaker's office, and they were put to use frequently during "legislative meetings." Jackman was a no-nonsense type who had little patience for some of the protocols of politics and government. He was the driving force behind a law requiring that contracts be written in plain language that everyday people—not just lawyers like me—could understand. "You had to be a student of Chaucer," he once said, to understand the language in a mortgage. Yes, he did reference Chaucer—it was not every day that lawmakers in Trenton cited a poet from the Middle Ages. Perhaps there was a side of Jackman we weren't aware of.

Once, during an Assembly Democratic caucus where he was whipping up votes to pass Governor Byrne's budget, he lost his patience with dissidents who were objecting to various priorities and projects. "Just vote for the damn budget," he blurted out. "We know it's as phony as a two-dollar bill." The budget passed, after some clucking about the speaker's candor and the two-dollar-bill gaff.

After a couple of years under Jackman's leadership, three young Democrats—Hudson County's Joe Doria, Essex County's Willie Brown, and myself—hatched a plan to replace Jackman with Middlesex County's Alan Karcher. We coordinated with the man who inspired me to a career in public service—Adam Levin, whose failed congressional bid got me started in politics in 1974. Levin was determined to make another run for it, and he wanted to have an ally in the speaker's office when congressional districts were redrawn in the aftermath of the 1980 census. It was a bold move, to be sure. Even casual students of politics know that if you're going to go after a leader, whether it's a county chair or the speaker of the House, you'd better succeed. Otherwise, you're put in time-out until you work your way back into good graces.

I had a very specific goal in mind, in addition to helping Levin: I wanted to chair the Assembly's Environmental Protection Committee. My experience working at my dad's factory at GAF was evidence enough to me that the environment, workers, and the public needed protection from toxic chemicals that were polluting the atmosphere, our waterways, and our bodies. But my more veteran colleague, Richard Visotcky from Bergen County, who sat next to me in the back row, also wanted the chairmanship. Jackman knew of the plot against him and sought to lure me to his side with an offer to chair the powerful Judiciary Committee. I wasn't having any of it. I gave my word to Karcher—and I made it a practice to never go back on my word. There was a lot of tension in our caucus, for it's a rare thing to move against an incumbent speaker. But my colleagues and I really believed that the time was right for new—and, yes, younger—leadership. We basically put our careers on the line, and that's no small commitment. Soon it was time to see where we stood.

Before the leadership fight spilled onto the Assembly floor, the caucus voted secretly and Karcher came out on top. That should have been the end of it, but Visotcky engineered a deal with the Republican minority to support Jackman. The GOP's votes, along with Democrats from Visotcky's Bergen delegation and Jackman's Hudson colleagues—except for Joe Doria, who hailed from Bayonne in Hudson County—would have been enough to defeat Karcher.

There was precedent for that unlikely alliance—future governor Tom Kean Sr. became speaker in 1971, even though his Republicans were in the minority. Four rebel Democrats cut a deal with Kean and gave him the votes he needed. I knew that if Visotcky delivered the speakership to Jackman, he'd get Environmental Protection and I would be relegated to oblivion, with no chance to climb back anytime soon. The moment came when I'd know whether I backed the winning horse. Visotcky rose in his chair, right next to me, to officially nominate Jackman as speaker. But Jackman, as solid a Democrat as there ever was, waved his hand down at Visotcky from the speaker's podium, indicating that he ought to stand down. At literally the last minute, Jackman decided he didn't want to be speaker if it meant cutting a deal with Republicans. Karcher became speaker, and I was appointed to chair the Environmental Protection Committee. The movement to clean up the Garden State after decades of pollution had found the champion it needed.

Hardworking people who lived in my election district of Elizabeth, Linden, Winfield Park, and Carteret—people like my dad and my relatives, neighbors, and friends—depended on the petrochemical industry that dominated the waterfront across from Staten Island. The pay was good and the jobs plentiful. But pollution from the petrochemicals created an environmental nightmare by the late 1970s and was particularly unhealthy for its workers. We were beginning to realize the impact of pollution after the first Earth Day in 1970, and as the decade progressed, many of us in public life and in the neighborhood realized it was high time for the industry to clean up its act. Given where I came from and the dangers that my constituents faced on a daily basis, it was only natural that I took up the cause of environmental protection at the very beginning of my time in the legislature. It was something I felt strongly about and saw—and smelled—on a regular basis. Anyone who traveled the New Jersey Turnpike from exit 14 in Newark, past exit 13 in Elizabeth, to exit 12 in Carteret, especially at night, knew that there was something in the air, and it wasn't good. And not all of the pollutants were in the air. The local bodies of water were also suffering from years of pollution and neglect. That was true near my current home, where the Elizabeth River was little more than a toxic stream, and it was true in seemingly more pristine places, like the Pinelands in South Jersey. The Arthur Kill was likewise polluted along the Elizabethport waterfront, where my father used to tell me he'd go fishing when he was younger. I once asked my dad on a visit to the Elizabethport waterfront why he didn't fish there any longer. He pointed to the nearby Exxon smokestacks and said, "That's why."

One of my first causes as a newly elected Assembly member was Governor Byrne's effort to preserve the Pinelands, or Pine Barrens, that vast and vital ecosystem in the southern portion of the state. It was unusual for a kid from Elizabeth to be concerned with an area on the other end of the state, but as a member of the Environmental Committee I was lobbied by environmental groups who educated me about the threat to and significance of the Pinelands' underground water supply. Plus, as a newly elected legislator, it made sense to support a priority of the governor. Byrne himself was a kid from Essex County who didn't know much about the Pine Barrens as a youngster growing up in West Orange. But as governor, he read John McPhee's wonderful book, called simply *The Pine Barrens*. Published in 1968, the book opened the eyes of people who had no idea of the importance of this vast wilderness in the most densely populated state in the country. Not only was the region unspoiled and beautiful, it provided safe, clean drinking water for millions of New Jersey residents. Byrne made saving the area from development a top priority and would later say that he believed that if he hadn't been in office in the 1970s, the fight over the Pine Barrens might have ended differently. "I'm not sure I can say that about anything else I did," Byrne said many years later. I was on board early with the governor on the Pinelands Preservation Act. I wanted to show my support for the environment and illustrate Governor Byrne's point about the importance of preserving the sources of our drinking water. It's something most of us take for granted—until there's a drought or a crisis like the recent problem of lead in the drinking water in Newark and several other New Jersey cities (and Flint, Michigan) or cancer-causing chemicals found in drinking water throughout the state. My goal was to draw attention to the pristine nature—and the importance—of waterways in the Pine Barrens, so I sponsored a canoe trip on the Mullica River for reporters. It runs for about fifty miles from Camden County southeast through Wharton State Forest, finally emptying into the Great Bay just north of Atlantic City. The watershed on either side of the river is a vital part of the Garden

State's natural infrastructure. The Mullica is navigable for about twenty miles beginning near Batsto in Burlington County. That's about where we launched the canoes.

Reporters who were more used to smoke-filled rooms—which did exist and were plentiful in the 1970s—looked a little out of place out on the river, in the middle of one of the great unspoiled places on the East Coast. And they were being led around by a guy from Elizabeth for whom the great outdoors meant a basketball court or a baseball diamond. And it showed. Despite never having been in a canoe before, I put faith in my athletic ability to carry me through and took the helm with two reporters trusting my ability. It was a misplaced trust all around. Within a few yards my inexperience showed, and I tipped the canoe once, and then again after getting back in. The reporters' notebooks were soaking wet. After the second tip, I got my bearings and was able to continue down the river, much to the surprise of the reporters. I was embarrassed, but I was young. I got over it.

The headline in the state's largest newspaper the next day was, "YOU CAN TAKE THE BOY OUT OF THE CITY BUT YOU CAN'T TAKE THE CITY OUT OF THE BOY." The full-page article educated the public about the pristine nature and importance of the Pinelands. Governor Byrne got his legislation passed by both houses and the Pinelands were preserved. Several years later, when I got to the state Senate, I sponsored the Pinelands Development Credit Bank to compensate property owners in preservation areas of the Pinelands by awarding them development credits to be sold for use in designated growth areas of the Pinelands. The Pinelands Development Credit Bank became one of the most successful transfers of development rights programs in the country.

After winning my Assembly seat, I became the darling of folks in Elizabeth who opposed Tom Dunn, the city's mayor since 1965. Not because I was an environmentalist, which was unusual for legislators from the district who had sided with industry leaders, but because I was a breath of fresh air, a "Ray of Hope" so to speak. While Dunn was a Democrat, he was in the mold of George Wallace, the racist governor of Alabama who supported segregation in the 1960s and whose presidential campaign in 1968 whipped up white supremacists around the country, just as President Trump did during his time in office. In 1972 Dunn supported Richard Nixon rather than the party's nominee, George McGovern. Other Democrats in the city were furious.

Even though I was consumed with the job of serving my constituents and working on public policy in Trenton, I couldn't stand by while Dunn was dividing the city of my birth on racial lines. I spoke out, early and often, against Dunn's harassment of the recent arrivals from Cuba who fled Fidel Castro's regime and were starting businesses along Broad Street and Elizabeth Avenue, just as they had done in Cuba before Castro confiscated their property.

The Cuban community appreciated my support. I was standing in line to board a plane at Newark Airport when an airline representative came from behind the reception desk and asked for my ticket. I gave it to him and wondered what was going on. He brought the ticket back and said, "Thank you for all you have done for the Cuban community." It was upgraded to first class. In the city's African American community, I was known simply as "Ray," not as "Assemblyman Lesniak," because I was seen not only as an ally but also as a friend because of my outreach to the African American community, a community ignored by Dunn. They weren't used to a politician reaching out to listen to their concerns as I did.

Dunn was up for reelection to a fifth term in 1980. There were no challengers committed to upsetting the status quo on the horizon, which bothered me. The other opponent of Dunn, David Conti, was in my opinion, and in that of most of the anti-Dunn faction, just another machine politician who wouldn't make the bold social justice changes we believed were necessary. So I decided to do something about it. I announced that I would be a candidate for mayor of my home city. It was not the wisest or most enthusiastic decision I ever made. Neither Ma Green nor my mom thought it was a wise decision either. But I saw it like a forced move in chess. I had no other choice. I had to make the move. It would lead to one of New Jersey's most epic feuds of the 1980s.

3 · SETTLING SCORES

Tom Dunn and I had a long history together. He was the dominant political figure in Elizabeth from my teens to my early forties, defeating my mom's candidate, incumbent mayor Steven Bercik, in 1964. I was too engrossed in sports to pay attention to politics at the time, but I know my mom was never a fan of Dunn. She believed he was mean-spirited, which was an insightful and accurate observation. But as he rolled to reelection victories through the turbulent 1960s and the depressing 1970s, he became something of an institution in my hometown. The high school sports auditorium is named after Dunn. For many people, Tom Dunn *was* Elizabeth. He was a divisive and polarizing figure, a lot like Donald Trump. He foreshadowed Trump's attacks on Spanish-speaking immigrants when, in the 1980s, he ordered city employees to speak only English at work. Elizabeth's hardworking Hispanic residents, who made up about a third of the city's population, took Dunn's edict as a personal attack. Which is exactly what it was. He was criticized, he was sued, but he refused to back down. In fact, like Trump, he doubled down, saying he would fire any worker caught speaking a language other than English while on duty.

Not far from Elizabeth's City Hall, many Cuban exiles who fled Fidel Castro's tyranny were opening up small businesses along Broad Street and Elizabeth Avenue, adding life to downtown. They and other Spanish-speaking immigrants didn't feel particularly welcomed in Tom Dunn's Elizabeth, which was ironic given that Dunn himself was the son of Irish immigrants and was as proud of his Irish heritage as I am of my Polish ancestry, and as Elizabeth's Hispanics are of theirs. Dunn even hosted an Irish music radio program on WJDM for years. But he, like so many other descendants of European immigrants, simply didn't see the irony of their opposition to new arrivals from South and Central America. They'd often say that their parents or grandparents or great-grandparents were "different." Not true. The Spanish speakers on Broad Street and Elizabeth Avenue, then and now, are no different from my Polish-speaking grandparents who came to the United States for a better life. Dunn didn't see it that way, but I did.

The mayor also projected a tough-guy image, again not unlike Trump during the protests following the death of George Floyd in Minneapolis in 2020. He saw himself as Mr. Law and Order. Early on in his tenure, deadly civil unrest broke out in Newark during five days in the summer of 1967 when a Black cab driver was beaten and arrested by two white police officers for a minor traffic infraction in Newark's Central Ward. The National Guard was called in, twenty-six people were killed, and parts of the city went up in flames. All these years later, the state's largest city still bears some of the emotional scars of those terrible days. Elizabeth borders Newark, and there was understandable fear in the city that the unrest might spill over. Dunn made a public show of issuing a "shoot to kill" order to police if they spotted anybody causing trouble. This illegal directive infuriated many people, but those who loved Dunn—and there were plenty of them—cheered him on. Many other people were outraged, although Dunn always said that his order prevented the unrest in Newark from spreading to Elizabeth. Despite all his tough talk, the police in Elizabeth weren't especially fond of Dunn, no doubt because he reduced the department's size by laying off their fellow police officers. At one point in his tenure, he was recovering at home from a medical incident following a triple-bypass operation and a call went out over the police scanner for an ambulance to respond to the Dunn residence. One wise-guy cop responded, "First one there's a rotten egg." Many residents were also not pleased with Dunn. One was particularly sarcastic during a snowstorm when the morning host on WJDM was taking calls from residents, many of whom complained about their streets not being plowed. The caller said, "I don't know why everyone is complaining. I live on Applegate Avenue and a plow's been up and down my street three times already this morning." Dunn lived on Applegate Avenue.

When I emerged on the political scene in Union County, Dunn attempted to get on Ma Green's good side by giving me a job as attorney with the Elizabeth Planning Department. I worked in City Hall, and often the mayor would bring me in for political discussions, most of which consisted of him telling me how to succeed in politics—one lesson was about the importance of being able to look people in the eye and lie to them. He also bragged about how he was able to get back at anyone who crossed him without them even knowing about it. This was supposed to impress me? More likely to keep me in line. I got out of there as soon as I could—but not before I rewrote the city's Land Use Planning Ordinance. I must admit Dunn never interfered with my work or the decisions of the Planning Board on which I served as attorney. My redraft of the ordinance was tough but fair, at least in my opinion, if not in the eyes of some developers who complained, but it sailed through Council and was signed by Dunn without a whimper. After completing that task, I left and started my own law practice in the downstairs apartment of my parents' home on Summer Street. I converted half the apartment into a law office and lived in the other half. If a client had to use a bathroom, they had to go into my living quarters. One time a matrimonial client did just that. She came back and whispered to my secretary, "I'm on welfare and I live better than my attorney."

Later, as a newly elected assemblyman, I was expected to show allegiance to the Democratic leader in my town—and that would be Tom Dunn. But I had very little respect for him and his disrespect for the city's Hispanic and African American residents. What's more, I was elected despite his support for another candidate, so it's not as though I owed him anything, although he would often mention the job he gave me at City Hall. I realized he had helped me, but that didn't stand in the way of my objecting to the way he ran the city. I served the city well as its Planning Board attorney, laying out a framework for its responsible economic development, and I wasn't about to stop there. I had bigger things to accomplish.

Dunn's enemies in the city noticed me during my early years in the Assembly, and they began to see me as someone who could take Dunn down in 1980—their "Ray of hope," as they put it. I was intrigued. Dunn had barely won reelection in 1976, scraping past an insurgent named David Conti by fewer than three hundred votes. There was a sense that the city was tired of Dunn and his hard-nosed antics. Still, running against an entrenched incumbent for any office is not something you do without a lot of thought. I knew I'd have the support of labor unions, African Americans, and Hispanics, and that would make up a formidable coalition in a Democratic primary. I was tempted, although in retrospect I realized that I allowed Dunn's enemies to talk me into doing something I might not otherwise have done. I decided to run for mayor.

It was a pretty bold move on my part, and while I was young and new to politics, I knew the chance I was taking. It was kill or be killed. I wasn't going to wait around for Dunn to come after me if I didn't follow his orders. But by the same token, I was well aware there would be a target on my head if I lost.

I demonstrated quickly that I was ready to upset the comfortable status quo in Elizabeth by naming Charles Harris to run with me for the citywide council at large position. Harris was a teacher in the Elizabeth public school district and was African American. No African American had ever run for citywide office in Elizabeth before. That was the point both of us wanted to make: it was time to ensure that this important and vibrant community was recognized on a citywide basis.

Harris was an honorable person who had one request of me before agreeing to run for the post. He asked for my commitment that we would campaign together, as a team, not only in the predominately African American First and Fifth Wards, but throughout the city. It was his way of saying that he had no intention of being a symbolic candidate. I wouldn't have had it any other way.

I knew all of this would trigger an explosive response from Dunn, and I was prepared for it. But I wasn't prepared for another kind of explosion. And neither was the city of Elizabeth.

It was ironic, in a terrible sort of way, that a business that turned a portion of Elizabeth into a toxic waste dump was known as the Chemical Control Corporation (CCC). Ironic, because the chemicals actually were out of control. On April 21, 1980, those chemicals—including cancer-causing compounds— blew up on a site owned by CCC near the neighborhood where I was born in Elizabeth. The explosion set off a catastrophic fire that enveloped CCC's two-acre facility along the Arthur Kill waterfront. Newspapers would later report that temperatures in the fire zone reached three thousand degrees, hampering efforts to bring the blaze under control. I rushed to the scene and watched from the waterfront on Front Street, horrified as I saw smaller explosions hurl fifty-five-gallon drums filled with toxins into the air, where they then blew up. It took ten hours to extinguish the blaze, and even that was something of a miracle and a tribute to the Elizabeth firefighters and those from other municipalities that offered mutual aid. Many firefighters were injured battling the blaze itself, and years later about twenty developed life-threatening cancers, lung issues, blood disorders, and other illnesses that they believed were connected to the toxic chemicals released into the air that day, not unlike the aftermath of the 9/11 attacks. Scary though it was, the Chemical Control fire could have been a thousand times worse had it broken out even a year earlier. The state had begun to clean up the site in 1979 after a grand jury indicted the company's president and two other officers on charges of illegal dumping. About eight thousand barrels, some of them leaking all kinds of toxic chemicals, were removed from the site in the months before the fire. Even more alarming, inspectors found six quarts of nitroglycerine placed on top of a pile of chemical barrels, along with nerve gas and cyanide. But even with the state taking action to clean up the site, tens of thousands of barrels were still stacked up on the day of the explosion. Months later, in a development that should have surprised nobody, the company's former president told investigators that a group of mobsters had taken over the property in 1977, ordering him off the site and saying that they were now in charge. Anyone who watched *The Sopranos* decades later could picture that scene—it was based on reality. The mob bosses controlled solid and hazardous waste disposal throughout the state, and anyone who crossed their boundaries could expect retribution ranging from vandalized trucks to bodies found in car trunks under the Goethals Bridge in Elizabeth to the murder of a competitor's wife, her body found floating face down in a pool. That all happened, and more.

Multiple federal charges were filed against the company, and a host of defendants wound up going to prison for their illegal storage of toxic chemicals. The fire and subsequent investigations of illegal dumping in New Jersey, especially revelations about the mob's influence, damaged the state's reputation and made it the butt of jokes—not all of them coming from comedians. A few years later, when former vice president Walter Mondale and Colorado senator Gary Hart were seeking the Democratic presidential nomination in 1984, Hart told a gathering that his wife, Lee, had been campaigning in California while he was campaigning in New Jersey, since both states would be holding primaries the same day. "I got to hold a koala bear," Lee joked. The senator smiled and said, "I won't tell you what I got to hold—samples from a toxic waste dump." That stung. Mondale called on Hart to apologize, but he refused to do so. For voters in the Garden State, Hart's words were a reminder of what we in New Jersey were up against—from both a policy perspective and for our image. I was Hart's New Jersey campaign manager. I liked his youthful presentation, but his putdown of the state sabotaged our campaign and we got creamed.

The Chemical Control explosion went beyond the borders of New Jersey. Breezes from the west carried airborne contaminants across the Arthur Kill toward Staten Island and the rest of New York City, affecting an estimated fifteen million people and reminding policy makers across the country that environmental hazards know no boundaries. There were reports of skin and eye irritation, intestinal discomfort, and other ailments throughout the metropolitan area. People and public officials were outraged. I was among them. The Chemical Control fire confirmed my worst suspicions of what was happening along my city's waterfront and more generally throughout New Jersey.

My mayoral campaign picked up momentum after the fire because Elizabeth residents were fed up with their city being treated as a dumping ground. People believed that surely the city government knew what was going on at Chemical Control all those years, but no one had the courage to stand up to the mob. And Dunn had his associations with mobsters. In the 1980s, he put Mafia soldier JoJo Ferarra on the city payroll as a municipal code inspector. JoJo was the personal protector of Giovanni "John the Eagle" Riggi, a member of the DeCavalcante crime family. Riggi was the leader of the "Elizabeth crew" in the family where he was a caporegime. Only in New Jersey.

There were three candidates in the mayoral race, complicating matters for an insurgent like myself. There was Dunn himself, of course. But like me, he was running without the support of the powerful Union County Democratic Party. The organization spurned the incumbent in favor of David Conti, who had come within a couple hundred votes of beating Dunn four years earlier. I suppose I could have dropped out of the race and backed Conti when the party gave him the nod, but the anti-Dunn faction saw him as a lesser version of Dunn. The Conti camp was interested in defeating Dunn, but not interested in social justice issues, a cornerstone of my campaign. I campaigned alongside Charles Harris and my other council at large candidates throughout the city and tried to emphasize the need for new blood in City Hall, but in the end Dunn carried the day. I finished a strong second, well ahead of Conti. That alone was a bit of a moral victory, since the party had resources I didn't have. And I obviously didn't have Dunn's power of incumbency. But still, it was a loss. I never liked losing, but then again, I wasn't terribly upset. I never really had my heart in the campaign. I felt worse for Harris and our supporters because they took the loss harder than I did. I knew I'd be returning to Trenton, where I'd be able to work for change in Elizabeth even though I wasn't mayor. It didn't occur to me, at least not right away, that Tom Dunn would be looking for revenge. I think he started planning it on Election Night.

I was up for reelection to the Assembly in 1981 and was pretty confident about my chances, especially as I emerged as a champion of environmental protection. The Chemical Control disaster prompted my sponsorship of legislation that required strict licensing requirements for transportation of solid and hazardous waste and drove organized crime out of the business. I was too young and perhaps too naïve to have any fear of retribution, nor was there any, other than a brick through the plate-glass window of my law office. The legislation is still referred to as a milestone in New Jersey's efforts to rid the state of unlawful, unregulated, and mobbed-up companies in the trash and hazardous waste disposal business. It was my second victory to protect the environment over powerful opposition. (My first victory involved the preservation of the Pinelands. More about that in a bit.) There were plenty more victories to come.

It wasn't only the mob that created thousands of toxic sites throughout New Jersey. Because of lax federal and state environmental regulations, New Jersey, with its huge petrochemical industry, was drowning in a sea of contaminated properties, many of which were abandoned. Others just went about their business contaminating land, water, and air without much of a peep from state and federal regulators. I changed that dynamic with the Environmental Cleanup Responsibility Act (ECRA), which required companies to clean up their sites before any sale of their property or before a cessation of operations. But there already were thousands of abandoned sites that needed to be cleaned up that didn't have a responsible party to pay for its cleanup. While ECRA was forcing responsible parties to clean up contaminated sites and put them back to productive uses, I sponsored a law placing surcharges on petrochemicals coming into the state, which provided a revenue source to clean up the abandoned toxic properties. Opposition from the national petrochemical industry was intense, but I had established the high ground on the need to clean up New Jersey from being a chemical wasteland. Opponents gained little support from my colleagues in the legislature or from Governor Tom Kean, but they were persistent and determined.

Opposition came not only from the petrochemical industry but also from the entire business community—bankers, developers, realtors, the New Jersey Business and Industry Association, and the Chamber of Commerce. They insisted that ECRA would ruin New Jersey's economy. The opposite was true.

With ECRA and the surcharge on petrochemicals, tens of thousands of contaminated sites were cleaned up. Without these two laws, New Jersey would be swimming in a toxic mess and our economy would have been ruined. By that time, because of the horrifying stories of contamination and pollution in the press nearly every day, I could have gotten a ham sandwich passed by the legislature if it was good for the environment. My victories made me a champion of the environment in a state and at a time that desperately needed an environmental champion. The petrochemical industry, however, did not give up after ECRA was signed into law. When Jim Florio, then a member of Congress, sponsored the federal superfund bill, the industry stopped making payments into New Jersey's fund, asserting federal preemption. I put on my lawyer's hat and filed a lawsuit—*Lesniak v. United States*—in federal district court, seeking a declaratory judgment that my law was not preempted. The court agreed. It was another notch in my environmental belt. In politics, the more notches in your belt, the easier it becomes to gather more.

Not only had I compiled a good record on environmental policy, but my legislative office helped many constituents with their needed services from government. People in Elizabeth knew they could come to my district office with their problems and complaints, and my political allies in the Union County Democratic organization knew that I was reliable and a person of my word—which is no small virtue in the world of politics. I assumed that record alone would get me support from the Union County Democratic organization as I prepared for reelection in 1981. The key to getting ahead in New Jersey politics is having the county organization's line. Running with the support of the party's machinery is important everywhere, but it's especially so in the Garden State, where our county organizations are stronger than in other states. I took nothing for granted, but I also had no reason to think that the county organization would turn its back on me. I should have been prepared. A Dunn ally, Dennis Estis, had become county chairman. I took a head count of my support as I moved into campaign mode. The organization's municipal chairs in Linden, Carteret, and Rahway were in my corner, which was the majority I needed to secure the organization line. Only Elizabeth, which was controlled by Dunn, was not on my side. Plus, I had other friends in the organization, thanks to Ma Green's legacy (she had passed away by this time) and my mother's decades of work on the party's behalf. What I wasn't counting on, but should have been, was Tom Dunn's determination to take me out. It was politics in its most basic and brutal form. I tried to beat him and failed. Now it was time for him to exact revenge.

Dunn played his cards perfectly. He was working against me behind the scenes, and I was blissfully unaware. On the night of the voting, the Rahway Democratic chair flipped against me, and Dennis Estis, the Union County Democratic chair, broke a tie in favor of Dunn's choice, who of course also had the vote of Elizabeth's chair. Estis told me I had no chance of winning and it would be in my best interest not to run. After all, he said, "don't you have a law practice to be concerned about?" A thinly veiled threat. Not running never crossed my mind. I was too stupid to realize I had no chance of winning. Dunn had arranged to dump me in favor of John Surmay, who was the city's director of health, welfare, and housing. And now I had all of two days to gather petition signatures so that I could run "off the line"—meaning on the equivalent of a third-party line. Of course I had to do all of this by myself and with my cadre of supporters without help from the Union County Democratic Party. The organization wasn't about to help me now that I was cast aside. I later learned that one of my presumed allies, the chair of Rahway's organization, had sided with the Dunn faction after being promised a ten-thousand-dollar-a-year part-time job as a legislative aide. *Malheureusement*, he never got the job because I defeated his candidate. If you wonder why politicians prize loyalty, that's why. Politics is a volatile business, and politicians need to know who will stand by them and who might not. The Rahway chair turned against me for a ten-thousand-dollar promise. Loyalty doesn't have a price tag.

Gathering signatures to get a ballot line, not just for me but for three candidates for freeholder, was a formidable task and was necessary to form a line and not be buried on the ballot. But I had a cadre of supporters who were upset with the treatment I got from the Democratic organization and got the number of petition signatures needed to secure my own line in the election. I turned over my petitions to a young volunteer, James Devine, who was an ardent enemy of Dunn because of a tussle Dunn had had with his dad. I gave him a train ticket to file my petitions with the secretary of state in Trenton.

After he returned, Devine said to me with an impish smile, "If Dunn was willing to promise the Rahway Democratic chair ten thousand dollars to knock you off the line, how much do you think I could have gotten to toss your petitions in a trash can and knock you off the ballot." We both laughed, but it was an indication of how Devine's mind worked. He would later become a controversial political consultant with a particularly devious side to him.

I knew I could count on many to work on my behalf and pound the pavement in Elizabeth and throughout the district, including organized labor activists who were on my side and who hadn't forgiven Dunn for supporting Richard Nixon in 1972. They also were grateful to me for my efforts to get a new exit ramp off the Turnpike into Elizabeth, a project that opened the area for development—which would include the Jersey Gardens Mall and Ikea—and create thousands of jobs. I also had the good fortune to have support from the most popular political figure in Union County. The day after I was knocked off the party line, my campaign got a big boost when respected Union County sheriff Ralph Froehlich announced he would be my reelection campaign manager, despite running himself for reelection on the organization line, an unheard-of action.

Froehlich, a former Elizabeth police officer, remembered I had supported him in his entry into politics against the Dunn political machine. It was an admirable position for Froehlich, a Marine veteran, but in military terms, it would be called an action above and beyond the call of duty. Dunn's candidate, Surmay, had the county organization on his side, but I had my supporters on the ground. And soon I had something more: In the aftermath of the Chemical Control disaster, more barrels of toxic waste were found in Elizabeth. Dunn got into a feud with environmental officials about how to handle the issue. I had a simple question: who was in charge of health issues in the city of Elizabeth? Wouldn't you know—that job was held by my opponent, John Surmay. I made sure to make that point. What's more, as chairman of the Assembly's Environmental Protection Committee, I was in position to investigate what was going on along the city's waterfront and pass legislation to clean up the mess. Governor Byrne, in appreciation of my support for the Pinelands Protection Act, sent DEP commissioner Jerry English to helicopter in for a campaign rally. Environmentalists from throughout the state volunteered and went door-to-door on my behalf. While I wasn't prepared to get knocked off the party line, I left no stone unturned during the campaign.

My Election Night party was at, of course, the Bayway Polish Home. Things were looking good. During the day, I received a call from a reporter with WPIX, the station that covered New Jersey politics, asking where I would be taking election results that night. I told him where and asked if he would be coming to interview me. The reporter said, "Actually, it's only a story if you lose." Yikes. Over at my opponents' headquarters, it was like a wake. Dunn's candidate, John Surmay, was devastated. He was told nobody runs off the line and wins, but the race was never about, at least in my mind, who would win, but about who would come in second to me. There were two Assembly seats in play, the other was won by Tom Deverin, not John Surmay. Thanks to my extensive support, my activism on environmental issues, and my mother's network of friends, I won a smashing victory, taking more than fourteen thousand votes to Surmay's seventy-five hundred. We were so confident that as a lark my campaign produced flyers touting my three county freeholder candidates who were on the ballot only to give me a line so I wasn't buried on the ballot. They had no chance of winning countywide. We distributed the flyers in the home district of the county chairman, Estis, just to get him riled up. Oh, the silliness of youth. And its arrogance.

Speaking of arrogance, when asked by a reporter how it felt to be knocked off the Union County Democratic organization line, I responded, "I *am* the Union County Democratic organization." Oops. Nevertheless, my victory surely was sweet vindication for me and a huge embarrassment for Dunn, who spared no moment campaigning against me, even firing a young campaign volunteer who was an umpire in the Elizabeth Recreation Softball League. His name was Chris Bollwage. Big mistake. So now it was my turn to go after Dunn. I had matured enough to wait for the optimum time to strike back. As the next battle in our feud began to take shape with the coming of a new decade—the 1990s—I was in a much stronger position and was about to get even stronger. By then I was in the state Senate (more on that later) and was up for reelection in 1991. I had continued to champion environmental causes, sponsoring the state's Safe Drinking Water Act, the Clean Air Act, and the Pesticide Control Act. Although I took nothing for granted, I had every reason to believe that voters would reward me with another term based on my work in Trenton and in the district. But I heard through the grapevine that Dunn was looking to challenge me in a primary. Dual office holding was commonplace in New Jersey back then and still is to some extent, although the practice has been severely limited. Dunn had held my Senate seat for four years in the 1970s while serving as mayor. Now he wanted it back. I don't think he was pining to return to Trenton so much as he wanted me out of the way.

Dunn would have been a formidable challenger. I was no fool—I knew that beating him would certainly be satisfying, but it would also take significant energy and resources. Maybe, I thought, there was a way to avoid this battle while also preparing for the next one. That's the hallmark of any good strategist: fight the battle you choose to fight, when and where it's most advantageous. I came up with a plan, and while it was a pretty crafty bit of New Jersey politics, it involved disappointing a friend and supporter.

Chris Bollwage, the young man who had been fired from his job as an umpire in Elizabeth because he supported me over Dunn's candidate in the 1981 Assembly race, was now a member of the Elizabeth City Council, representing its Fifth Ward. He was not just an ally but a friend, and remains one all these years later. Chris wanted to run for an Assembly seat that became vacant because of redistricting. He understandably expected my support for his bid to become one of my two legislative running mates. I had another idea, and I knew it was not what Chris wanted to hear. My plan was to offer Dunn the Assembly seat in exchange for him agreeing not to run against me for Senate. A sell out? I'd call it practical. If I had to fight Dunn again, I wanted it to be on a field of my choosing, and at a more advantageous time. Besides, I was also setting a trap.

Dunn took the bait and agreed to run for the Assembly with my support. This wasn't the kind of news you break to a friend over the phone or, these days, by text message. I wanted to look Chris in the eye and tell him the truth—the opposite lesson that Dunn tried to teach me years earlier, when he talked about being able to look people in the eye and lie to them. I invited Chris to a Devils hockey game at the Meadowlands Arena. Sitting in the box of team owner John McMullan, I got around to shop talk. "Chris," I said, "you're not going to be my choice for Assembly." He hadn't seen this coming. He was stunned. "Who is it?" he said, sounding very disappointed. I didn't hesitate. "Tom Dunn," I said. His jaw dropped. It took a moment for Chris to make sure he had heard correctly and maybe to look into my eyes to see if I was playing some kind of cruel practical joke. "What?" he said. "Why, Ray? Why? What about me and why Tom Dunn?"

That's when I let him in on my cunning plan. "Chris," I said, "you're going to run against Dunn for mayor next year. And when you do, you'll be able to attack him for holding two offices at the same time." Chris and I both knew that Dunn almost lost his reelection in '76 when Conti attacked him for being mayor and state senator at the time. Pretty good plan, I thought. But Chris still was shocked, and at the moment, it's safe to say he didn't see how this was going to work out. But work out it did. Dunn went on to win the Assembly seat, and I was reelected easily, but I hadn't forgotten Dunn's threat to challenge me. It just had to wait for the right time, as the poet Lady Mary Montgomerie Currie wrote: *Tout vient a qui sait attendre.* All good things come to those who wait.

Back to the Assembly—I returned to Trenton in 1982 after my victory over John Surmay, determined to continue my work on environmental issues and to support my running mates, State Senator John Gregorio and Assemblyman Tom Deverin. Both were to the right of my liberal beliefs, so we agreed to disagree on some issues while uniting on others as we fought on behalf of our constituents. One issue we did agree on led to a vote to reinstate the death penalty—a vote I later came to regret and which I felt the need to repent and repair. New Jersey, like other states, was considering passage of legislation reinstating the death penalty after the U.S. Supreme Court reversed its previous position that it constituted cruel and unusual punishment. State death penalty statues had been tossed out in 1972 in the Court's *Furman v. Georgia* ruling, which faulted how, when, and where capital punishment was applied. All death penalty sentences reverted to life in prison after

the *Furman* decision. But then in 1976, in *Gregg v. Georgia*, the Court reinstated the death penalty because it found sentencing guidelines had improved
and made its application less capricious. But new state death penalty laws had
to be written to comply with the *Gregg* decision.

The death penalty was popular—national polls at the time showed that
about two-thirds of the country favored capital punishment. Many cities
were experiencing high murder rates, which people believed were the result
of not having the death penalty. New Jersey was no different in that regard.
There was a clamor to return to the days of capital punishment, and legislation to do just that made its way to the Assembly floor. It gave many lawmakers the opportunity to brandish their "law and order" credentials—a senator
from South Jersey, Joe Maressa, spoke in favor of the death penalty bill on the
Senate floor but argued that capital punishment didn't go far enough. Only in
New Jersey.

Not long thereafter, Maressa decided not to run for reelection after he and
several other New Jersey politicians got caught up in the Abscam debacle.
Maressa was prosecuted for taking ten thousand dollars from a supposed
Arab sheik. Maressa came up with a novel argument to defend himself: he
said it was "patriotic" of him to take the money because it meant money from
OPEC would come back to the United States. Only in New Jersey.

I took the politically expedient route and voted to reinstate the death penalty. Years later, after a spiritual conversion, I championed abolishing the
death penalty. It was an evolution of my soul that changed my position. I cast
another important vote during my Assembly years, and this was one I never
regretted. I was the deciding vote on a bill to increase the drinking age from
eighteen to twenty-one. States were under pressure from the federal government to raise the drinking age to twenty-one in the early 1980s. I was on the
fence about the issue—I saw merit in both sides of the argument. We had
sent eighteen-year-olds to the battlefields of Vietnam back when I was young,
and we continued to recruit young people still in their teens for our armed
services. Were we really saying that somebody eighteen, nineteen, or twenty
was old enough to die for our country but not old enough to buy a beer?
Then again, studies seemed to show that at least some of the carnage on
our roads and highways—more than fifty-one thousand Americans died in
car accidents in 1980—could be reduced significantly if we raised the drinking age.

I was still sorting things out one Sunday night—the night before the vote—
as I drove home from a ski weekend at Hunter Mountain in the Catskills. My
car broke down on the way to the New York State Thruway. Luckily I had one

of the first car phones. It had to weigh ten pounds. I called a gas station, whose owner came by and picked me up in his tow truck. After some small talk, I told him I had to get back to New Jersey the following day to vote on a bill to raise the drinking age. I still wasn't sure how I was going to vote, and I told him that. I was just making conversation, so I wasn't expecting what came next. The driver was quiet for a second and then he started crying. He reached up to his visor and showed me a picture of his daughter. She looked to be about eighteen years old. He said his daughter was dead, killed several years earlier by a drunk driver. A teenage drunk driver. "You've made my decision for me," I told him. "I'm going to vote yes." The driver said, "Thank you. Thank you. Thank you." He fixed my car that night, and I was in Trenton the following morning. The bill passed with no votes to spare.

Even though I wasn't exactly a political veteran in Trenton, I didn't shy away from flexing some political muscle, even when the battle was with other Democrats. I was determined, even then, to leave a mark and to earn a reputation as somebody who could withstand intense political pressure. After the 1980 census, New Jersey, like every other state, had to draw up new maps for its congressional and state legislative districts, which the legislature had to approve.

At one point late in the process, the legislature was presented with a congressional redistricting map that had the support of Governor Byrne, Assembly Speaker Jackman, Senate President Merlino, and the entire Democratic congressional delegation. But I had a problem with the map, even if all those Democratic leaders liked it. The man who helped inspire me to enter politics, Adam Levin, was getting ready for a rematch in 1982 with Congressman Matthew Rinaldo, who beat Levin in 1974. I had told Levin that I would support a new map only if Rinaldo's district, the Seventh, was drawn in a way that made it more competitive for Democrats. But the map the Democratic leaders drew up did not accomplish that goal. The lines may well have been drawn up by Rinaldo; if fact they were. Rinaldo had more Democratic than Republican friends because he crossed party lines often. So I balked, and I wasn't alone. I had become close friends with my colleagues Bob Janiszewski of Hudson County and Bill Flynn of Middlesex County. We shared a summer house in Point Pleasant, which had a cast of friends—Jim McGreevey, my best friend Marilyn Lennon, Senate Democratic flack Jim Manion, state Senator John Russo's daughter Carol Russo, and Paul Byrne. I also shared a ski house at Hunter Mountain with Janiszewski and Flynn, and together we formed a caucus of three working on Levin's behalf. Along with the legislature's

Republicans, we stonewalled the leaders' map. Republicans hoped for a stale-mate, which would throw the map making into the court where they believed, understandably, they would get a better shake. We wanted a map that would give Levin a fighting chance against Rinaldo. That's how politics works, and it has served us well for more than two hundred years, never mind what took place on January 6, 2021. Governor Byrne was puzzled that the map that the entire Democratic leadership supported had not been approved. He sent his chief of staff, Harold Hodes, to ask what I wanted in exchange for my support for the map. I told Hodes that nothing would change my commitment to Adam Levin. He then went to Janiszewski and Flynn, and they pointed to me. Hodes went back to the governor's office in something less than a good mood. Years later Hodes told me he told Byrne that I wouldn't change my mind even if the State House fell on my head. And he was right.

The map was amended to make it friendlier for Levin, or any Democrat for that matter. It was invariably described as looking like a fishhook—the district included Elizabeth, ran down the Route 1 corridor to include several Democratic municipalities in Middlesex County, and then moved south to Princeton before finally curling up to take in parts of Republican Monmouth County. It's not just Republicans who gerrymander districts. Levin wound up losing the rematch despite all that effort. But my toil on Levin's behalf and my willingness to stand up to the governor, my own legislative leaders, and the Democratic congressional delegation earned me credibility in the State House and in the broader world of New Jersey politics. My candidate lost, for which I was very sorry, but I emerged a winner because I was willing to take a stand and fight for my position. People noticed.

I switched positions in the State House in 1983 when I won a special election for state Senate when the incumbent, John Gregorio, resigned from the Sen-ate and from his job as mayor of Linden after he was convicted of income tax evasion, hiding his financial interest in two go-go bars in the city. (At my request Governor Tom Kean later pardoned Gregorio, who made a remark-able comeback, winning election as mayor again in 1990. More on that later.)

Gregorio was well respected in the Senate, and while he was on trial, Sen-ate Majority Leader Tony Scardino pulled me into a walk-in coat room at Lorenzo's Restaurant in Trenton, a favorite gathering spot for legislators and lobbyists, and said, "We're going to have a conversation that never took place. If Gregorio goes down, will you be his replacement?" I said yes. "Okay," Scardino replied. "This conversion never took place." Scardino was afraid Gregorio would find out that he was asking about his replacement while he was fighting in court to save his seat. I've used Scardino's phrase now and then in the years since: *We're going to have a conversation that never took place.* My election to replace Gregorio after his conviction was without much drama other than some procedural craziness. I ran at the same time in both the special election to fill Gregorio's seat until the end of his term the following January and also for the Democratic nomination for the entire term, which was for two years. (In New Jersey, Senate terms are for four, four, and two years to correspond to the ten-year census.) I had different candidates running against me in the two elections on the very same day. Voters had to vote in two voting machines that were adjacent to each other. I cut through any confusion with a campaign theme, "For Clean Air and Clean Water, on Election Day, you can vote twice for Lesniak for Senate" and "For Job Creation, on Election Day, you can vote twice for Lesniak for Senate." It was a brilliant campaign message created by political consultant Hank Sheinkopf, who was later instrumental in the successful political campaigns of Mike Bloomberg and Andrew Cuomo in New York.

My transition to the Senate was seamless. After my farewell speech to the Assembly, I was sent off with the running joke when a member of the Assembly went to the Senate: the average IQ of both Houses went up. As I walked through the corridor to the Senate chambers, I was stopped by a very outspoken senator, Frank Graves, who jokingly said, "Lesniak, there's not room enough in the Senate for both of us."

I remained friendly with my Assembly colleagues and continued to hang out with my Assembly buddies Bob Janiszewski, Bill Flynn, and Dennis Riley at the shore in the summer and at local ski resorts in the winter. Inevitably, given my own work ethic, there was some mixing of business with pleasure. For example, I wrote significant parts of the Environmental Cleanup Responsibility Act (ECRA) while drinking beer—I hadn't discovered wine yet—during a weekend at Riley's Elk Mountain resort home in the Poconos. Our favorite hangout at Hunter Mountain was the Hunter Village Inn, where, in addition to featuring local rock-and-roll bands, a mug of beer cost twenty cents! We used to buy five at a time for a dollar to bring to our group of revelers.

Not long after I got to the Senate, my colleague Dick Codey—a lifelong teetotaler—shamed me into settling down. "Ray," he said, "you're in your mid-thirties and you're still partying as a teenager." That really got to me. It truly was time to settle down. I bought a retirement home for my parents in Monmouth Beach, where I could go on weekends in the summer, and gave up my winter and summer party rentals at Hunter Mountain and Point Pleasant. My friend Don Petroski would bring his thirty-five-foot boat to the canal off the

Shrewsbury River to the Monmouth Beach home and would take my dad and me to cruise by the tall ships when they docked in the Hudson River. We circled the Polish ship and saluted its sailors. It was a special treat for my dad.

But I still had to settle a score with Tom Dunn.

I was in a perfect position to influence Democratic Party politics throughout the state and especially in my hometown and my district. Governor Jim Florio, who succeeded Tom Kean in 1990 and had been a champion of environmental issues when he was in Congress, named me as chairman of the state Democratic Party in 1992. He knew he was going to be in the political fight of his life the following year because of the outcry against tax hikes he rammed through the legislature to close an enormous budget deficit. He needed a warrior on his side to ward off a primary challenge. Florio decided I was that warrior.

But before Florio hit the campaign trail, there was another election that meant a lot to me: the mayoral contest in Elizabeth. Tom Dunn was intent on winning an eighth term. And I was equally intent on making sure that didn't happen. As state Democratic chair, I had the resources and power I needed to make sure it didn't happen. My candidate was Chris Bollwage, the young Council member I had disappointed a year earlier when he wanted to run for Assembly. He got over it and now was all-in with my plan to bring real change to the city we both called home. Needless to say, throwing the weight of the state party behind an insurgent against a Democratic mayor of the state's fourth-largest city was an extraordinary and risky move on my part. Dunn, of course, was furious. He asked the state attorney general to investigate me for using state Democratic Party funds to support Bollwage. I did no such thing, but I did use my considerable political power to raise campaign funds for Bollwage. Dunn didn't like it, to say the least. Too bad. It was perfectly legal. If Bollwage lost, I was a goner as state chairman, and Dunn would come back at me again. But putting aside the personal animosity and rivalry between us, I believed that Dunn's policies and politics belonged to the past, if they ever actually belonged at all, and that it was time for a mayor who was connected to the new Elizabeth of the late twentieth century. Our first poll, by John Anzalone of Frederic Schneiders Research, showed that we had our work cut out for us. Dunn came in at 30 percent, another candidate, Councilman Bob Jaspan, had 21 percent, and Bollwage was third at 17 percent. Some people were understandably worried about it, but I took one look at the cross-tabs, smiled, and said, "We're going to win." If you looked past the top-line numbers, it was clear to me that Dunn and Jaspan didn't have enough support to move beyond the numbers they already had. Only Bollwage had room to grow. And he did. Bollwage was a fierce door-to-door campaigner and out-worked them both. Bollwage also had a great message: nobody should be mayor for more than twenty-eight years. (Ironically, Bollwage was reelected in 2020 to his eighth four-year term.)

We put together a diverse team of at-large Council candidates, including Patricia Perkins, who would go on to become the first African American to win a citywide race, and Orlando Ehreida, who would become the first His-panic elected official in Elizabeth's history.

Dunn decided to go after me personally in the late stages of the campaign, sending out multiple mailings that attacked me for raising campaign contri-butions from out of state for Bollwage and other attacks against me person-ally. It was unusual, to say the least, for a campaign to attack someone other than the opposition candidate. We didn't know how to respond, or even if we should. So I decided to call one of the smartest political consultants I had met through his work with me at the State Democratic Party, James Carville. James was working for Bill Clinton's presidential campaign, but he took the time to hear me out as I explained the situation. Carville took it all in and then asked, "Are you on the ballot?" The answer was obvious. "No," I said. "Then don't do anything," replied Carville. We didn't. We ignored the may-or's attack and instead kept the focus on Dunn. There was no need for me to get into a contest with Dunn when I wasn't even on the ballot. Dunn was just wasting campaign funds.

It was clear as Election Day approached that Bollwage had momentum and posed a real threat to Dunn's long tenure—there were adults in Elizabeth who had never known anybody else but Dunn as their mayor. On the day before the election, Florio's chief of staff, Joe Salema, asked me how I thought the vote would go. "We'll win by about fifteen hundred votes," I said. "Good," Salema said, with a knowing look in his eyes. "That's good." Salema and I both knew the consequences if I was wrong. I would have had to resign as state chairman, which would have been bad not only for me but also for Flo-rio, since I was his protection against any insurgent Democrats thinking about challenging the governor the following year. On the night before the election, some of our young and mischievous campaign volunteers celebrated the end of an arduous few months with some playful shenanigans. The may-or's campaign slogan that year was "If it ain't broke, don't fix it," which was pretty much the only message he had left after nearly a quarter century in office. A few volunteers pasted bumper stickers across Dunn's signs, reading, "It's broken."

I had the usual Election Day jitters as the polls closed, and we waited for returns at the home of our supporters, John and Joann Malone. The first results were from my own home election district—Dunn took it by twenty-two votes. I was pretty shaken up because these were my neighbors and friends. Bollwage noticed that I had gotten quiet, and he reminded me that it wasn't just my district, it was Dunn's home base as well. "He should have carried it by fifty votes or more," Bollwage said. He was right. My mood brightened. An hour later, we were ahead by a thousand votes with just four districts left to count. There was no longer any doubt. I grabbed Bollwage and John Malone (a future superior court judge) and we shared a big group hug. The victory party went on for hours. Cars drove past our party at the Cedars Restaurant on North Avenue in Elizabeth (now the site of a school named after my former teacher, Chessie Dentley Roberts, an Elizabeth education and civil rights trailblazer) honking their horns. I saw a lot of happy faces that night, but none as happy as mine. Elizabeth had a new mayor, and my nemesis was beaten for good.

4 · ELECTIONS MATTER

Campaigns and elections are what drive our conversations about politics. They're all about promises, attacks and counterattacks, and speculation. No doubt campaigns are more fun to talk about and engage in than policy making. Drafting a bill, cajoling colleagues to support it, and seeing it through to passage take patience, determination, and lots of old deal making and an occasional arm twisting.

Journalists and political junkies love to talk about elections. Most, though not all, are less inclined to dive into the details of public policy. I consider myself a policy wonk. I enjoy the details and hard work required to make government more responsive to the people, especially those like our LGBTQ community, people of color, and poor folks whose needs and basic rights have been ignored at best and denied outright at worst and our animals that roam the wild are our companions and provide the food we eat, but have no voice of their own, and who are often subject to cruelty and extinction, or safeguarding the environment that often needs protection from human "progress."

Here's something I learned very early on in my career: you cannot bring about the changes you support and you cannot influence policy in ways you'd like if you don't have power. And in a democracy like ours, power flows to those who can mobilize people and resources in order to win elections.

Camden County's George Norcross, who wields tremendous political influence in South Jersey, provides a great example of how to mobilize and use power on behalf of a cause or a constituency, in his case the city of Camden. Norcross, through his ability to raise serious campaign funds, his aggressive campaign tactics, and his control of a solid South Jersey body politic, has established himself as the most formidable political power broker in New Jersey.

I became close with the Norcross power structure when I supported South Jersey senator Steve Sweeney for Senate majority leader over Bergen County senator Paul Sarlo in 2008. I was floor manager for Sweeney, which meant I had the responsibility of lining up votes. During the Democratic caucus when the vote for majority leader was about to take place, I received a call from *Star-Ledger* State House reporter Josh Margolin, who said he heard Sweeney and Sarlo made a deal—Sarlo would be majority leader and Sweeney budget chairman.

I told Margolin it takes more than two people to make that deal and sought out Sweeney, grabbed this mountain of a man by his traditional suspenders, and said, "There's no deal! I have the votes for you for majority leader." So Sweeney became majority leader, which positioned him to replace Dick Codey as Senate president two years later. I saw Sweeney as the future of the Senate's leadership. He's been there now for more than twelve years—it's good to have friends in powerful positions.

Sweeney has held the post of Senate president longer than anyone else in state history, and the reason is clear—he has been a senator's senator. He always helps his colleagues when asked, including Republicans. That's why Governor Murphy's staff made a mistake when they tried to unseat Sweeney after Murphy took office in 2018. Sweeney had an ace in the hole. He would have gotten the support of Republican senators if necessary. (Remember, Tom Kean had Democratic support when he became Assembly speaker decades ago.) But Sweeney didn't need to go that way. He retained the support of a majority of Senate Democrats.

It's not possible to wield power without being controversial. The more power you wield, the more controversial you become. For every friend you make, you're sure to have made an enemy or two. I've been more than a tad controversial myself. Win, and you can achieve things. Lose, and you can only complain as bills become law without your input. Winning elections often, though not always, requires something more than mere resources—it also requires the right candidates who can win. That's something reformers sometimes don't understand. High-minded ideals are great—I have them myself—but you can't act on those ideals if you don't have power. And that means finding and supporting candidates who can win.

Beginning in the early 1990s I was involved in a number of local, state, and national campaigns, more often than not on the winning side. I saw firsthand the importance of charisma and personality in winning over persuadable voters. Sure, sometimes you can win on a message alone, which would explain Christie Whitman's victory over Jim Florio in 1993. Sometimes money plays a big role, as it did for Jon Corzine in his Senate and first gubernatorial campaigns and in Phil Murphy's gubernatorial campaign. Neither Whitman nor Corzine nor Murphy knocked people over with their personality and charm, but Whitman overcame it with a tax-cutting message and Corzine and Murphy buried their opposition with huge campaign expenditures.

Absent a compelling message or a huge campaign funds advantage, a winning candidate needs a certain "it" factor. Michael Dukakis didn't have it. Neither did Al Gore. They lost to candidates who had seemed to have more personality and vigor, and as fate would have it, both were defeated by candidates named Bush. If Gore had been able to project a sense of humor or empathy instead of campaigning and acting like an inside-the-Beltway robot in 2000 he would have won the nail-biter election for president. I got Gore to let his hair down once. We were backstage with President Clinton before an event. Clinton and I went to the bathroom. When I came out, I said to the vice president, "I guess you could say I just had it out with the president." Gore hesitated for a second and then burst out laughing.

Gore was well qualified but not a good candidate, which was unfortunate for the country and the world. Climate change would be at the forefront and not denied, as President Trump did. We wouldn't have thrown the Middle East into turmoil, and hundreds of thousands of American and Iraqi lives would have been saved. When Gore accepted his presidential nomination at the Democratic Convention in Los Angeles in 2000, I was standing alongside him onstage. Because of my prolific fundraising, I was hoping to be President Gore's ambassador to France. C'est la vie. Political observers, including yours truly, believe Gore lost because he refused to accept help from President Clinton, a result of the Monica Lewinsky matter. And yet Clinton left the presidency with the highest approval rating since FDR. (And let's remember another reason Bush won—Ralph Nader siphoned off Gore votes in Florida.)

As a competitive person by nature, I wanted to win elections and was disappointed by Gore's loss. As a politician who wanted to achieve change, I wanted power not for its own sake but to influence policy. Beginning in the early 1990s, I got a taste of both by supporting candidates like Chris Bollwage and Bill Clinton, who had what it took to win. The Bollwage victory in Elizabeth captured the attention of the state's politicians and journalists. The notion of a Democratic state chairman actively campaigning against a seven-term incumbent Democratic mayor of the state's fourth largest city and former state senator was unheard of. The fact that my candidate not only won but won impressively made me a genuine New Jersey power broker. But Chris Bollwage wasn't the only winner I backed as Democratic state chair. There also was that young governor from Arkansas who caught my attention early and often.

The Democratic primary field heading into 1992 was not especially promising. Incumbent president George H. W. Bush seemed destined for a second term, in part because of the success of the Persian Gulf War in early 1991. Bush's approval rating reached an astronomical 90 percent, the highest in the history of the Gallup poll, after America and its allies drove Saddam Hussein's Iraqi forces out of Kuwait with minimum casualties. Some of the party's top stars—Mario Cuomo and Bill Bradley, among others—decided not to challenge Bush. That left the party with what seemed like the B team, consisting of former and future California governor Jerry Brown, Nebraska senator Bob Kerrey, former Massachusetts senator Paul Tsongas, Iowa senator Tom Harkin, and Clinton. None was a household name at the time—Brown was probably the best known for dating Linda Ronstadt and already had tried for the party's nomination in 1976 and 1980, with unimpressive results.

It was clear to me very early in the process that Bill Clinton was the class of this field, even if few people had ever heard of him as the campaign got under way. I was struck by his appearances on television, impressed not so much by the specifics but by how he presented himself. He had that quality so many good politicians have—he gave you the impression that he was speaking directly to you. In person, he left people with the impression that he really was listening, that what you were saying was important to him.

I had the feeling—as voters did—that Clinton understood me, and yes, that he felt my pain. He related to me as no other candidate did since John F. Kennedy in 1960, when I was a kid. So I decided I'd try to help this promising young governor from Arkansas in his quest to become the youngest president since JFK. Again, it wasn't just so that I could be part of the pageantry of a national campaign. It was because I saw Clinton as someone who could win and go on to become the leader of a new generation of Democrats in Washington.

I was much more liberal than Clinton. We disagreed on LGBTQ rights and criminal justice, but the Clinton years would go on to see the longest peacetime economic expansion in American history (eat your heart out, Donald) and peace in Northern Ireland. And at least he tried to get Israel and Palestine together, something Donald Trump had no interest in achieving. Trump's diplomacy drove them further apart.

With my growing connections to Democrats around the state and region, I figured I could be a valuable asset to the Clinton campaign by bringing in campaign contributions. Fundraising is an essential part of our political system, far more than in any other democratic country. Reformers have been trying to change the system for decades, but many well-meaning reforms have made matters worse. I know, having sponsored what turned out to be super PACs for legislative leaders that entrenched them in power and didn't create the diffusion of power from county party chairs that reformers thought it would.

So until public financing of elections is put in place, those of us who have access to wealthy would-be contributors are king. With the internet and email, small-dollar donors now are also important, as demonstrated by Bernie Sanders and a host of others who raised tens of millions of dollars from donations of less than a hundred dollars as candidates for the Democratic nomination for president in 2020. It's good that small-dollar donors can impact political campaigns as they do, but big money will always find its way into politics, as my bundling of thousand-dollar checks did back in 1992.

Bill Clinton didn't know me in early 1992, but he soon had good reason to notice this state senator from the city of Elizabeth. That's because I began soliciting thousand-dollar checks for the Clinton campaign from my friends, contacts, colleagues, and anybody who wanted to be part of a winning presidential campaign. Because of my position as state chair, I was able to raise hundreds of thousands of dollars quickly. And that was when hundreds of thousands of dollars was real money.

It's important to bear in mind that at the time campaign contributions were limited to personal checks of no more than one thousand dollars and no corporate donations were allowed. That all changed in 2010 with the Supreme Court's *Citizens United* decision, which reopened the gates to big money and corporate donations and the power of super PACs funded by unlimited amounts of undisclosed donations. After all, according to the U.S. Supreme Court, corporations are people just like you and me.

I became heavily involved in the Clinton campaign when he was at the lowest point of the campaign cycle. It's been nearly three decades since Clinton's emergence as a candidate, so it's understandable if people have forgotten—and younger people simply do not know—how unlikely his nomination seemed in early 1992. He had won some good press in the early going in the summer and fall of 1991, but as the primary season got under way in earnest, Clinton seemed like a lost cause, getting less than 3 percent of the votes in the

Iowa caucuses. That actually wasn't quite as bad as it might seem, given that Iowa U.S. senator Tom Harkin was in the race and won nearly 80 percent. Harkin's win was expected. But Clinton finished behind Paul Tsongas, and that was definitely not expected.

His campaign was in trouble. Next on the calendar was the fabled New Hampshire primary, where he would once again face a local hero, Tsongas, from neighboring Massachusetts. Another dismal performance would probably spell the end for Clinton. Supporters were worried and would-be donors were skittish.

During those weeks, I quickly raised a hundred thousand dollars for the campaign to help get it get back on message about the economy, a critical topic in recession-ravaged New Hampshire. How was I able to raise that kind of money for a candidate reeling on the ropes? I was able to by telling contributors it was important to me that they contribute. That's what works.

Clinton began to address the hardships endured in the Granite State, where unemployment was more than 7 percent. Plus, he got a nice boost when he appeared on the Johnny Carson show and played the saxophone. That humanized him and made him more likeable. It was a pretty smart move—maybe I should have played accordion during my gubernatorial campaign.

On the Republican side, commentator Pat Buchanan was giving Bush a run for his money in the GOP primary based on a populist economic message.

Clinton had been given up for dead, with the smart money turning to Nebraska senator Bob Kerrey, a Medal of Honor winner during the Vietnam War. But Clinton never disappeared, campaigning at a frantic pace, spending his money wisely, and winding up a strong second to Tsongas and well ahead of Kerrey, Brown, and Harkin. That's how he earned his nickname as the "Comeback Kid." (And, in a sign of trouble for Bush, Pat Buchanan won almost 40 percent of the vote on the GOP side, a moral victory for a candidate with no experience running against a supposedly popular incumbent.)

Clinton picked up momentum so quickly that, as usual, the New Jersey primary in June meant nothing because the race was over by then. But my role as a fundraiser remained critical, thanks in part to New Jersey's wealth. My success at bringing in donations and my stature as the party's state chair gave me more than a little standing when I suggested—firmly—that the Democratic National Committee (DNC) commit resources to the Clinton effort in New Jersey for the general election. The state had not voted for a Democratic presidential campaign since Lyndon Johnson's landslide win in 1964 (something that seems hard to believe all these years later, with New Jersey firmly blue in presidential years) and the folks at the DNC thought a Democrat

Southern Baptist could not win New Jersey, and there was no reason to believe that would change in 1992. But I persuaded them otherwise.

Money and resources began pouring in from the DNC by October, and the national campaign held a final preelection rally in the Meadowlands Arena on the Sunday before Election Day. I was in the front row, sitting beside the evening's main entertainer, Shania Twain. That was cool. Two days later, Bill Clinton won the presidency in an Electoral College landslide, taking 370 electoral college votes to Bush's 168 and even carrying New Jersey.

I was overjoyed for lots of reasons—I believed Clinton would be good for the country as well as the party, I felt I had made a valuable contribution to a historically significant campaign, and, for the first time, a fellow baby boomer would be in the White House. The Clinton presidency, I hoped, would mark a new beginning in American politics, and I was proud of having helped bring it about.

That sense of accomplishment and pride became even more pronounced on the night before Clinton's inauguration, when I was given a second-row seat at Barbra Streisand's concert in honor of the incoming president. At one point I took a look behind me and saw Senator Ted Kennedy two rows back. I had a better seat. Wow!

Not long afterward my secretary, Lucy McGrath, received a call from the White House—President Clinton, the caller said, wants to meet with Senator Lesniak. Lucy was pretty excited, needless to say, and called me to let me know. I quickly found a few openings in my calendar and asked Lucy to let the White House know when I was available. Lucy called back and gave a few proposed dates and times to the White House. The White House staff couldn't stop laughing. When the president wants to meet you, you're not the one who decides when or where. The person on the other end of the phone said: "Tell the senator that he will meet with the president on Friday at three o'clock in the White House."

I had met Clinton during campaign events, but this was a one-on-one coffee in a room just outside the Oval Office. The president expressed his gratitude for my help and suggested if I needed any help myself, I should contact the assistant to the president for political affairs, Rahm Emanuel, who would go on to serve as chief of staff to President Obama and then mayor of Chicago.

I didn't take full advantage of the president's offer, although I did ask that he make a personal appearance at fundraisers in my home for the Democratic Assembly candidates and for U.S. senator Bob Menendez. I also asked if I could fly on Air Force One with the president when he flew to New Jersey to greet Pope John Paul II, the great Polish-born pontiff, in 1995. About a year after the election, I secured an invitation to the first state dinner of the Clinton era, when he hosted South Korean president Kim Young-sam. I was interested in attending because my law firm was general counsel to Samsung North America, a subsidiary of the giant South Korean–based company. On the receiving line, I shook Clinton's hand and said, "Mr. President, I don't know a soul here." The president nearly burst out laughing.

With Bill Clinton in the White House and Chris Bollwage in the mayor's office in Elizabeth City Hall, I was on a roll as the next campaign season—the race for governor of New Jersey—heated up in 1993. In some ways the campaign had a familiar look, because my candidate, Governor Jim Florio, was an underdog, like Bollwage was, and was just about counted out, as Clinton was in early 1992. My job as state chair was to revive the governor's prospects and get him started on the comeback trail. It figured to be a formidable task.

Jim Florio was a well-intentioned politician who had the bad luck to become governor in the middle of a national economic downturn. The glory days of the 1980s were over when he was elected in 1989, and it was clear he was going to have to make some tough decisions about spending and taxes to keep the state solvent.

He also had the bad luck to succeed one of the most popular governors in modern New Jersey history, Tom Kean, a Republican who won his first term in 1981 by beating his Democratic opponent by fewer than two thousand votes out of two million cast. The candidate on the losing end of that heartbreaking race? Jim Florio. He missed the good times of the 1980s by fewer than two thousand votes and then won in a landslide in 1989 for the right to preside over hard times.

Florio inherited a budget deficit that became even more difficult when the state's top court ordered the legislature and governor to spend more on public schools in order to comply with the New Jersey Constitution's mandate to provide a "thorough and efficient" education for every child. While this edict caused agita in politicians who were compelled to raise taxes, it lifted our public education to the top of measurements of the quality of public education nationwide and is one of if not the most significant reason why families choose New Jersey as their residence.

Florio decided, understandably, that he would never have as much political capital as he had at the start of his tenure, after winning more than 60 percent of the vote. So he went all-in with a plan to raise taxes by $2.8 billion. That included raising the state's top income tax bracket from 3.5 percent to 7 percent, a huge increase, and hiking the state sales tax from 6 to 7 percent.

And, infamously, Florio said the sales tax would apply to a broader range of goods—and as critics quickly discovered, that included toilet paper. You could not have handed opponents a better one-liner. Yes, the governor now wants to tax toilet paper.

The Florio proposals were something less than popular. The governor won praise from liberal Democrats across the nation, and he eventually was honored with a Profiles in Courage award from the Kennedy School at Harvard University, but for those of us in the legislature who'd have to vote on it—and would be expected to support our fellow Democrat in the governor's office—the plan was a nightmare. Many of us understood that the state was in bad financial shape and that unpopular measures had to be taken. Florio definitely had the courage to face the challenge head-on rather than look for halfway measures that really wouldn't solve anything. The problem was that he simply didn't explain his plan to the people who mattered most—the voters.

Florio was elected to Congress in the Watergate-wave year of 1974. His district, which took in portions of South Jersey, was tailor-made for a Democrat, just as other districts in the state were drawn for Republicans. Like most other members of Congress, and most members of the state legislature, Florio had a safe seat and so was rarely pressed to explain or defend a vote. Safe seats and gerrymandering are the bane of reformers, and having engaged in some politicking over district lines myself, I understand the criticism. But I also know that politicians have a strong preference for safe seats and friendly district boundaries for obvious reasons. Yet those noncompetitive races can come back to haunt you: if you no longer feel you need to explain how you vote or why you supported a certain project rather than an alternative, you invariably lose touch with your bosses—the voters.

Florio was as authentic as they come. There were parts of his story I could relate to—he grew up in Brooklyn, wasn't a particularly motivated student, and without any clear path in life, he joined the Navy. Then he found himself, got his GED, went to the old Trenton State College, got his law degree from Rutgers, and set out on a career in public service. He was a street kid.

But having a safe seat can lead to complacency, and I think that's what happened with Florio. He didn't try to explain to voters why tax hikes were necessary. He reformed parts of the teachers' pension system without consulting the very powerful teachers' union, the New Jersey Education Association. He didn't get buy-in from the teachers on the tax hikes, most of which went to fund education. The result was a disaster. Groups from around the state, but particularly in the South, organized into a coalition called Hands Across New Jersey to rally against the tax hikes. Talk-show hosts at New Jersey 101.5

FM—until then a relatively minor voice in state politics—seized the issue and whipped up the protests. The NRA got involved because Florio also had the temerity to support a ban on assault weapons.

Suddenly everybody hated Jim Florio, from the teachers' union to the don't-take-away-my-gun folks (even if it's an assault weapon designed for combat). As a result, the midterm legislative elections in 1991 were a bloodbath for Democrats. We lost both houses badly—in the Senate, we were left with just twelve members in the forty-person chamber. We held our caucuses in a small room in the State House basement. That was humiliation. And that's how we felt. It was my job, as state Democratic chair, to figure out a way to get Jim Florio reelected in 1993.

My first order of business was to protect Florio from serious challenges from within the party. I had vivid memories of the last time a seemingly unpopular governor sought a second term—that was Brendan Byrne, in 1977, the year I won my first election. As mentioned earlier, Byrne faced an absolute revolt among his fellow Democrats, and it worked to his advantage. He had ten challengers, which actually helped him prevail in the primary. Had he faced a single strong challenger, he likely would have been defeated.

Remarkably, Florio probably was more unpopular in 1993 than Byrne was in 1977. Polls showed him with an 18 percent approval rating, which is pretty bad but is no longer an all-time low. That record belongs to Chris Christie, who had an approval rating of 15 percent during his last few months in office in 2017. Many readers will remember just how unpopular Christie was on his way out. That should give you an idea of how bad it was for Florio, and unlike the lame-duck Christie, Florio was about to embark on a reelection campaign.

I successfully blocked an attempt by powerful senator John Lynch to recruit George Zoffinger to run against Florio. Zoffinger was a business leader, not an elected official, but he was a former state commerce commissioner and bank president and would have been a formidable opponent. I managed to neutralize the threat from Lynch by lining up the big county Democratic chairs for Florio. Lynch quickly folded his tent and Zoffinger was no longer a threat.

Less familiar and more unpredictable was a highly publicized challenge from a very nontraditional candidate who had cofounded the anti-Florio Hands Across New Jersey movement, John Budzash, a postal worker from South Jersey.

Budzash was a political novice, but he was at the head of a powerful movement and had the support of the crowd at New Jersey 101.5, which promoted him and assailed Florio every minute of every day, or so it seemed. In a sign that state politics had truly turned upside down, Budzash had the support of the teachers' union, because it opposed Florio's changes to the teachers' pension system, and the NRA, which had one of its typical fits when Florio signed a ban on assault rifles.

Although Budzash wouldn't have defeated Florio in the Democratic primary, he would have gotten upward to 40 percent of the vote. And that would have inflicted a mortal wound to Florio's reelection campaign against Christie Todd Whitman, who was promising tax cuts and seemed to be a moderate in the mold of Tom Kean. It was up to me to try to find a way around a potentially embarrassing primary. Luckily, Budzash all but handed me the weapon I needed: an insufficient number of petitions.

Candidates need to submit a certain number of valid petition signatures from registered voters in order to qualify for the ballot. Budzash was required to have at least a thousand signatures—as a rule of thumb, experienced candidates turn in many more than required, knowing that some will be deemed invalid. Budzash turned in just 1,140 signatures. He was, after all, an amateur. It was clear to me that he didn't have enough valid signatures, so I filed a lawsuit, *Lesniak v. Budzash*, seeking to have Budzash disqualified.

My legal challenge was not without controversy within Florio's inner circle. Some advisers thought it looked petty of us to knock this neophyte off the ballot. I asked, "How will it look if Budzash gets 40 percent of the vote?" My point was made. Florio, who was in the room, looked at me and said, "You'd better win." "I will," I replied. The New Jersey Supreme Court determined that 279 of those who signed the petitions were not registered voters, that 108 of the signatories were registered Republicans, and that 409 were unaffiliated voters, not registered Democrats as the rules require. Budzash's candidacy came to a crashing end.

I also had a hand in stopping a Republican effort to repeal Florio's assault weapon ban. Thanks to their victories in the midterm elections of 1991, Republicans had veto-proof majorities in both the Assembly and Senate, and they used their new muscle to pass repeal legislation, to the delight of the NRA. Florio vetoed the legislation, but the Assembly voted to override it. Now it was up to the Senate, where there were just a dozen Democrats left. Before we voted, I commissioned a dramatic mailing that I hoped would turn public opinion in our favor. The mailing, which went out to hundreds of thousands of New Jersey voters in Republican districts, showed an assault weapon pointed at the recipient and a postage-paid tear-off that recipients could mail to their Republican senators urging them to sustain Florio's veto. The senators were inundated with the tear-offs.

The override vote, which had seemed like a cinch, wound up failing dramatically. Twenty-six senators, well more than half of the chamber's forty members, voted to sustain the veto, nowhere near the two-thirds required to override. Fifteen Republican senators who had originally voted for the bill changed their minds. That's an effective mailer. It went on to win a Pollie Award from the American Association of Political Consultants given for the most effective political mailers of the year. With that achieved, it was time to focus on raising Jim Florio from the political dead. I hired the newest star in the political consulting business, James Carville, who first came to national attention when he guided Democrat Harris Wofford to victory over Richard Thornburgh in a U.S. Senate race in Pennsylvania. He then, of course, became a household name for his role in helping to elect Bill Clinton as president in 1992. Carville brought with him a younger colleague, David Plouffe, who coordinated the campaign with our congressional candidates. Plouffe went on to be Barack Obama's presidential campaign manager. Both Carville and Plouffe were terrific to work with and, obviously, very bright. Not surprisingly, though, it was Carville who was the dominant figure given his personality, his media exposure, and his record. I often found myself on the receiving end of a rambling, hours-long "talk" with Carville, but inevitably came away with a gem of advice or two. He advised me to be flexible in my campaign plan, advice Donald Trump should have used when the coronavirus hit during the 2020 campaign. He continued to rely on his campaign plan to stress the economy and, as a result, downplayed the pandemic. Big mistake. In my opinion, it cost him his reelection (thank God).

There was no such melodrama in the general election, but there was drama, something few would have expected only a few months earlier. Florio began picking up momentum as voters reconsidered his actions and began to conclude that while his tax hikes may not have been well executed, they were a brave attempt to solve the state's fiscal woes. His ban on assault weapons was also seen as brave, taking on the powerful NRA. Whitman, on the other hand, went around promising to cut taxes by 33 percent. That was about the extent of her platform, and some people were beginning to realize that beyond a tax cut, she had nothing else to say. In the end, Jim Florio lost his bid for reelection, but by only 26,000 votes out of more than 2.4 million cast.

His approval rating by Election Day had shot up to 50 percent, an almost incredible feat.

Immediately after the election, Whitman's campaign manager, Ed Rollins, who had served as national campaign director for Ronald Reagan's two victorious presidential runs, bragged on national television that Whitman won because her campaign had suppressed the Black vote by, in essence, paying off African American ministers. He said: "We went into the Black churches and basically said to ministers who had endorsed Florio: 'Do you have a special project? We see you have already endorsed Florio. That's fine. But don't get up in the Sunday pulpit and say it's your moral obligation to vote on Tuesday, to vote for Jim Florio.'"

Suddenly the race for governor of New Jersey was national news. Whitman hit the ceiling, insisting it never happened. Democrats in New Jersey were equally angry, but for different reasons. They believed Rollins.

I immediately filed suit in federal district court to overturn the election. That wasn't an easy decision because it meant that I, as state Democratic chair, had to allege that African American ministers accepted bribes from Whitman's campaign to suppress the vote, so I hired Ted Wells, a prominent African American attorney, to handle the case.

The governor-elect was furious. At some point during the transition, she met with Florio and asked him to step in and exert some control over his state party chair. Florio was amused. "Control Lesniak?" he asked. "Good luck."

And so I filed a lawsuit in the federal district court. We brought in Rollins for a deposition in late November, and the national press corps was out in full. A couple of intrepid reporters, hoping for an exclusive, slipped notes for scoops under the door where we were interrogating Rollins. I ignored them. Rollins, under oath, said he made up the whole story. It never happened, he said. He had ruined his career and there were times, he said, that he wanted to put "a gun to my head." We tried to get him off that story, but he stuck to it. He took full responsibility for telling a lie, he said. He had been irresponsible. He had no excuses. We hammered away to no avail. There was no smoking gun to be had.

During a break in the proceedings I paid a visit to the men's room, and there was Rollins straddling an adjacent urinal. It was very awkward to say the least. Rollins tried to break the tension. "You're a tough adversary," he said. I replied, "But we can't break you." Despite tough questioning by attorney Jerry Krovatin from Ted Wells's firm, Rollins stuck to his story that he made it all up. We were both right. I was a tough adversary but couldn't break Rollins.

The case was dismissed, although the larger issue of voter suppression remains very much a part of American political life.

My experience with voter suppression, true or not with Rollins, led me to champion legislation that is at the heart of battles between Democrats and Republicans to this very day—making it easier for our citizens to participate in our democracy. On June 30, 2009, Governor Corzine signed my legislation making everyone eligible to vote by mail, not just those with disabilities or those who will be out of state on Election Day. Little did I know that voting by mail would be the controversy it would become during the Trump-Biden presidential campaign.

Taking it one step further, on January 12, 2010, I introduced same-day voter registration, but Governor Christie was in office so it went nowhere. If we are to pride ourselves as the world's greatest democracy, we need to have greater voter participation. The United States has a lower percentage of voter partici-pation than twenty-five other countries, as diverse as South Korea, Hungry, Mexico, and Spain. Voting by mail and same-day voter registration will go far to boost our democracy. The Republican Party has been going out of its way to depress voter turnout, closing polling locations in minority neighbor-hoods and in some places basically making people vote in person at the height of the COVID-19 pandemic. They would be better off supporting pub-lic policies that give citizens a reason to vote.

I didn't seek reelection as state chair after Florio's defeat. It seemed like the right time to step back from running the party so I could devote more time and energy to policy making in the Senate. However, I did manage to find time to further my relationship with Bill Clinton through the 1990s. It's always nice to have a friend in the White House. There's nothing in politics quite like getting a phone call and hearing a voice say, "Please hold for the president."

One of those opportunities came on October 4, 1995, when Pope John Paul II flew into Newark Airport to say Mass in the city's Sacred Heart Cathe-dral (which he was about to designate as a basilica, an honor given to few churches by a pope). The president and his entourage were going to fly in Newark aboard Air Force One so they could be on the tarmac to greet the pope when he arrived by plane. I was invited to be part of the greeting party. I live ten minutes from Newark airport. I could have met the president there once he landed and joined the welcoming party waiting for the pope. But I wanted to be on the president's plane when it landed in Newark and among the dignitaries who emerged from Air Force One and accompanied the presi-dent down the stairs to the tarmac. I drove from my home in Elizabeth to Penn Station in Newark, took a train to Washington, D.C., and then a cab to the White House, all so I could board a plane to fly back to Newark. There may be some kind of Polish joke to be made about my convoluted journey, but for me it was all worth it.

I sat with the president and his other special guests—Ray Flynn, the U.S. ambassador to the Vatican, and Tim Wirth, an undersecretary of state—for the short flight. At one point Clinton became self-conscious about the tie he was wearing. It had bright colors. He asked us if it was too loud for such an occasion. It was, and we all knew it. But we left it to Flynn, the former mayor of Boston and a consummate Irish American politician, to come up with a discreet answer. He was, after all, a diplomat. "It's not one I would have chosen, Mr. President," Flynn said. We all nodded our heads in agreement. Clinton called his staff, who brought a box of ties, and he chose one with subdued colors. We all nodded in agreement. When I walked off the back of the plane, I was in seventh heaven. (Only the president and the first lady walk off the front, something that later miffed House Speaker Newt Gingrich when he was not allowed to walk out at the front of the plane with the president.) To think this young man from the streets of Elizabeth who grew up with Polish lineage was with the president to greet the first Polish pope on his visit to the United States. It was an experience I could not have imagined just a few years beforehand.

The president and I continued to keep in touch throughout his first term, especially after Republicans took control of the House in 1994 thanks to Gingrich's Contract with America campaign. That didn't bode well for Clinton's reelection in 1996. So he turned to New Jersey to hold his first reelection fundraiser, which I took as a sign of his appreciation for what we had done in 1992 and how we could be of help in 1996. I was by now a certified Friend of Bill, a nickname for those who were both political and personal friends of President Clinton, and was often invited to the White House for social occasions with other key supporters. The tables were turned at one point when the president would come to visit me in my house in Elizabeth for fundraisers I hosted for other officeholders. At one point Clinton was asked why he came to New Jersey to raise money for local campaigns. "Because Ray Lesniak asked me to," Clinton said. "That's why." We bonded over politics, but that eventually spilled over into another mutual passion, golf, which is a great way to enjoy competition and the comradeship that comes with it. We decided we ought to get together for a round not long after he left office.

I'm a member at Suburban Golf Club in Union Township, just down Morris Avenue from my home in Elizabeth, but I thought Clinton might enjoy playing at one of the world's premier courses, Baltusrol in nearby Springfield, which has played host to several U.S. Open and PGA Tour championships. I called a friend, George Ring, another big fundraiser for Clinton and a member of Baltusrol, and asked if he would be able to join Clinton and myself and make the necessary arrangements to play at the legendary club. Ring called back to say that it would not be possible. The day Clinton was in town happened to be a members-only day at Baltusrol. Even a former president would not be welcome. I kid you not.

We are not so picky at Suburban, a hidden gem of a club, so I was able to arrange a tee time there. It turned out for the best, as Clinton and everyone at the club had a great time. He took pictures with everyone—caddies, groundskeepers, waitresses. He left after purchasing two armfuls of mementoes from the club.

Clinton was a little tired when he arrived, for he had just gotten back from a European trip. A staff member told me that Clinton probably wouldn't make it through all eighteen holes because he was exhausted. Well, perhaps he was, but he didn't show it. Some political figures (and others who live public lives, like actors) find another level of energy when they're with other people. Donald Trump wasn't the first president to feed off the energy of adoring fans. With the exception of introverts like Richard Nixon, they all do. Trump just took it to an extreme, as he did with everything else.

When we got to our golf cart, Clinton immediately swung into the driver's seat. "You don't mind if I drive, do you, Ray?" he asked. There could be only one answer, "No, Mr. President, I don't mind." As we finished the ninth hole and headed back toward the clubhouse, I was prepared to hear Clinton say he was done. But he said nothing of the kind. We drove over to the tenth tee near the clubhouse and soon found ourselves in a conversation with a few other members, all of whom wanted a word with the former president. One member in particular was intent on asking Clinton about the peace process in Northern Ireland, which the former president had done so much to achieve. I tugged at Clinton's arm, trying to get him away from the crowd, but he brushed me off and continued to engage in conversation. He was articulate and intelligent, and more than anything else, he listened to my fellow members of Suburban. There's a reason the man left office more popular than he was when he started, even though he had been impeached. A remarkably talented and caring person.

In the spirit of the golfer's code of honor, I should be sworn to secrecy about the president's game (and my own), but Clinton would have none of that. I have a framed scorecard from that day, signed by Bill Clinton. He wrote:

"To Ray: You beat me." I did. And I had to grind out a one-stroke victory to do it. I have said I am a competitor, haven't I?

Speaking of presidents and golf, I played with my friend Mike Scierra and the Donald at his club in West Palm Beach, Florida, some years ago. Trump is a better golfer than Clinton, but not nearly as good as he thinks and says he is. After the round, Scierra and I had lunch in the clubhouse, and we both ordered clam chowder. Trump came by and said, "Look at that clam chowder. We have more clams in our clam chowder than any restaurant in the world." I kid you not.

More than twenty years into the twenty-first century, it's hard to think of New Jersey as a hospitable place for Republicans. Never mind Chris Christie's two terms as governor—they were the exception to the all-Democratic rule in the Garden State these days. But not so long ago—the late 1990s to be exact—New Jersey Republicans were riding high. Christie Whitman was governor, the legislature had Republican majorities, and the GOP was well represented in the state's congressional delegation. Democrats weren't exactly a vanishing species, but it's fair to say we were a little demoralized and were looking to revive our fortunes. One of the state's U.S. Senate seats was up for grabs in 2000 as longtime incumbent Frank Lautenberg announced he wouldn't seek a fourth term. (Later, it turned out he wasn't quite done with the Senate after all. Lautenberg replaced Bob Torricelli as a candidate for senator just before the election in 2002 because Torricelli was mired in a political scandal.) The state's Republicans hadn't elected a U.S. senator since Clifford Case's final reelection in 1972, so they were chomping at the bit for a chance to break that losing streak. Many people expected Whitman to run for the seat since her second and final term would expire in 2001.

I was no longer state chair, but I still was a force in Democratic politics because of my fundraising abilities and my connections. There weren't too many other state senators who could get the president of the United States to an intimate fundraiser for local candidates at their home. In fact, there was only one, and that would be me. Given that Republicans would have a big fundraising edge because they controlled all of state government, I was looking for a candidate who would be able to self-finance, at least in a substantial part. And I wasn't shy about saying so. One day Rahway mayor Jim Kennedy asked me who I thought we would run to replace Lautenberg. "Some rich guy from Wall Street," I replied. "What's his name?" Kennedy asked. "I don't know," I said. "I haven't found him yet." My quest would soon be fulfilled.

Torricelli introduced me to a Summit resident who was interested in running for the Lautenberg seat. His name was Jon Corzine, and he had recently been forced out as chairman of Goldman Sachs. When the company went public not long after he left, he made a tidy four hundred million to go along with the millions he already had. Corzine was not exactly a candidate from central casting. He was soft-spoken and introverted. He had no background in retail politics. He was from Illinois and seemed very much the midwesterner even after years in the grittier, scrappier Northeast. And he had a beard. It was a handsome beard, as beards go. But conventional wisdom and polling suggested that facial hair on politicians went out of style in the late nineteenth century.

Still, Corzine's background as the head of a well-known Wall Street firm and his willingness to part with a portion of his wealth made him an attractive possibility. He clearly was aligned with Democratic positions on social justice, on government's role as a regulator to protect health and safety, and even on issues of income inequality, a rarity on Wall Street. I was impressed. But I still wasn't so sure about the beard.

Two developments shook up the race: Whitman decided not to run after all and became head of the Environmental Protection Agency under President George W. Bush, so the eventual Republican nominee was longtime House member Bob Franks, a good candidate but not exactly a household name. And then Jim Florio announced that he would seek the Democratic nomination. Even though I had worked hard for Florio as state chair and admired his toughness, I thought this was a mistake. He'd inevitably be on the defensive about his tax increases at a time when Democrats were trying to get away from our image as the party of taxes. We wanted to put the toilet paper tax in our rear-view mirror. A new Florio candidacy would put the issue front and center, even if it had nothing to do with U.S. Senate business.

So I got behind Corzine and prepared for a primary fight against Florio. Corzine got some of the best talent money could buy. He brought on legendary political consultant Bob Shrum, pollster Joel Benenson, who would later work for Barack Obama and Hillary Clinton, and local political whiz Steve DeMicco. We came together for the first time at the prestigious Manhattan Club to plot out our campaign against Florio. Before we sat down with the candidate, the others pulled me aside for a private talk in the men's room. They had done a poll that showed Corzine, who was utterly unknown in New Jersey, had no chance of beating the better-known Florio. In some ways, my work in rebuilding Florio's reputation during the 1991 campaign against Whitman was coming back to bite me. Florio was now much more popular than he had been during the depths of the tax revolt. Shrum, Benenson, and DeMicco were going to show Corzine the poll, and they asked me to support them in their recommendation that he not run.

So we sat down with Corzine to deliver the less-than-inspiring news, and we held our tongues when we realized that Corzine was more familiar with New York politics than New Jersey's. He thought his primary against Florio would be held in September as in New York, not in our June primary election. After absorbing the bad news about the poll, Corzine turned to me and asked for my opinion. I chose not to simply repeat what the consultants already said. I told him I wanted to see the poll myself before offering an opinion, which I said I'd do the following morning. The meeting broke up inconclusively—it wasn't a particularly auspicious beginning, to say the least. I brought the poll home with me and looked over its findings. There was a big flaw, in my view, in how it presented Corzine. It portrayed him as a rags-to-riches businessman, trying to draw a contrast with Florio, a lifetime politician. I felt that wasn't the issue to push. Instead, Corzine should be cast as the candidate of big, progressive ideas with the determination to turn those ideas into reality. I learned from Bill Clinton that successful campaigns talk about the future, not the past. That's how I thought Corzine could win. I told Corzine exactly what I was thinking and that he ought to commission a new poll, which, I added, would cost him sixty thousand dollars. He didn't hesitate. The new poll, repositioning Corzine as a bold liberal, had him beating Florio, recast as a candidate of the past. Those findings helped us reframe the campaign, and Corzine went on to win the nomination by sixteen points.

The party came together for the general election, and it certainly didn't hurt that Corzine was not afraid to spend money. He would eventually part with sixty-two million of his own money, making the campaign the most expensive Senate race in the nation's history at that point.

During the campaign against Franks, Corzine's campaign manager, Steven Goldstein, the legendary fighter for LGBTQ rights in New Jersey, asked me to speak to Corzine about changing his opposition to the death penalty. His position wasn't polling well, and while it wasn't a Senate issue per se, it was one of those emotional wedge issues that can determine a close election. Goldstein himself opposed the death penalty, but as Corzine's campaign manager, his job was to win, and he felt the death penalty was making his job much more difficult. By that time I too opposed the death penalty, but as part of the campaign team, I felt obliged to bring up the topic with Corzine. He wouldn't hear of it. "Ray, I'm not changing my position against the death penalty just to get elected to the U.S. Senate," he said. I admired that. I also felt the need to offer some unsolicited advice on a less controversial subject. I told Corzine to shave his beard. We learned from focus groups that people weren't keen on facial hair—maybe they associated beards with radicals or artists, not that there's anything wrong with artists. It's just that they weren't considered to be good candidates for governor. Once again, Corzine said he wasn't going to change just to win an election. He was who he was, he said. I had to admire that also, even if I didn't agree and feared that he was hurting his chances.

It turned out Corzine was right. The beard made him look professorial, in contrast to Franks, a lifelong politician. In the end, I think the beard had something to do with his margin of victory, which was only 3 percent. Only Jon Corzine, beard and all, could have won that race in 2000. And that victory would have repercussions in New Jersey politics in the years to come.

5 · WORKING TOGETHER

The nation's capital has been in the grip of partisan gridlock for a generation. That's no secret. Long gone are the days when President Ronald Reagan, a Republican, and House Speaker Tip O'Neill, a Democrat, were able to put aside their differences and enjoy each other's company when the business day was done.

That didn't mean they weren't partisan or that they were anything less than aggressive in pursuing their policy goals, which were diametrically opposed. In fact, early on in the Reagan years, O'Neill said in a television interview that the president had "no regard" for the "little man." Reagan, who was famously even-tempered in public, lashed out at the speaker, accusing him of "sheer demagoguery." Back in 1981, those were fighting words, and Reagan called O'Neill to apologize. O'Neill wasn't offended. "Old buddy," he said, "that's politics—after six o'clock we can be friends, but before six it's politics." Can you imagine a conversation like that between Donald Trump and Nancy Pelosi? It would have been more likely for Trump to start a "lock her up" chant at a rally.

While local politics has taken on some of the toxicity we've seen in Washington since the 1990s and the emergence of Newt Gingrich's us-against-them extremism, for the most part Trenton remains a place where Democrats and Republicans can find common ground. Indeed, sometimes it's more difficult for Democrats to find common ground among themselves. It's true that earlier in my career there seemed to be more of an emphasis on solving problems than in scoring political points, but still, compared to Congress, New Jersey's legislature is more willing to come together for the sake of the common good. It's also a place where the whole idea of partisanship can be stood on its head: I've seen Democrats turn on other Democrats. In fact, a fellow

Democrat who happened to be one of my best friends turned on me in the most dramatic way possible. More about that in a bit.

I don't make a secret that some of my best friends are Republicans. And some of the most contentious debates I've seen through the years were between various factions of the Democratic Party during Brendan Byrne's two terms, when we controlled both houses of the legislature. I was on both sides of that intraparty battle, fighting the party establishment over congressional redistricting but supporting the governor on Pinelands protection. The idea that one-party government leads to unchecked power and unanimous consent on just about anything is just not true. While it seems that way in the abstract, in the real world, one-party control can be just as bitter and confrontational as divided government. Byrne, for example, had huge difficulties getting his fellow Democrats in the legislature to support his income tax bill and the Pinelands Protection Act. The governor, who had a keen and sometimes biting wit, told me privately that the bigger the Democratic majority in both houses, the more difficult it is to get things done.

I wasn't in the legislature for the income tax debate, but from what I've gathered, getting the Pinelands Protection Act passed was even more contentious than the income tax issue because it limited the development rights of property owners, thereby reducing property values. South Jersey Democrats were furious over what they saw as a Trenton power grab. Local control has always been a big deal in New Jersey. To take a recent example, homeowners on Long Beach Island whose properties were flooded during Superstorm Sandy went to court to prevent the state from constructing dunes that would protect the island from flooding because they obstructed their view of the ocean from ground level. Thankfully for the inland residents whose properties were also flooded, the shoreline property owners lost. In an effort to ease some of the concerns about the Pinelands, I sponsored legislation establishing the Pinelands Development Credit Bank, which granted development credits to property owners. It allowed them to transfer for value their prior development rights to growth zones in the Pinelands to ease the Pinelands Protection Act's economic impact.

The best years of bipartisan cooperation during my career were during Tom Kean's eight years as governor, from 1982 to 1990. I had a few contentious moments with Kean, but we were able to resolve them amicably. One would think we had nothing in common. Kean was a descendant of one of New Jersey's first families, a genuine, blue-blooded American aristocrat with an accent that was not exactly Jersey. I was a second-generation Polish American whose grandparents came through Ellis Island and were working-class folks.

But Kean never flaunted his privileged upbringing and never talked down to those of us in the legislature. In fact, during his State of the State messages, he took great pains to name individual legislators—Democrats and Republicans alike—and give them credit for many of the achievements he touted. That was in stark contrast to a later governor and fellow resident of Livingston who, ironically, claimed that Kean helped inspire him to a life in politics, Chris Christie, who rarely gave anyone credit, which helps explain why nobody offered him a helping hand when he was floundering during his second gubernatorial term or his campaign for the Republican nomination for president. During his keynote speech at the 2012 Republican National Convention, Christie famously talked more about himself than the party's nominee, Mitt Romney. No one in New Jersey was surprised.

Knowing how and when to flatter, sweet talk, and, if necessary, berate your colleagues in government is part of the art of governance. President Clinton was a master of all. I overheard Clinton on his cell phone speaking with a Democratic congressman during the debate over the North American Free Trade Act (NAFTA). Clinton was incensed as the congressman was trying to explain his commitment to Richard Gephardt, House majority leader, who opposed NAFTA. "Next time you want something, ask f****n Gephardt," Clinton yelled and hung up.

Kean was definitely a specialist in the art of governance. I think there's little question that his eight years in office were the age of enlightenment for environmental protection in New Jersey. He made that priority clear in his inaugural address, declaring that "our children and grandchildren deserve the right to live and work in this state free from the fears of poisons in their air, water and earth." As chair of the Assembly Environmental Protection Committee, I found him to be good to his word. Despite our partisan differences, I worked closely with Kean's commissioner of the Department of Environmental Protection, Bob Hughey. His agency initiated the concept of the Environmental Cleanup Responsibility Act (ECRA), which I sponsored, the most significant environmental protection law in any state in the country at the time. It had the support of Democrats and Republicans alike, thanks to the cooperative way Kean approached the issue as he worked with both parties. That cooperative bipartisan effort was necessary to overcome intense opposition from the business community.

On the other hand, I sometimes found legislators in my own party unwilling to take on these kinds of issues because of their own parochial concerns. My effort to pass the Safe Drinking Water Act in the mid-1980s ran into opposition from Senate president Carmen Orechio, a fellow Democrat who also was chairman of the North Jersey District Water Supply Commission. He seemed to be more concerned about possible rate increases to pay for removing toxic chemicals than providing consumers with safe drinking water. I called my friends in the environmental movement, and they mobilized their allies across the state, bombarding Senate offices with phone calls.

Orechio bowed to public pressure and the bill passed the Senate, but he was not happy about it. He took me aside and asked if I had been behind all the calls. "Not at all," I fibbed. I don't know whether or not he believed me. What mattered is the bill passed both Houses and Kean signed it into law, marking another bipartisan victory for New Jersey's environment.

Governor Kean and I definitely shared an interest in repairing New Jersey's image as an environmental dumping ground. But that important cooperation didn't always extend to political considerations, as opposed to public policy. We had a falling out early in his administration when I used an unwritten political rule known as senatorial courtesy to block Kean's appointments that required Senate approval. I needed to keep a promise to my mentor, Ma Green, and Kean was standing in the way. This is how politics works—or, as some would say, shouldn't work.

In New Jersey, any state senator can block a gubernatorial nominee requiring Senate approval if the nominee lives in the senator's county. You don't even have to explain why. It sounds wrong, but this unwritten rule helps balance the immense power vested in the governor's office.

Ma Green had asked me on her deathbed to get John Pisansky, an attorney of Polish heritage, appointed to the superior court. It's a gubernatorial appointment, and Kean objected to Pisansky's nomination. So I in turn exercised senatorial courtesy over all his nominees who lived in Union County. As the standoff dragged on, I went to see Kean's chief counsel, Gary Edwards, in his office in the State House. I had in my hand a list of Kean's stalled nominees, and with a flourish I tossed the list into his wastebasket. "I'll sign off on them only when the governor appoints Pisansky to the bench," I said. Kean was incensed and issued a press release attacking me as "the king of senatorial courtesy." I guess he thought that was an insult, but to me, all I was doing was using the rules to fulfill a deathbed wish of the person to whom I owed much of my political success. My battle with Kean made headlines in the *Star-Ledger*, New Jersey's largest newspaper. This all unfolded right before a reelection campaign, so having an immensely popular governor criticizing me at such a moment wasn't the best politics. But that didn't matter to me. Ma Green made me promise to make Pisansky a judge, and that was all that mattered. Kean finally asked to see me in an effort to break the deadlock. He had a solution: he said he couldn't appoint Pisansky to the bench while I was holding his nominees hostage. That simply wouldn't look or be good. So he proposed a face-saving deal: if I signed off on his appointments, he would eventually do right by me. I trusted him. And for his part, he knew that he had given his word.

So we did a deal, not as Democrats and Republicans but as two human beings who were willing to look each other in the eye and pledge our word. These kinds of deals almost seem impossible these days because nobody trusts anybody and because two people from different parties rarely get the chance to sit in the same room and figure out a compromise, even sometimes two from the same party. I didn't consider Tom Kean an enemy to be crushed and humiliated, and he felt the same way about me. That's how politics gets done—when it gets done. Kean and I crafted another deal, again based on trust, when I intervened on behalf of an old friend, colleague, and supporter, John Gregorio, my predecessor in the Senate and the former mayor of Linden. Gregorio had been convicted of hiding income from a Linden go-go bar operated by his son. He had to resign from the Senate and the mayoralty, and under terms of the conviction, he was prohibited from holding public office again. He made a mistake, no question about it. But I thought the prohibition against holding office again was too much. His transgressions didn't touch the office of mayor. Gregorio loved his city, and the city loved him despite his run-in with the law.

Gregorio was another of the many Damon Runyon–type figures in New Jersey politics. When a reporter questioned him about nepotism in Linden City Hall, he proudly replied, "In Linden, if you're kin, you're in." As mayor, Gregorio raised money to help Linden residents in dire straits. Often he took money out of his own pocket to help. My friends didn't think I should intervene on Gregorio's behalf because they were convinced he would want his old Senate seat back—the one I now occupied. I told them that would never happen. So I went to Kean's office as he was on his way out in late 1989 with an offer: a pardon for Gregorio in exchange for my approval of a last-minute appointment he wanted to make for his longtime secretary, an appointment I could have blocked using senatorial courtesy. We struck the deal in the final hours of the Kean administration. Kean pardoned Gregorio just before midnight his last day in office, allowing him to be reelected mayor of Linden several months later, holding the job for another sixteen years. And he never did run against me for the Senate. There are politicians who can be trusted to do the right thing. Oh, and of course, I signed off on the appointment for his secretary.

Kean was succeeded by Jim Florio, who had the same contentious relationship with his Democratic-controlled legislature as Byrne did. Then again,
that was to be expected given that Florio, like Byrne, sought a bold and unpopular solution to the state's financial problems. For Byrne, it was the income
tax. For Florio, it was the infamous $2.8 billion tax hike, which included
increases in the income and sales taxes. The difference was that Byrne managed to hold on and win a second term, while Florio did not. But what's forgotten is just how close Florio came to pulling off a Byrne-like miracle in 1993.
The lesson of Florio's failed reelection is not that you can't support unpopular
positions. It's that you have to lay the groundwork and build support, however grudgingly, for unpopular positions. In Byrne's case, it certainly helped
that the state's Supreme Court ordered the schools closed until they were
properly funded—that sent a loud and clear message to voters.

Florio's defeat led to Christie Whitman's election and a Republican surge
in New Jersey. And given that I led a legal challenge against her election because
of the Ed Rollins episode, I didn't expect a good deal of interaction with the
new governor. My instincts were correct. Nevertheless, Whitman signed one
of my most significant initiatives, a bill providing tax increment financing
needed to get the Jersey Gardens Mall constructed. The mall has the most
visitors from out of state of any attraction in New Jersey and has generated
millions of tax revenues for the city of Elizabeth and state of New Jersey and
thousands of jobs. Getting that done, however, required all the political skills,
personal relationships, and influence I could muster.

The mall was built on what was an abandoned toxic garbage dump. Its
location adjacent to the Turnpike and Newark Airport made it an attractive
site for retailers big and small, but first it required intensive remediation of
contamination and needed a discharge permit from the Joint Meeting of
Essex and Union counties, a wastewater treatment facility. The developer,
Peter Aggar, applied for a discharge permit to clean up the contamination on
the site, but the Joint Meeting's executive director, Michael Brinker, denied it
because the facility was reserving capacity for its suburban Essex County
towns of Maplewood and Millburn, both Republican towns at the time.
(Maplewood is now solidly Democratic.) The Board of Trustees of the Joint
Meeting was dominated by members from Democratic towns, so I went over
Brinker's head, making the case for Aggar's permit directly to the board.
Brinker flipped out and cursed at me. Not a very diplomatic move. At my
insistence, the board fired Brinker and replaced him with my choice, Brian
Christensen, who had been executive director of the Passaic Valley Sewer
Commission. The discharge permit was issued in short order. A friend, Tony

Sartor, principal of a large engineering firm, PS&S, hired Brinker at my request to ease the transition and give Brinker a soft landing. A good life lesson—don't ask anyone to do what they feel uncomfortable doing, unless you can give them a reason that satisfies their conscience. Getting Brinker another job made the decision to replace him easier on the board members.

There was one other obstacle in the way, and it was a considerable one: the project cost was $260 million. Raising that kind of money required not only some legislative creativity but also powerful allies from across the aisle. Fortunately, I had a friend in Republican Senate president Don DiFrancesco, who also represented a piece of Union County. Obviously I was not plugged into the Whitman administration, but DiFrancesco was (and he would eventually succeed her as governor when she resigned to become EPA administrator in 2001). He and I sponsored legislation to finance the cleanup—the city of Elizabeth would pledge the future mall's incremental increases in property taxes as security for financing the cleanup, a practice known as tax increment financing.

Whitman signed the bill, and the mall—with this creative legislative tool to finance its cleanup costs—was eventually developed by the Glimcher Company. For the want of a discharge permit, however, it could not have been built. And but for my cross-party friendship with DiFrancesco, it wouldn't have gotten the financing needed to get it built.

Years later, when it seemed as though DiFrancesco would run for governor against another friend of mine, Jim McGreevey, State House insiders came up with a running gag. Who would win a race between DiFrancesco and McGreevey, they asked. Answer: Ray Lesniak. If you're looking to get things done instead of simply scoring partisan points, the bridges you build can benefit not only you politically, but more importantly your constituents and the entire state. Indeed, Joe Biden was criticized early on in his 2020 presidential campaign for speaking highly of fellow Republican senators. Civility is an effective means of getting things done, as well as an admirable trait for life in general. I once publicly had kind words to say about Joe Kyrillos, a Republican state senator who sat on the Economic Development Committee I chaired while he was running for the U.S. Senate against incumbent Bob Menendez, a fellow Democrat, in 2012. Menendez noticed. He called and said, "Look, I know the two of you are friends, but can you wait to say nice things about him until *after* the election?" Fair enough. Menendez won in a landslide but was taking nothing for granted.

Unlike my old nemesis from Elizabeth, Tom Dunn, I've never crossed party lines to endorse a Republican, even one I got along with, like Kyrillos.

I'm a Democrat and I believe in my party's principles. But I've tried not to let partisanship stand in the way of cooperation with Republican officeholders.

My friendship with DiFrancesco again came in handy after he succeeded Whitman as governor in 2001. I was looking to secure commutation of a sentence handed down to my friend, Saul Leighton, owner of Bayway World of Liquors, after he pled guilty to a kickback scheme. Saul and I were close friends. When I was named "Man of the Year" by the Jewish National Fund in the early 1990s, Saul served as chairman of the awards ceremony. The following year Saul was "Man of the Year," and I was his awards ceremony chairman. We went on a mission to Israel together to help preserve its water supplies.

Saul got in trouble for taking kickbacks from distributors and entered a guilty plea in 1996. His business partner, Harry Hammer, kept copious notes about the kickbacks in a notebook he kept on the premises. Law enforcement seized the notebook during a raid on the store, and that was all the evidence the prosecution really needed. Stupid, stupid, stupid. Bayway World of Liquors was and is the second largest retail liquor store in the country. Its location near the Goethals Bridge in Elizabeth attracts huge business from Staten Island and elsewhere in New York in addition to its New Jersey customers. It remains an important business in Elizabeth. Saul and Harry paid a two-million-dollar fine and were lifetime barred from working in the liquor industry under the terms of their sentence. I saw that Saul and Harry were victims of a stupid, anticompetitive law that I later changed. Alcohol was not allowed to be sold by distributors below a price floor. It was a vestige of post-Prohibition years. So owners of liquor stores regularly would get kickbacks from distributors, effectively lowering the price for consumers. Saul and Harry got caught, and so did others in the industry, including Matty Feldman, a former Senate president. Harry left the industry, but Saul wanted back in and deserved to be able to return. He paid a hefty price for violating an outdated law that hurt consumers.

Will Rogers, the political humorist of a century ago, famously said that he was not a member of an organized political party. He was a Democrat. There were times when I knew exactly what he meant, and what's amazing is that his joke remains timely all these years later.

You'd think that the election of a Democratic governor and a majority Democratic legislature would lead to a disciplined, coordinated agenda and a relative consensus on legislative and policy priorities. Wrong! Jon Corzine's difficult single term as governor once again showed that partisanship is a lot more complicated than many realize, at least when you're dealing with a party that contains multitudes, to borrow a phrase from a former resident of Camden, Walt Whitman.

Corzine didn't help himself in forming his administration. When I recommended Hudson County freeholder Bill O'Dea, a brilliant mind and expert in economic development as chief of staff, Corzine said he didn't want anyone with institutional ties to a party organization. Yikes! So he brought in a Goldman Sachs ally, Bradley Abelow, a nice, smart man who had no governmental experience and no institutional ties. Not an auspicious beginning.

Corzine, who was elected governor in 2005 after serving less than a full term in the U.S. Senate, probably had an even more difficult time than Brendan Byrne did with his Democratic colleagues in the legislature. There were several factors at play during those years. First of all, Corzine was no Brendan Byrne, in the sense that Byrne was a professional politician, and I use that phrase in the best way possible. He had spent his life in and around government, while Corzine was a well-meaning amateur whose career had been spent in the private sector. As the chief financial officer and senior partner at Goldman Sachs, Corzine didn't have to negotiate with the private-sector equivalent of legislative leaders—and, more to the point, treat them as coequals. The inevitable tug of war between the executive and legislative branches was new to Corzine as it would be for any other business leader with no political experience, as it was when we elected a president with no such experience in 2016.

Second, the Democratic Party in New Jersey and elsewhere is no more organized than it was in Will Rogers's time, and that's actually a good thing. The party is diverse, perhaps not diverse enough for some, but it is so much more diverse than it was during the Byrne years. That diversity brings strength, but it also makes it difficult at times to coalesce around a bill, an idea, or even a candidate. On the other hand, the Republican Party, both locally and nationally, is more of a monolith, no doubt because it simply is not as diverse as the Democrats. And not coincidentally, Republicans seem to have a much easier time putting aside their differences and rallying behind their party's leader. Look how the GOP got behind Donald Trump, even after he insulted and defamed John McCain, the Bush family, Marco Rubio, Ted Cruz, and so many other Republicans, even after he lost reelection! It's hard to imagine how Trump, the ultimate amateur in politics, and Mitch McConnell, a lifelong politician, understood each other. But these two older white men figured out how to get along with each other.

Meanwhile, with Corzine as governor and solid Democratic majorities in both houses, we managed to force a government shutdown—the first in state history—in 2006, less than a year into Corzine's term. The dispute was over a tax hike, as usual. The state faced a $4.5 billion deficit and Corzine proposed, among other measures, an increase in the state sales tax from 6 percent to 7 percent. Some of us who remembered how Jim Florio's tax hike was simplified, ingeniously, into a "toilet paper tax" were concerned about the governor's plan, and there was an outright rebellion in the Assembly, led by Speaker Joe Roberts. When the Democratic majority in the Assembly refused to pass a budget with the tax hike, the Democratic governor ordered nonessential state operations to close on July 1, the first day of the new fiscal year. Among other things, Corzine's order forced the casinos in Atlantic City to close because they were heavily monitored by the state's Casino Control Commission. Roberts, who was a key part of George Norcross's South Jersey machine, was irate over the casino closure. Corzine famously said, "Pigs will fly over the State House before there is a realistic level of new taxes or spending cuts that can fix this mess." I never knew pigs could fly, but they did.

After four exhausting days, the dispute was settled when Roberts and his allies accepted the sales tax hike as long as Corzine agreed to designate half of the new revenue to property tax relief. The governor agreed, and the budget passed. But it was an ugly and divisive process that pretty much set the tone for the remainder of the Corzine years. The governor didn't help his cause when he proposed huge toll hikes on the Turnpike, Garden State Parkway, and Atlantic City Expressway that would take effect every four years beginning in 2010 and ending in 2025. Corzine had taken my cost of living proposal increases to eliminate the state's pension debt and put it on steroids to eliminate the entire debt of the state. Corzine bit off more than the public could chew. There's an unfortunate political axiom that Corzine chose to ignore: don't do today what you can put off until tomorrow. To which I would add: don't do today what you can put off until your second and final term as governor.

Corzine, of course, did not get that second term, in part because of his missteps and in part because he simply was not a particularly riveting personality. But there was something else at work: powerful fellow Democrats abandoned him or even quietly supported Republican Chris Christie. Essex County's Democrats, led by County Executive Joe DiVincenzo, stood down in the campaign, depriving Corzine of the support he needed in that Democratic bastion. The day after his election, Christie celebrated with a visit to the North Ward Center in Newark, home of legendary Democratic power broker and DiVincenzo ally Steve Adubato Sr. DiVincenzo's son later got a top job at the state Department of Education under Christie. So it seems fair to say the

Republican Christie and the Democrat DiVincenzo certainly found common ground. The question, though, is whether that common ground was for the common good. It certainly served DiVincenzo well in getting funding for his pet projects in Essex County and a job for his son. There's Tip O'Neill again—all politics is local.

It would be fair to say that Chris Christie and I didn't get along, and as should be clear based on my relationships with other Republicans, it wasn't a matter of party affiliation. And that was clear from the very beginning of our non-relationship. Shortly after Christie's election in 2009 we were, by chance, dining at the same restaurant, Benito's, in Union Township, a great restaurant that many politicos frequent. A mutual friend introduced us. Shaking Christie's hand and congratulating him on his victory, I said, "We've never met." Christie responded only half jokingly, "You should be grateful about that." Christie, of course, had been the U.S. attorney for New Jersey before his election as governor and had made a name for himself by going after several leading political figures in the state. So with his first words to me, Christie couldn't help but remind me of his power and his unearned sense of self-righteousness.

It turned out that I was indeed on Christie's radar during his years as a prosecutor. He tried to get at me through my onetime best friend and colleague Bob Janiszewski, who had begun working as an FBI informant in 2001 after he was caught taking bribes. Janiszewski and I were very close—he was a top-notch policy wonk, as I think I am, and we spent long hours talking about legislation, regulations, taxes, and all manners of policy issues. We rented a summer home together at the Jersey Shore and a winter home at Hunter Mountain in the Catskills every year. Though I knew him well, I had no idea of the double life he was living beginning in the 1990s, when he started taking bribes through his position as Hudson County executive. He was elected to that post as a reformer who would finally rid the county of its bad apples, but it didn't take long for the rot to set in. The FBI videotaped him taking a payoff involving a contract for psychiatric services in county facilities. The feds asked him to cooperate, and he agreed, wearing a wire while meeting with friends and associates, including me, it turned out.

At some point in 2001, after Christie took over as U.S. attorney, I attended a meeting in Bareli's restaurant in Secaucus to discuss the privatization of the Secaucus Sewage Authority, a deal that required millions of dollars to finance. The meeting was set up by a municipal bond banker, Jay Booth, a direct descendant of John Wilkes Booth, representing Red Horse Securities, which was financing the deal. I was there in my capacity as a lawyer for U.S. Water

Company, which wanted to purchase the authority. Also at the table were Secaucus mayor Dennis Elwell, a highly decorated Army veteran who would later be found guilty of bribery, and—to my surprise—Janiszewski, who was invited by Mayor Elwell. The fact that my friend didn't tell me he would be at the meeting probably should have set off an alarm bell, but I didn't think much of it at the time. Afterall, he was Hudson County executive.

After the meeting, Janiszewski and I went to the bar. Nothing unusual there. As I drank wine—I had become quite the wine snob by this point—and Janiszewski had a beer, I asked him why he was at the meeting. There was no apparent reason for him to be there, and what's more, he never gave me a heads-up about it. He paused for a moment, and then said, "I don't feel comfortable taking four hundred thousand dollars to facilitate this transaction." I had heard a lot and seen a lot in my years in New Jersey politics, but never something like this. Four hundred grand? To "facilitate" a deal? We lawyers call that bribery. "You can't take anything for this transaction," I said. "You're chief executive of Hudson County." "Yeah," he replied. "I don't want to go to prison for four hundred thousand dollars." "You assh-le," I said, as discreetly as I could after a couple of glasses of wine, "What the f-ck's wrong with you? You don't want to go to prison, period."

Janiszewski then left abruptly, leaving me to wonder what the hell was going on. Whatever it was, it wasn't good, so I told my client and Red Horse Securities this deal wasn't about to happen. Sometime later, a mutual friend, Paul Byrne, who also got into legal trouble, told me he got a video of my conversation with Janiszewski from discovery in his case. I then realized what was going on. I found out that Christie's office had set up the meeting and the conversation I had with Janiszewski and that it was videotaped. Presumably Christie was hoping I would incriminate myself somehow in a conversation with a friend I trusted. No such luck, Chris.

Some years later, Byrne confirmed the setup during a long interview with NJTV's chief political correspondent, Michael Aaron. In discussing Janiszewski's turn to crime and his desperate but ultimately futile attempt to avoid a prison term, Byrne told Aaron, "Janiszewski even tried to entrap his best friend, Ray Lesniak." Byrne himself was an only-in-Jersey character, a bon vivant figure who would light up a room when he entered, loudly saying, "Top of the morning to you." For the uninitiated, he was not related to Governor Brendan Byrne.

Paul Byrne was part of Janiszewski's bribery schemes and eventually was indicted and convicted. But after years of bad health, including diabetes that robbed him of his sight, he died less than a week before he was due to be sentenced for his crimes. The FBI actually checked his casket at the funeral parlor to make sure he was dead. Paranoid? Maybe not—years before, Hudson County state senator David Friedland, who was under indictment, faked a fatal boating accident. He was found years later operating a marine shop in the Maldives. You could make a TV miniseries about New Jersey politics. But would people believe it? Maybe they would. After all, it is New Jersey.

Christie and I had several battles—over marriage equality, criminal justice reform, and animal welfare—which will be detailed in a later chapter. With other Republican governors, like Tom Kean and Christie Whitman, we could disagree without being disagreeable. Not so with Chris Christie. When I called for a special prosecutor to investigate Christie's involvement in Bridgegate, when lanes were blocked on the George Washington Bridge to tie up cars, school buses, and emergency response vehicles for hours in Fort Lee, Christie called me a "crazy quack" and a "lunatic." I chose not to respond in kind. "I think the governor needs a good meditation practice," I said. "Or at least a vacation. He's had a bad year."

We clashed on another issue that was less about party affiliation and more about politics: keeping Rutgers University insulated from political dominance. Christie made a deal with South Jersey Democrats like George Norcross and Senate President Steve Sweeney, who wanted a bigger say in Rutgers' governance and sought to stack my alma mater's Board of Governors with their political appointees. I could not let that happen. Rutgers has a treasured history with being independent of political pressure. In 1965, with American troops dying daily in Vietnam, Rutgers professor Eugene Genovese said during a "teach-in": "I do not fear or regret the impending Vietcong victory in Vietnam. I welcome it." Despite the remarks going viral before things went viral, and even though they took place during a gubernatorial campaign, Governor Richard Hughes refused to pressure Rutgers to fire Genovese, citing academic freedom. Richard Nixon, who was campaigning in New Jersey for Hughes's opponent, Wayne Dumont, called the governor "a commie sympathizer." Despite this pressure, Governor Hughes stood firm and won reelection handily.

To uphold Hughes's insistence on academic freedom, I resisted the political interference with the university's governance with all the political might I could muster. The appointments were related to a battle between the school's Board of Trustees—a separate entity from the Board of Governors—and the South Jersey Democrats over a plan to merge Rutgers–Camden with Rowan University in Glassboro. The South Jersey delegation wanted the merger, but the trustees, who get to appoint seven of the fifteen members of the Board of Governors, did not. Sweeney wanted to disband the trustees, but that didn't happen, and neither did the merger he wanted.

I saw the maneuver as an attack on the university's independence, so I worked with Senator Bob Smith, who represents the district in which Rutgers is located, and Peter McDonough, Rutgers' senior vice president for external affairs, who had Rutgers alumni call their legislators to vote against the maneuver. Some people automatically equate bipartisan cooperation with good government. Not so. In this case, a Republican governor and some Democratic leaders were cooperating to achieve a bad public policy goal, at least in my view. The vote failed to pass the Senate, and Rutgers' independence was preserved.

I had a mixed success with Christie on several other issues that I detail in other chapters, but I suffered an extremely disappointing loss when I challenged Christie's settlement of a lawsuit against ExxonMobil over the company's legacy of pollution in New Jersey.

The state had pursued a case against the oil giant for years, over the administrations of four governors representing both parties. New Jersey wanted the company, successor to the old and infamous Standard Oil, to pay for the damage it caused along the Arthur Kill waterfront and throughout a northern portion of the state. The case finally went to trial in 2014, a decade after the state sued the company, with New Jersey seeking $9 billion in damages. But just as a ruling seemed imminent, the Christie administration announced it would settle with the company for $225 million. Peanuts.

And there was more to it: the settlement also let the company off the hook for more than $1 billion in liability for which it had conceded responsibility and for sites included in the settlement that were not part of the litigation. The fact that Christie's office reached the settlement very quietly, with no announcement, told me everything I needed to know.

I filed a lawsuit seeking to block the settlement, joined by allies in the state's environmental movement. In my argument to the court to establish legal standing—the first step for such a challenge—I recalled that my father had brought me to the piers off the Arthur Kill in Elizabethport, adjacent to one of the company's plants. He talked about how much he enjoyed fishing off those piers as a youngster. I asked him why he had never taken me fishing off the same spot. He pointed to the plant's nearby smokestacks. "That's why," he said. He knew—we all knew—that the company now known as ExxonMobil was a hazard to our collective health and to the health of our state and our planet. You didn't have to be a scientist to figure out that the sludge in the wetlands along the waterfront and the colored smoke in the air had to be bad for human, animal, and plant life. Surely the company knew that, but it did nothing, despite all its financial resources and technical know-how.

I also told the court that my home in Elizabeth was subjected to flash flooding because the buffers provided by marshlands and wetlands were depleted by ExxonMobil's pollution and they would not be restored if Christie's settlement were allowed to stand. It was to no avail. The state Supreme Court ruled that I did not have standing to challenge the settlement—actually, it ruled that no one had standing to challenge a settlement by the state.

The settlement was a massive giveaway to ExxonMobil, which contributed half a million dollars to the Republican Governors Association when Christie served as its chairman in 2014. The settlement also included an illegal deferral of the company's obligation under an administrative consent order to restore the natural resources in and alongside Morses Creek, which flows into the Arthur Kill. This restoration was estimated by expert testimony at the trial to cost in the neighborhood of $700 million. The settlement allowed the company to put off restoration until it could do so without disrupting a discharge permit at the site—in other words, it will be decades before Morses Creek gets cleaned up, if it ever happens. This deferral violated New Jersey's Spill Act, but since the court ruled no one had standing to sue, ExxonMobil got a huge gift from the state.

Christie's giveaway also included a release from liability for restoration of natural resources at sixteen other industrial plants not included in the litigation. The Department of Environmental Protection refused my Open Public Records Act request to produce its assessment of natural resource damage at these sites. How badly were the natural resources damaged? We'll never know, and ExxonMobil will never be held accountable. As an extra added bonus, Christie let the company off the hook for natural resource damages at sixteen hundred of its gasoline stations. Admittedly, it's not likely that a gasoline station would do extensive damage to natural resources, but one must ask why ExxonMobil wanted them included in the settlement. Christie's giveaway shocked the conscience of many New Jersey residents. Apparently it didn't shock Christie's.

6 · THE NATURAL

The Saga of Jim McGreevey

Jim McGreevey was a natural.

He had that "it" factor from the very beginning—he had charisma, he was smart, and he knew how to connect with voters, with donors, with colleagues. He was equally at home giving a speech in front of a large crowd as he was in a more intimate setting with supporters at a fundraising event. And he was as ambitious as anybody I've ever met.

He popped up on my radar screen in the 1980s, as he established himself in politics right out of Georgetown Law School by volunteering to work with the Middlesex County Democratic organization and landing a position with the Assembly Oversight Committee, where he wrote a report on parole reform. Union County Democratic chair Christopher Dietz, who was chairman of the State Parole Board, was impressed with McGreevey's report and appointed him to be its executive director. McGreevey had also been corporate spokesperson for Merck, the pharmaceutical giant headquartered in Rahway. At the time, Merck was regularly voted the most admired corporation in America. It was easy to see this young man had a future in politics.

McGreevey was elected to the state Assembly in 1989, and within two years he decided to take on the popular incumbent mayor of Woodbridge, Joe DeMarino, who was yet another colorful New Jersey character. McGreevey's upstart campaign showed what many of us already knew—he had big plans, and he wasn't about to wait in line. DeMarino was an ex-Marine and former detective renowned for his unorthodox approach to law enforcement. He famously spent several nights sleeping in a cemetery in order to catch somebody who had been stealing brass markers and urns. They called him "Kojak," after the television detective, and sure enough, DeMarino kept an autographed picture of actor Telly Savalas, who played the lollipop-sucking sleuth, in his office.

But like so many other "colorful" characters in state politics, DeMarino also had a run-in with the law. He was indicted on bribery charges just as he was getting ready to run for reelection. When McGreevey was given the opportunity to vouch for DeMarino, who had been something of a mentor to him, he declined. DeMarino was furious and arranged to strip McGreevey of the Middlesex County Democratic party's line in the upcoming legislative election—just as a vengeful Tom Dunn took away the Union County organization's line from me in 1981. Another bad move by a veteran politician.

DeMarino may have assumed that McGreevey would just go away after losing the line. If so, he clearly did not have the measure of the man. Not only did McGreevey refuse to go away, he announced that he would challenge DeMarino's reelection bid. That took some nerve. McGreevey was basically betting his career on beating an established and almost legendary incumbent who, to be sure, was under indictment. But still—it was a pretty fearless act because if he lost, he was toast.

I had to admire him. McGreevey reminded me of my younger self in the 1980s. I saw in McGreevey a politician with the talent and fire in his belly to become governor and, yes, possibly even president. My law firm, led by my partner, Paul Weiner, threw its support behind him. We raised campaign funds and drafted his campaign literature. DeMarino was acquitted of the bribery charge in October, but it was too late. McGreevey outworked him as he outworked every political opponent he faced. And he built support within the Middlesex County Democratic organization so that he took control of the township's local Democratic committee, overthrowing DeMarino.

Yes, Jim McGreevey was a natural. He never stopped campaigning, making it pretty clear that he had no intention of spending too much time waiting to move up the political ladder. As Democrats began to think about who might take on the very formidable task of running against Christie Whitman in 1997, I had my eye on one person and one person only—Jim McGreevey. I wasn't alone. My Senate colleague John Lynch, whose power base was in Middlesex County, had also noticed the ambitious mayor of Woodbridge, and, to be sure, McGreevey noticed us. We became even better acquainted when McGreevey won election to the Senate in 1993, joining the ranks of mayors who also held positions in the state legislature.

McGreevey quickly established himself as a can-do mayor. On his first day in office he fired three public works employees who were under indictment.

He brought in a forensic accountant to straighten out an insurance scandal under the DeMarino regime, attracted economic development, including FedEx, into Woodbridge, built a new Town Hall, and kept property taxes down. He accomplished all this by putting together a very talented and young administrative team that included Paul Weiner as law director, Gary Taffet as chief of staff, John McCormac as finance director, Tim Dacey as public works director, Steve Goldin as planning director, and Marvin Corwick as business administrator.

While we knew Jim McGreevey the politician, we didn't know—no one did—Jim McGreevey the person. He kept his inner self locked away, allowing no one, perhaps including himself, to enter. We saw a hardworking, hard-driving political animal who always seemed to be performing. What we saw is what we thought we were getting. Of course, as we all know now, there was so much more to Jim McGreevey than the smiling, backslapping natural politician who seemed destined for great things in public life. All along, going back to his formative years, he struggled to please his strong-willed mother and equally strong-willed dad, a former Marine drill sergeant who served in World War II and the Korean War. He was brought up in a traditional, post-war Irish Catholic household where homosexuality was considered not just a sin but a perversion of God's will. It must have been so difficult for him.

McGreevey, it seems clear now, was driven to seek the approval and acceptance through political achievements he couldn't get by being true to himself and his sexual feelings and desires. The famously long hours on the campaign trail or in the office were a sign of ambition for sure, but they were also a way for McGreevey to avoid coming to terms with who he was. Again, while this seems clear now, it certainly wasn't at the time. I was one of the last to realize that McGreevey was gay, not that it would have mattered to me in the least. I saw what McGreevey wanted me to see: an untiring, upbeat, and ambitious politician with great promise. Being upbeat has always been an important character trait to me. The word Pollyanna has sometimes been used to describe me. I try to look on the bright side of life, as in the Monty Python song in *Life of Brian*.

When Lynch and I gravitated to McGreevey as our choice to run against Whitman in 1997, the only other major Democrat who seemed interested in the nomination was Rob Andrews, a popular member of Congress from South Jersey who had no base of support and no name recognition north of the Driscoll Bridge. South Jersey political leader George Norcross, who was not quite yet the powerful boss he would later become, wasn't keen on Andrews, but he stood by him as a fellow South Jersey Democrat.

It's never easy running against an incumbent, particularly an incumbent governor of New Jersey, because our governor's office is among the most powerful in the nation. Whitman had made good on her promise to cut state income taxes by 30 percent, she was a moderate on cultural and social issues, and she had a decent record on the environment. So we knew that McGreevey had his work cut out for him, but we also knew that nobody would work harder. If Whitman was going to get a second term, she'd have to earn it. But first, there was the matter of winning the nomination, and it proved to be more difficult than we expected. McGreevey was a better candidate than Andrews, and McGreevey had Lynch and myself in his corner while Andrews had only the perfunctory support of Norcross. Still, McGreevey was having a hard time lining up the organizational support he needed, even in the northern portion of the state. Complicating matters was the presence of another candidate, Morris County prosecutor Michael Murphy, who seemed to be draining support from McGreevey.

As the date for filing primary nomination petitions approached, I picked up intelligence that the Essex County Democratic organization was preparing to endorse Andrews. That would have been an unmitigated disaster for McGreevey. Thus far the county organizations were splitting along geographic lines, which worked to McGreevey's advantage because Lynch and I would get out the vote in the North and Norcross wouldn't dispatch the troops enthusiastically in the South. But if Essex went with Andrews, the map would change, and not in McGreevey's favor. We had to put a stop to that.

I went to see Steve Adubato, the powerful leader of Newark's North Ward. Adubato's passion and the source of his political strength was the North Ward Cultural and Civic Center, a nonprofit community development organization located near the city's Branch Brook Park. The center served thousands of residents with adult day care, sports teams, and other activities. It was Adubato's pride and joy. Joining me for the trip to the North Ward was a close friend of mine, Dick Kinney, who was chair of the corporate foundation of giant pharmaceutical company Schering Plough.

Adubato, who died in 2020 at the age of eighty-seven, always was his own best cheerleader—he loved to show off the North Ward Center's work to a new audience. The center is based in an old Queen Anne–style mansion on Mt. Prospect Avenue, but at the time it was expanding to create a state-of-the-art charter school, which Adubato would name after one of the city's colonial founders, Robert Treat. I could see that Dick was impressed with Adubato's presentation. He told Adubato that the North Ward Center was just the kind of organization the Schering Plough Foundation wanted to support. Its mission of service and empowerment was a perfect match for the foundation, Dick said. Adubato's eyes lit up. You could sense the calculations taking place in his head.

Adubato quickly met with Newark mayor Sharpe James and persuaded him to support McGreevey over Andrews. James was a shrewd politician who knew just how influential Adubato could be. It was good politics to stay on his good side, especially since James was up for reelection the next year and had a young Cory Booker looming boldly to challenge him. So the mayor used his enormous influence over the Essex County Democratic organization to get it behind McGreevey rather than Andrews. It was the key moment during the primary. And the Schering Plough Foundation came through with a half-million-dollar contribution to the North Ward Civic Center.

I remember Election Night well. Andrews was in the lead when I got a call from Union County's clerk, Joann Rajoppi, who told me McGreevey carried my home county by 14,000 votes. I told Joann not to release the number until I called her. Jim Florio said during a television interview from Andrews's headquarters that his candidate was on his way to victory, and he proceeded to outline how Andrews would go on to defeat Whitman. The mayor of Cherry Hill, Susan Bass Levin, was with Florio at the time. She later told me she didn't feel it was the appropriate time to declare victory. Was she ever right. After I heard Florio's announcement, I called Rajoppi and asked her to release the Union County results. That announcement stopped everything in its tracks, and all of a sudden it seemed as though Andrews was not, in fact, the winner. McGreevey wound up with a slim victory, finishing just 9,993 votes ahead of Andrews out of about 370,000 votes cast. I was credited with bringing McGreevey to victory.

I admit it was a little naughty to hold back the Union County results, but it was fun. When McGreevey was declared the winner, George Norcross ran out into his backyard and screamed "Yeah!" to nobody in particular. He was not a fan of Andrews, but because of Andrews's popularity in South Jersey, Norcross had to keep his feelings under wraps. He let it all go that night when McGreevey was declared the victor.

At the start of the general election campaign nobody thought McGreevey had a chance against Whitman. The question was not whether Whitman would win but by how much—some people were thinking double digits, maybe even as much as 20 percentage points. It was understandable. Whitman had a lot going for her, at least on paper. The economy was humming along nicely. (Thank you President Bill Clinton, the last president to run a budget surplus!) Whitman had done a decent job persuading voters that she was a

Republican in the mold of Tom Kean, not of Ronald Reagan. And there seemed to be—and I emphasize *seemed to be*—no pressing issues for McGreevey to exploit.

Or so most thought.

The first thing we needed was deep-pocketed financial contributors. I convinced super Democratic fundraiser Orin Kramer to be McGreevey's finance chair by assuring him that the pundits were all wrong. The margin would be less than four points, I told him. Kramer, a New York City–based hedge fund manager and former speechwriter for President Jimmy Carter, probably thought I was nuts, but he signed on anyway. Orin likes challenges as much as I do. Kramer didn't know what I had learned years earlier about McGreevey's tenacity. He was only relying on my prediction that the election would not be a Whitman blowout, as most believed. During the campaign, Orin learned that McGreevey was a tireless campaigner, a Jersey guy who knew how to connect with ordinary people and their concerns in ways that Whitman, an elite Republican from New Jersey's horse country, could not. She seemed more than a little surprised when McGreevey seized on an issue that really wasn't in the Whitman playbook for 1997: car insurance rates.

Any politician who seeks public office in New Jersey knows all about the state's property tax burden. Most years we're number one in that department nationwide. But in the mid-1990s, we also were number one in car insurance rates. And people were pretty fed up about the combination of property taxes and car insurance.

McGreevey was completely focused on those two issues. If you asked him about the weather, he'd find a way to bring the conversation back to the high cost of car insurance. No other issues mattered, and within two weeks of Election Day, we were closing in on Whitman. We just needed a final push.

That final push was supposed to be provided by an Atlantic City casino owner named Donald Trump. He was furious at Whitman for proposing to spend $220 million to build a road and tunnel to Atlantic City's Marina District, where a casino that didn't bear the Trump name was going up. Steve Wynn, the casino magnate who had walked away from Atlantic City a decade earlier, was planning to return with a new Las Vegas–style place away from the city's famous boardwalk. The tunnel project would take people directly to the Marina District from the Atlantic City Expressway.

Wynn and Trump were bitter rivals at the time, and Trump was furious with the plan to use public dollars to benefit his competition. So he threatened to sue in a futile attempt to stop the tunnel project. At the groundbreaking ceremony for the new casino, which eventually became the Borgata,

Wynn told reporters he was prepared for a long battle with Trump. "He's had zero success," Wynn said of Trump's lawsuit threats, just as Trump's legal challenges to overturn Joe Biden's victory had zero success. A Washington, D.C., law firm representing Trump Hotels & Casino Resorts Inc. informed several state and federal agencies that it intended to sue over the environmental permits issued for the tunnel. Can you imagine Trump raising environmental issues to stop economic development? It was probably the first and last time Trump showed any concern about the environment.

To get back at Whitman for her support of the tunnel, Trump had committed to fund a half-million-dollar television campaign against the governor focusing on the misuse of taxpayer dollars involving the project. We were aware of the plan, and of course we were delighted to have Trump raise the issue as the race drew closer. But Whitman's campaign caught wind of the plan and was determined to stop it. Whitman's husband John met with Trump and read him the riot act. Trump was aware that meant the casino gaming regulators would constantly be looking over his operations. Trump had three casinos—all which eventually went bankrupt—in Atlantic City, and he certainly didn't want regulators looking over his shoulder. So he went back on his commitment. The ads never aired, depriving McGreevey of a good issue as the race was reaching its climax.

In New Jersey, campaign twists are expected, but none of us could have imagined the twist that unfolded in late October 1997. Two weeks before Election Day, a hooker in Perth Amboy named Myra Rosa was arrested and told the arresting officer that Jim McGreevey was one of her johns. (Wait, isn't McGreevey gay? Apparently it's more complex than that.) The officer didn't mention that in the arrest record, but word quickly got out and the press was beating the bushes to interview her. Every time the phone rang in campaign headquarters my heart sank into my stomach thinking someone had the story. I had Rosa bailed out and sent to Disneyland for two weeks, all expenses paid. Lynch called me in a panic, "She flew the coop, Ray." I said, "I know. We sprung her and flew her to Disneyland." Lynch breathed a sigh of relief. The press was pissed off at me for years. Five years later, when McGreevey was governor, Myra Rosa was killed by gunfire on the streets of Philadelphia. A sad ending to her troubled life.

Even without the Trump bump, it seemed for a while like McGreevey would pull off an upset. He was leading in the early returns on Election Night, and at some point after the polls closed a contingent of state troopers arrived to serve as security for the prospective governor-elect. The dean of New Jersey's press corps, Michael Aaron, sensed that it was turning into a nail-biter. He interviewed me at McGreevey's Election Night party at the Sheraton Hotel in Woodbridge and asked me how I thought it would turn out. "It's in God's hands," I said. Aaron was surprised by reference to the Almighty—it wasn't a common reference point in politics at the time.

The mood in the room changed, however, when votes came in from the state's Republican-dominated northwest counties. Whitman soon overtook McGreevey and opened a small but insurmountable lead. She wound up winning by a single percentage point. My friend Orin Kramer, remembering that I predicted the margin would be less than four points, laughed and told me, "Well, you beat the spread." It wasn't me who beat the spread. It was Jim McGreevey, the natural. We knew he would be back for another try.

Having run such a strong race against Whitman, McGreevey was the presumptive Democratic gubernatorial nominee four years later, but as you might expect, McGreevey didn't rest on his laurels. He formed a nonprofit organization named the Committee for Working Families, largely funded by developer Charlie Kushner, which worked closely with President Clinton's Democratic Leadership Council. Even as he continued to amass a good record as mayor of Woodbridge, he spent the next four years campaigning for other Democratic candidates, raising funds for the state party, and hosting policy-making forums.

As 2001 approached, the Democratic nomination for governor was his for the asking, until a ten-thousand-pound gorilla named Bob Torricelli threw his hat into the ring. Nobody saw that coming. Torricelli, a longtime member of Congress and U.S. senator, was a well-known personality in Washington circles, where it was simply assumed he would win the Democratic nomination over the supposedly "unknown" mayor of some place called Woodbridge. The Beltway gang forgot that all politics is local, especially in New Jersey. Torricelli also had celebrity power. He was dating Bianca Jagger (after her divorce from Mick) and I, without thinking, called Torricelli and invited him and Bianca to join me in a box at Giants Stadium for a Rolling Stones concert. Oops. Torricelli said, "Ray, really?" He declined the invitation.

Torricelli did have some significant backing, particularly in the form of the Democratic state chairman, Tom Giblin, who was also the Essex County Democratic Party chair. To add a surprising twist to this complication, Giblin held the state chairmanship thanks to McGreevey, who got him the job after Essex County withdrew its support from Andrews in 1997. McGreevey wanted Giblin inside his tent, thinking that when the time came for the 2001 governor's race, Giblin would be in his corner. Nobody was even considering the possibility that Torricelli might want to leave the Washington spotlight for the governor's office in Trenton. His bid posed a considerable—and, some thought, insurmountable—obstacle for McGreevey.

Once again, Sharpe James came to the rescue. I arranged for McGreevey and me to meet with Sharpe at his son's Newark nightclub. Joining us were the mayor's right-hand man, Calvin West, the Democratic chair from South Orange, Cathy Willes, and McGreevey's campaign comanager, Regena Thomas, who would become secretary of state in the McGreevey administration. Willes explained that she and others in the Essex County organization wanted to support McGreevey, but they couldn't because their county (and state) chair, Giblin, was supporting Torricelli. Thomas, an outgoing, ebullient personality, couldn't contain herself. "Giblin?" she stood up and exclaimed. "That white boy isn't going to tell us what to do. We'll tell that white boy what to do!" McGreevey and I loved it. "You go, girl," we said in unison.

Giblin was concerned about chatter that McGreevey was gay and was caught in a compromising position in a graveyard with another young man. It was, as often is the case, a permutation of an actual encounter McGreevey had at a rest stop on the Garden State Parkway, where he was questioned by a police officer for flashing his headlights, a signal that he was looking for sex. The officer let him off with a warning, but the story was making the rounds. That set the stage for me to take Mayor James outside for a walk.

It was just the two of us walking side by side in deep conversation. I know it sounds like a sinister scene from a movie about politics, but it wasn't. I knew that Sharpe James could help McGreevey, and I had an idea about how I could help Sharpe. His son's nightclub was not doing well. During our walk outside, I put my arm around Sharpe and mentioned that I knew his son's venture was in trouble. I told him I'd bring in one of my clients to help figure out where the club was leaking money. "And if, and when, your son needs financial help, he'll get it, as long as he straightens out its operation," I said. As favors go, this wasn't much—I was giving away ice in the wintertime. This stuff was in my client's wheelhouse. Sharpe shook his head, knowingly. "The boy is strong-headed, just like his dad," he said. Then he paused, looked at me, and said: "Now let's go back inside and get McGreevey elected governor."

When we returned to the meeting, Sharpe told the group that they would persuade Giblin to go with McGreevey rather than Torricelli. "McGreevey's our guy," he said. We all hugged each other. I smiled and thought, "Mission accomplished." Within three days, Sharpe pulled together the Essex County delegation, including Tom Giblin, for McGreevey. A deflated Torricelli dropped out, paving the way for McGreevey to become the Democratic candidate for governor.

And that's how politics works at its most basic level. People may argue that this is not the way politics ought to work, but those critics don't understand the human element in politics. Personal relationships are part of the dynamic in any workplace. Politics is not an exception. In fact, it's an integral part of politics. Bear in mind that in my dealings with Steve Adubato and Sharpe James, no commitments were made. The deals were sealed with trust that we would do what was right for each other. And, by the way, the nightclub went bankrupt and Sharpe never called on me for help. But when he pledged his support to help McGreevey, he knew he could count on me. Trust is more important than commitments.

With the Torricelli obstacle removed, McGreevey had a relatively easy path to victory. New Jersey was beginning to turn a darker shade of blue by the turn of the twenty-first century, and the Republican candidate against McGreevey, Bret Schundler, was not a typical Tom Kean–Christie Whitman Republican. He was socially conservative and not all that familiar with grass-roots state issues. McGreevey beat him in a landslide, although he worked as if he were a dozen points behind. When he took office in 2002, I thought it was not the end of his journey but just the beginning. He was destined to go places.

At around the same time, another character was emerging in New Jersey's political landscape. His name was Chris Christie, and President George W. Bush had recently appointed him as U.S. attorney for the state despite his utter lack of qualifications for the post. But Christie's brother, Todd, was a big fundraiser for Bush, so the job as the state's top federal prosecutor went to the fundraiser's brother. If the Bush team had done a little research, they might have thought twice about Christie. It was common knowledge in Republican circles that Christie was abrasive, self-righteous, and more concerned about himself than his party (sounds an awful lot like a former president). He was sued for defamation after saying that political opponents in a race for Morris County freeholder—fellow Republicans!—were under investigation.

Actually, the local prosecutor had simply opened an inquiry that led to nothing. The suit was settled out of court and Christie had to apologize. Suffice it to say that Chris Christie didn't make many friends nor did he influence many people during his time in Morris County. But through the magic of patronage, he became the federal government's chief law enforcement officer in New Jersey just as Jim McGreevey was emerging as the political power in the state. In my view, there was no question that Christie was intent on collecting as many indictments of politicians as he could before making his inevitable next move. It seems clear he had his eye on the new governor from the very beginning, and there's no question that the McGreevey years were tumultuous. And some of that tumult was self-inflicted, especially the astonishing series of events that led to his resignation.

That's how McGreevey's time as governor is remembered, but I think that's unfair in many respects. McGreevey had a pretty solid record of achievement in his two and a half years in office. And some of those accomplishments we now take for granted—those of us who have been in elected office know that voters have short memories of the good done by politicians. That's why we work so hard to remind them of things we've done that they may have forgotten.

For example, McGreevey inherited an enormous mess at the old state Department of Motor Vehicles. Granted, it would be hard to find a state where motorists just can't wait to visit their local DMV office. But McGreevey basically blew up the old model, rebranded the agency as the Motor Vehicle Commission, and insisted on a new culture of customer service. The system he implemented served motorists well at its time and was far better than the old way. It subsequently crashed again when Murphy was governor, but its systems hadn't been updated in more than a decade. McGreevey also was handed a broken E-Z pass system that the Whitman administration mishandled. He managed to right that ship, a major victory not just for motorists, who no longer had to wait in line to pay tolls, but for the environment—no more miles and miles of cars idling while in line. McGreevey also cut down the number of toll booths on the Garden State Parkway (even less idling and wasted time), preserved portions of the state's magnificent Highlands region, and made good on his promise to reduce New Jersey's auto insurance costs. McGreevey would have been good to go for reelection in 2005, except for the extortion plot of Golan Cipel.

7 · CHRISTIE, GOLAN CIPEL, AND THE KUSHNER CONNECTION

The McGreevey era, short though it was, did not lack for the kind of drama any governor would prefer to avoid. He had more than his share of bad newspaper headlines back in the days when print headlines still mattered. But he also compiled a solid list of achievements, so much so that his reelection campaign in 2005 would have had plenty of ammunition to deflect all of those bad headlines. But there would be no reelection campaign.

The trouble actually started even before McGreevey took office. Gary Taffet, McGreevey's chief of staff, and Paul Levinsohn, the governor's chief counsel, had owned a billboard company, and it was alleged that they used their political influence in the months before McGreevey's inauguration to win approval for thirteen billboards in localities where they had been prohibited by zoning ordinances. They sold the company before taking their new jobs. U.S. attorney Chris Christie took the rare step of announcing that his office was investigating the two of them. That made for a big headline. In the end, both resigned. Christie's investigation came to nothing—although he didn't announce that. Strange, but typical, for a U.S. attorney with his eyes on public office like governor and president, à la Rudy Giuliani, although Christie hasn't self-imploded as Giuliani has representing President Trump's folly.

After the billboard investigation, which came to nothing, there was the infamous "Machiavelli" episode involving a land deal in Middlesex County and a Democratic donor in early 2004, McGreevey's third year as governor. The convoluted details aren't worth reprising. Suffice it to say it was alleged that McGreevey had used a code word—Machiavelli—to indicate that the fix was in. Christie's office wired one of the participants in the deal and announced that the governor had indicated his knowledge of a corrupt scheme by using a preplanted code word and that it was all on tape. McGreevey denied any wrongdoing and was never charged, although in the forty-seven-page indictment there are repeated references to the involvement in the deal of "State Official 1," later revealed to be the governor.

It is worth noting that in his investigation of the land deal, Christie made a great show of issuing subpoenas to the governor's office rather than asking more quietly for the documents they wanted, as they would normally do. But a quiet, low-profile request for information would not have suited Christie's style. Or his ambition. Christie went to great lengths to cultivate his image as a corruption fighter.

A couple of years later, when Jon Corzine was governor, Christie made a spectacle of raiding the home of Corzine's Department of Community Affairs commissioner, former Assembly speaker Joe Doria. Alerting the press to the morning raid, Christie staged a scene with his investigators carrying boxes of "evidence" out of Doria's home. It was great theater for television and the print media, which learned only much later that the boxes were empty! What a nice guy.

Christie's investigations no doubt cast a cloud over McGreevey's tenure. But that was nothing compared to the powerful storm that went by the name of Golan Cipel. He was Jim McGreevey's secret gay lover, a part of his life that few knew about. In the aftermath of his fall, many people said that they suspected McGreevey was a closeted gay man and was having an affair. I didn't, and I don't deny that maybe I was blind to what others saw or suspected. One thing's for certain: I didn't know about McGreevey's relationship with Golan Cipel.

Cipel was in his early thirties, a native of Israel and a veteran of the Israeli Defense Forces. He served in various capacities in the Israeli government through the 1990s, including a stint in the Israeli consulate in New York City, and met McGreevey when the future governor visited Israel along with other mayors in 1999. There was an immediate and strong connection between the two. McGreevey was falling in love with this young, attractive, ambitious Israeli. At some point, McGreevey introduced Cipel to his largest financial supporter, real estate developer Charles Kushner, future father-in-law of Ivanka Trump. Kushner was a major player in New Jersey politics, and by going all-in for McGreevey, he certainly had a friend in the governor's office. Although "friend" might be the wrong word, because someone like Charlie Kushner had a more practical view of his relationships with other people, especially if they happened to be politicians. McGreevey was somebody who could be useful to him, an ally of convenience—not really a friend, although Kushner and McGreevey have kept their cordial relationship to this very day. Strange, considering the turmoil between the two over the years. As recently as 2018, Kushner raised campaign contributions at McGreevey's request for the gubernatorial campaign of Jersey City mayor Steve Fulop. There's a typical New Jersey backstory there, but first on to Golan Cipel.

Cipel returned to the United States to live in 2000, to work not for the Israeli consulate but for Charles Kushner. On his visa application, he listed Kushner as his sponsor, making it clear that the two of them knew each other well through the McGreevey connection. Cipel went to work for Kushner as a public relations person. McGreevey and Cipel hooked up to the extent that McGreevey helped Cipel find an apartment in Iselin, a section of Woodbridge, and even helped with its decorating. McGreevey then got him a job with the state Democratic Party as he campaigned for governor.

Once McGreevey won, Cipel got a job with the administration as a special assistant for homeland security. It raised eyebrows because Cipel didn't seem qualified. One reporter actually asked McGreevey if he was involved in a romantic relationship with Cipel. "Don't be ridiculous," McGreevey replied. In truth, McGreevey was in love with Cipel. Not long after the appointment, Cipel ran into trouble because, as an Israeli citizen, he could not get a security clearance from the U.S. Department of Homeland Security. The press got wind of the story and speculated there was more to the Cipel-McGreevey relationship than met the eye—and there was, but nobody could prove anything.

Under continuous pressure from the press, McGreevey asked Cipel to resign in August 2002, after serving about six months. It was not, of course, the end of the story. Just the beginning. McGreevey tried to help Cipel land on his feet, getting him a job at the hefty salary of $150,000 a year with one of New Jersey's best connected lobbying firms, MWW, which represented Kushner along with many well-known New Jersey powerhouses. After a month of being nonproductive at MWW, he moved to State Street Partners, another firm well connected to McGreevey, for another job paying $150,000 a year. He developed a reputation as something less than a productive worker in both offices and was again terminated. While all this was going on, Cipel's sponsor to the United States was getting into deep trouble.

What Charlie Kushner wanted most from Jim McGreevey was to head up the powerful Port Authority of New York and New Jersey. McGreevey took the first step toward that goal almost right away, appointing Kushner to the Port

Authority's board in February 2002, a month after taking office. A couple of months later, the governor announced that Kushner would indeed be his choice for chairman—by agreement, New Jersey's commissioners get to select the Port Authority's chairman, while New York names the authority's executive director. Such selections generally are not contentious, but this one became so because a former employee of Kushner Companies filed a lawsuit charging that Charlie was making improper donations to political candidates from his businesses. That accusation set off alarm bells in the office of a certain federal prosecutor named Chris Christie.

Republican lawmakers, particularly my Senate colleague from Atlantic County Bill Gormley, also had deep concerns. Gormley chaired the Judiciary Committee, which had jurisdiction over gubernatorial appointments requiring Senate consent. Gormley didn't have control over who became the chairman—that was up to the board—but he was a crafty politician and knew how to use his authority. He called upon Kushner to testify before his committee about the campaign contribution allegations. Kushner refused. Gormley said he would issue a subpoena, leading Kushner to withdraw his name from consideration and quitting the Port Authority's board entirely. But that was hardly the end of Kushner's troubles. In fact, they were only just beginning.

Charlie was also being sued by his brother Murray, again over the use of company funds for campaign contributions. Christie began a formal investigation into what seemed at first like a run-of-the-mill family feud. He sensed, correctly, that there was bad business afoot at Kushner Companies. But even he could not have foreseen just how bad this business would get. As it is so often in politics, it's not the first wrongdoing that's the problem, but the cover-up. And boy did Kushner concoct an unusual cover-up—unusual and dastardly.

Charlie wanted to prevent his brother Murray, his sister Esther Schulder, and Esther's husband Bill Schulder from cooperating with Christie's investigation. So he came up with something that sounds like a plot from a B movie: he paid ten thousand dollars to a Manhattan-based call girl to lure Schulder to a motel room, where they were secretly videotaped. Charlie then sent the tape to his sister, making sure it arrived on the day of a family party. What a diabolical mind.

The message was clear: Charlie was capable of anything, and if his siblings knew what was good for them, they'd keep their mouths shut. Instead, they told Christie about the tape and the FBI tracked down the call girl, who gave them information about the devious liaison Kushner had set up. Years later, Christie would say that Kushner committed "one of the most loathsome, disgusting crimes" he had ever prosecuted. On that point, I have to say I agree with Christie. It was truly reprehensible—and it offered an insight into Kushner's soul.

While all of this was going on behind the scenes, Kushner and McGreevey had a huge blowup in late 2003 over the developer's attempt to buy the New Jersey Nets NBA team. Kushner was competing with a very well-connected New York developer, Bruce Ratner, who wanted to move the team to Brooklyn, where he planned to build a new arena. According to a report in *New York Magazine*, Kushner was determined to beat out Ratner and keep the team in New Jersey. He asked McGreevey and two officials from the New Jersey Sports and Exposition Authority for a twenty-five-million-dollar subsidy from the state to help seal his deal. McGreevey said no, and as the magazine noted, that wasn't a word that McGreevey said very much, especially to big donors. Kushner was furious—he was well known for his volcanic temper, but even with that knowledge, people on the call were stunned at his over-the-top tirade. According to the magazine piece, when Kushner hung up, McGreevey said, calmly, "Well, I guess I won't have to put up with Charles Kushner anymore." He was right. They stopped speaking. For a while, anyway.

On July 13, 2004, Christie's office announced a criminal complaint against Kushner, charging him with conspiracy, obstruction of a federal investigation, and interstate promotion of prostitution, among other counts. Quite a bit more serious than the original investigation of campaign contributions. Kushner surrendered at the FBI's Newark office and was arrested. It was an astonishing humiliation. At about that time Golan Cipel suddenly threatened to go public with a claim that McGreevey had sexually assaulted him. The timing was extraordinary. Cipel, who had seemingly disappeared after he left McGreevey's administration, was demanding fifty million dollars to keep quiet about his allegations. It's not clear why he took this drastic step—conventional wisdom has it that he was angry over losing his jobs at MWW and State Street Partners and saw an opportunity to get rich quick. Or maybe there were other forces at work. More about that in a bit.

I knew something serious was up when McGreevey called me on a Friday evening and said we had to get together. He and I were friends, but we didn't often get the chance to spend nongovernmental time together. Plus, I detected some urgency in his voice. "Fine," I said. "Let's have dinner on Monday." McGreevey said Monday wasn't quick enough. We had to meet the following day. What's more, he said, we had to meet in private, at my shore house. Now I knew for sure that this wasn't going to be a run-of-the-mill get-together. But why? Maybe, I thought, he wanted to confide in me about his differences with the state treasurer, John McCormac. There was talk that McGreevey was getting ready to fire McCormac, which would have been a pretty big deal.

McGreevey showed up at my house in Ocean County the following morning, by himself. McGreevey had a unique arrangement for a governor. He had private drivers—friends of his—instead of a state trooper. Insiders took notice and wondered why that was necessary. The plot thickens. I could tell right away that this meeting wasn't going to be a conversation about the state treasurer's future. McGreevey looked troubled. His face was drawn, and he had the tired eyes of somebody who wasn't getting enough sleep. I asked my girlfriend and future wife, Salena, to take our dog Brittany for a walk while we spoke privately. Once Salena left, McGreevey got to the point—no pleasantries, no chit-chat about the weather at the shore. He said that Cipel called him and was ready to accuse him of sexual assault if he wasn't paid fifty million dollars to make it go away. McGreevey said he hired a D.C. lawyer, Bill Lawler, to negotiate with Cipel's lawyer, but the talks had gotten nowhere. McGreevey wanted my political insight along with my legal expertise. I felt like Obi-Wan Kenobi when Princess Leia said, "Help me Obi-Wan. You're my only hope."

Needless to say, this was shocking news. And yet I immediately went into lawyer mode, detaching myself from the personal trauma McGreevey was experiencing. All these years later, I still can't reconcile how that happened, how I didn't take a moment to comfort McGreevey or offer some words of empathy. At the time, all I saw was a problem that needed to be solved, and I was the one who had to solve it. "Okay," I said. "We can handle this." And by "we" I meant "me." I prided myself on being able to solve any problem, big or small. Plus, I never liked bullies, and Cipel clearly was trying to bully McGreevey. Cipel's threat got my Polish up and I went into full battle mode. I told McGreevey to relax and get a good night's sleep. We would assemble at the governor's residence, Drumthwacket, the following morning with his chief of staff, Jamie Fox, a really smart New Jersey character who once was Senator Bob Torricelli's chief of staff. He had lots of experience dealing with politicians in hot water. McGreevey nodded, let out a sigh of relief, and returned home. His mood seemed a little brighter, maybe recalling that I had gotten him out of jams in the past. But this, of course, was no ordinary jam. Again, I saw this as just another legal matter that came across my desk, not as an existential crisis for McGreevey's tenure and career. Salena returned from walking Brittany and asked, "Okay, what's up?" She knew this was no ordinary visit from the governor. I told Salena what was going on. "No problem," she said. "You'll handle it. Should I open a bottle of Caymus or Stag's Leap?" And that was it—no further discussion. She, too, was confident that I'd somehow find a way out of yet another McGreevey problem.

At Drumthwacket the following morning, I told McGreevey and Fox I arranged through a lawyer, Timothy Saia, who had represented Cipel when McGreevey was getting him to resign his state position, a meeting with Cipel's lawyer, Alan Lowy, in his Manhattan office. The arrangement was made—the first step in my attempt to figure out what Cipel really wanted and how I might save McGreevey's career. The meeting with Lowy took place shortly thereafter, and it did not start well. Lowy opened with an accusation. "Why are you stalking my client," he asked me. He said Cipel had spotted me in the neighborhood. I was astounded at Lowy's rudeness. Cipel, it turned out, was living in an apartment in the Hell's Kitchen (or, as it's called now, Clinton) section of Manhattan, near West Fifty-Ninth Street and Ninth Avenue, and he had spotted me one day while I happened to be in the neighborhood. Like many areas of Manhattan, Hell's Kitchen has been gentrified in recent decades, so it's not a cheap place to live. And yet an out-of-work Golan Cipel was living in a high-rent apartment in Manhattan. How could that be? Therein lies a clue to what was driving Cipel. We'll probably have to wait for Cipel to write a book to find out.

I should have been put off by Lowy's accusatory tone, but I simply explained that Cipel must have spotted me when I was in town to attend Mass at a friend's church, St. Paul the Apostle, at West Sixtieth and Columbus Avenue. It was a special place for me. The priest during the Sunday noon Mass would burst out into modern-day tunes like the Beatles "Something" when speaking about the Blessed Virgin Mary. The avant-garde presentation of the Mass appealed to me so much I would drive from New Jersey to attend his service. So besides being an extortionist, Cipel was paranoid. I brushed aside Lowy's accusation, and we quickly reached a settlement for five million. I would have had to form a legal defense fund to raise the money but believed it was doable. I also demanded that Cipel sign one of those now notorious nondisclosure agreements. But first, I insisted that Lowy give me what we lawyers call a proffer of proof demonstrating that Cipel had a genuine claim for damages. A proffer is an outline of the evidence that would be presented in court to prove a case. Lowy claimed he had pictures of McGreevey and Cipel together. I knew what he meant, that they weren't innocent pictures, but Lowy refused to produce them.

I immediately called off the discussion. Without a proffer of proof, Cipel's demand would be an extortion, pure and simple, and not a legitimate claim. I would have nothing to do with that. I often wonder why Lowy wouldn't produce the proffer. It's standard practice in tort claims such as this. Perhaps there was a good reason why.

I left Lowy's office in an unhappy mood and called McGreevey and told him about the failed negotiation. McGreevey was stoic. He didn't react one way or the other. I drove from Manhattan directly to Drumthwacket to speak to him personally. When I got there, McGreevey came outside, sat me down, and said, "Ray, I think I'm gay." I responded, "You THINK you're gay?"

We laughed and embraced before going inside to plan what to do next. The magnitude of the situation still hadn't hit me. In my mind the meeting with Lowy was just a setback in a larger battle. It didn't work, so it was on to the next move. I was raring to take on the challenge: I wanted to expose Cipel as an extortionist and go on the attack.

Once we knew we couldn't convince Cipel to remain silent, several of McGreevey's close advisers assembled the next day in the equivalent of a war room to figure out the governor's options. It was all decided in one meeting, in the library in Drumthwacket, which was a pretty gloomy place. Joining me were McGreevey, Fox, political guru Steve DiMicco, New York political consultant Hank Sheinkopf, whom I brought in, and Curtis Bashaw, a close friend of McGreevey. It wasn't long before the "r" word was mentioned—resignation. I counseled against it, recommending that McGreevey expose Cipel as an extortionist and fight his allegations. But I was the lone voice against resignation, other than McGreevey's first wife, Kari, who called in from her home in Vancouver, Canada. McGreevy's second wife, Dina, was not involved. She was in a state of shock throughout the ordeal.

Everyone else believed McGreevey would face impeachment and removal from office, not because he put his lover on the state payroll—that certainly wouldn't have been unique in politics—but because he put Cipel in a sensitive homeland security position not long after 9/11.

Fox then raised an additional concern: the specter of Chris Christie. The ambitious prosecutor might seize the moment to launch a full-fledged investigation of the McGreevey administration. That would make it almost impossible to govern.

Fox's arguments won the day. He had a Svengali-like influence over McGreevey. Broken and exhausted, or perhaps because Fox and he knew more about the proof of the illicit relationship with Cipel than they let on, McGreevey agreed. He would make the announcement the next day, August 12. The political consultants left to leave the details of the announcement to McGreevey's close circle of friends and advisors.

McGreevey's chief counsel, Michael DeCotiis, walked into the room and saw and felt the doom that engulfed it. He looked around at Curtis Bashaw, gay, Jamie Fox, gay, Jim McGreevey, gay, and me and asked what was going on. McGreevey responded, "Tomorrow I'm going to announce I'm a gay American and resign." DeCotiis was stunned. And I said, flailing my arms,

"Michael . . . and I'm gay, too!" The entire room broke out in laughter, lightening the atmosphere for a moment.

A little later, McGreevey brought me up to the bedroom on the second floor of Drumthwacket to help him break the news to his wife. McGreevey had kept Dina at arm's length during the ordeal, but she knew generally what was going on. She also suspected what was going on between her husband and Cipel but played the dutiful wife throughout. When McGreevey told Dina he was going to announce his resignation the following day, she looked at me and said, "Where are we going to live?" It actually was a very pertinent question because Jim was never about making money. He was a policy wonk. They literally had nowhere to go. I assured her not to worry, Jim will announce he would stay in office forty-five days, until mid-November. That would give us time to set everything up. I said this not knowing of the political firestorm a delayed resignation would set off. McGreevey had a request for Dina. "Be strong," he said. "You have to stand by my side tomorrow and be strong." Even at such a moment, McGreevey was all about hiding his feelings and refusing to show vulnerability. A lifetime in the closet will do that to you. It was clear that Dina was shellshocked. The next day was going to be an ordeal, and by the look in her eyes, I wasn't so sure she wanted to stand by her husband's side. After McGreevey spoke, I said to her: "Do what you feel is right for you." I left the McGreeveys and went downstairs in search of a good bottle of wine. I needed a drink after all that tension. I found a bottle in Drumthwacket's cellar. I remember it well, a California Cabernet, Ridge 1997, a great vintage. It must have been left over from the Whitman years. McGreevey wouldn't know a bottle of Ridge from a jug of Gallo.

The following morning was like none other in my career. News outlets had gotten wind of McGreevey's impending announcement of his resignation, although not known was that he would use the occasion to tell the world he was a gay American. As I was pulling into the State House parking lot to attend the speech, my car phone rang. It was the lawyer, Timothy Saia, who set up my meeting with Alan Lowy. Saia said, "Tell McGreevey not to resign. All that's needed to keep Cipel quiet is approval of Touro Medical School." Touro College, based in New York City, had applied to the New Jersey Board of Medical Examiners for approval to start a medical school. Charlie Kushner was on the school's board of trustees, and he wanted to name the medical school for his mother, the Rae Kushner School of Medicine. I had no idea what that was all about, but I had a two-word answer: "F-ck you," as I slammed down the phone. Luckily smartphones weren't yet invented or I would have smashed it into pieces. The die was cast for McGreevy's resignation, and this last-second gambit wasn't going to change that. I still was upset as I walked into the State House. The first person I saw was Jamie Fox. When I told him about the phone call and the request, he immediately said, "Kushner!" I often wonder if Fox knew more about the McGreevey-Cipel-Kushner relationship than he let on. Fox died in 2017, and we'll likely never know. McGreevey refused to speak to me about this book, and Cipel is a ghost in Israel.

McGreevey gave his "I am a gay American" speech in the Assembly chamber with Dina by his side looking like a deer in the headlights. In the long history of New Jersey, nothing like this had ever happened before. The eyes of the nation were on Trenton, on McGreevey. They heard something no governor of any state had ever said. McGreevey became the country's first openly gay governor, although the circumstances were not celebratory.

When the announcement was done, the political intrigue began. New Jersey didn't have a lieutenant governor at the time, so by law the Senate president would serve as acting governor until a new one was chosen. That meant Dick Codey would succeed McGreevey. The question was how long Codey would get to serve.

Under McGreevey's announced time line, he would quit effective November 15, and that's when Codey's tenure would start. He would serve the remaining fourteen months of McGreevey's term and could, of course, run for a term in his own right the following year, 2005. Not everybody was on board with that plan. Codey had made some powerful enemies in New Jersey politics during his decades in the Senate, and they were not happy with the idea of Codey anywhere near the governor's office. They wanted to keep his tenure as short as possible.

If McGreevey could be persuaded to change his mind and leave before September 3, the state would call a special election in November to choose a new governor who would serve for a little more than a year. U.S. senator Jon Corzine was not shy about expressing interest in running, as he was bored being one of a hundred in the Senate. He was used to being a top executive at Goldman Sachs.

Corzine had a lot of support from some powerful people. They told McGreevey that if he didn't leave by September 3, he would face financial ruin. Nobody in either the public or private sector would hire him. They had that kind of power, or at least they were perceived to have that kind of power. They didn't count on me—I told McGreevey he could join my law firm.

Still, the pressure was intense. With a few days to go before the deadline for a special election expired, I went to see McGreevey to check how he was holding up. "Ray," he said, "they could tie me up, tar and feather me, and drag me through the streets of Trenton. I'm not resigning early." I breathed a sigh of relief. I had no dispute with those pressuring McGreevey to resign early. I just wanted him to leave office on his terms with whatever dignity he could muster. And he did. He left on November 15 as he planned, turning the office over to Codey, who went on to serve the remainder of the McGreevey term. Corzine got his chance to get out of the Senate in 2005, winning election as governor; Codey, afraid of Corzine's money and the personal attacks that would come from his political enemies, chose not to challenge Corzine in a Democratic primary. I supported Codey over Corzine to the end. Codey did a good job filling out the remainder of McGreevey's term and deserved a full term of his own. I admired him for saying he would punch out shock jock Craig Carton for making fun of his wife's mental illness. I would have my own run-in with Carton years later. More about that later. In the end, Codey decided to serve as Senate president rather than challenge Corzine.

And so ended a drama like no other in New Jersey history. In the years since McGreevey left office, he has rebuilt his life, come to terms with who he is, and emerged as a very public advocate for prisoners reentering society. He even forged a bond with Chris Christie on issues like prison reform and treatment for those caught up in the opioid epidemic. Redemption? I think so. Jim McGreevey's second act as a public person has been a credit to his character and his commitment to others. There's no happy ending here. The McGreeveys had a nasty, publicly played-out divorce. But at least Jim McGreevey was able to rise again from his downfall, which is a lesson for all of us.

Still, though, there are lingering questions some of us ask all these years later, and they focus on the complex and intriguing relationship between Charlie Kushner and Jim McGreevey.

There's no question that Charlie Kushner was and is an enigma. Those of us in New Jersey politics were familiar with his Jekyll and Hyde act years before he emerged in the public eye. A religious man, Kushner stopped work at Kushner Companies twice a day to give his Orthodox Jewish employees an opportunity to pray. But he's also the guy who set up his brother-in-law with a sex worker to intimidate and shame him in front of Kushner's sister, an act that's certainly incompatible with religious faith.

Kushner is soft-spoken and low-key, but he can become the most mean-spirited person imaginable when he doesn't get his way, something I saw first-hand when my law firm represented Kushner and another developer, Roseland, at some point during the McGreevey years. We had an agreement with our developer clients to waive any conflicts based on who contacted us first for a specific development. Both Kushner and Roseland's principal, Carl Goldberg, were interested in a huge development opportunity on the waterfront in

Perth Amboy. My thought was to bring them both together. The development was that big. Goldberg thought it was a good idea. Not Charlie. He figured his close connection to McGreevey would give him the upper hand. At a meeting I arranged, Kushner went into a tirade, cursing and threatening Goldberg with the wrath of God, using every profanity imaginable. Mr. Hyde emerged.

Even Al Gore felt Kushner's wrath during his presidential campaign twenty years ago. We had scheduled a fundraiser for Gore in New Jersey and tagged on a tour of Kushner's office building in Livingston, where he would greet employees. The tour was Kushner's idea, and it was designed to pump up his ego. As the day neared, Gore's campaign staff decided the tour wasn't a good idea. They called me to say Gore wasn't going to do it. When I broke the news to Kushner, he said, "Tell Gore the fundraiser's canceled." Gore took the tour. That's the kind of power Kushner had, and it was clear he wasn't shy about using it. His support for McGreevey in both 1997 and 2001 wasn't from the goodness of his heart. He was expecting things, like the chairmanship of the Port Authority, a subsidy to keep the Nets in New Jersey, designation as master developer for lucrative projects like the Perth Amboy waterfront, and support in his effort to build a medical school to be named for his mother. He was not happy that he couldn't cash in his chits.

Which leads us to the question—did Kushner set up Golan Cipel to take down McGreevey?

At that time there was speculation to that effect. The various entanglements were more than enough to get people whispering—there was the visa sponsorship, the job Kushner provided Cipel, the fact that Cipel lived in an expensive Manhattan hotel with no source of income and that McGreevey and Cipel sometimes disappeared to spend a weekend at Kushner's home in Florida. Was this how Lowy got "pictures"? And why did McGreevey have personal friends, Jason Kirin or Teddy Peterson, drive him rather than a state trooper? Could this be the reason why Cipel's attorney wouldn't give me proof of his claim—because it would expose Kushner's role in the extortion plot? The most telling Kushner connection was that phone call minutes before McGreevey's resignation speech, when I was told the governor wouldn't have to quit if he approved Touro College's application for a medical school to be named for Kushner's mother. We'll likely never know if Kushner was behind the extortion plot. There's certainly plenty of circumstantial evidence to suggest a connection. Kushner proved he's capable of doing anything. Then again, Cipel could have been acting as a free agent on Kushner's behalf.

On ne sait jamais.

Chelsea Clinton and Senator Lesniak discussing her book *Don't Let Them Disappear*, Kean University, Union, New Jersey. Private photo.

Volunteers at St. Hubert's Animal Welfare Center with workers and Lesniak's to-be-adopted dog, Sammy, St. Hubert's, Madison, New Jersey. Private photo.

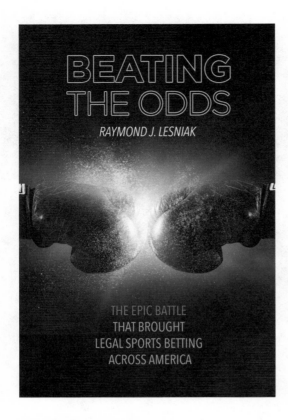

Front cover, *Beating the Odds.*

Letter from the Hon. Philippe Duron, chairman of the Human Rights Competition in Caen, France, won by Senator Lesniak.

Stephanie, Marge, and John Lesniak dining. Private photo.

Lesniak's niece Suzanne Devanney, his nephew Dan Devanney, his sister Marge Devanney, President Clinton, his mom Stephanie Lesniak, Raymond Lesniak, his nephew George Devanney, and his nephew Chris Devanney at Lesniak's home in Elizabeth, New Jersey. Private photo.

Stephanie Lesniak, at a young age. Private photo.

Katherine "Ma" Green. Private photo.

8 · FIGHTING INJUSTICES

I grew up in a working-class environment where everyone was supposed to know their place in life and that's where they stayed. And that was okay. Life was good. My dad provided my mom, sister, and me with a nice home, and we knew how to make do with what we had. Women became homemakers without even thinking about going to college. Young men out of high school took the many decent-paying working-class jobs that were available and got on with their lives. What made me different, I don't know. I was one of a few in my high school graduating class who went to college. Perhaps it was an aversion to work or because I saw my dad's great intellect go underappreciated in his job. I didn't have dreams of being prominent in anything, other than baseball. I breezed my way through classes with no ambition other than to show up and do the minimal work required. I was not an inspired student. I never thought about the future other than which team we were playing next, but I did have this nagging feeling of injustice that my dad's skills were not fully recognized because he had to drop out of school in the eighth grade to help support his family. It bothered me. It wasn't fair. And looking back through the years, I think that witnessing that unfairness—seeing my father's frustration when others were willfully blind to his intelligence simply because he lacked a full formal education—opened my eyes to the broader, systemic, and more serious injustices that so many less fortunate people face in our state and our country.

And when I experienced firsthand a small version of the injustice, unfairness, and outright bigotry that far too many Americans know all too well, it led me to redouble my advocacy for people who've had it far tougher than I had. In early 2007, two radio personalities at New Jersey 101.5 FM, Craig Carton (who had already gained "fame" by attacking Governor Dick Codey's wife) and Ray Rossi, decided to attack me based on my heritage and what they presumed to be my sexual orientation. They were known as the "Jersey guys," which was an insult to all of the decent people in the Garden State, and they specialized in the kind of humor that only an overgrown and not particularly bright frat boy would find amusing. They specialized in cruelty, bullying, and outright bigotry—they had "outing days" when they named public figures they thought were gay and, of course, made fun of them. Disgraceful.

Their attack on me started off as banter that went off the rails of decency. They saw a picture of me with my arm around another man with fire engine red hair dressed in a leopard skin outfit. Their presumption was that I must be gay. Here's what the Jersey Guys didn't know, or didn't care to know: that red-haired guy was a Polish rock performer who was a guest of honor at a house party I threw after a performance at the Ritz Theatre in Elizabeth. The party was part of my efforts to promote Polish culture, something that would make Ma Green and my mother proud.

Carton and Rossi went on a rant about the picture and then referred to me as a "gay Polack." I wasn't upset at being called gay, although I'm not, because that's not derogatory. But use of the ethnic slur "Polack" drove me to take action. I wrote a widely circulated op-ed in the *Star-Ledger* condemning the hatred of the Jersey Guys for their demeaning of my heritage. I called the station manager to explain why "Polack" was such an offensive term. My father, a brilliant man and the son of Polish immigrants, had to endure that kind of name-calling—being called "Polack" by those who wanted to demean him. I learned as a child what people meant when they called me or my dad a "Polack." It wasn't pretty, and it wasn't pleasant. And to hear it said on the public airwaves, directed at me personally, got my Polish up.

My complaints led Carton and Rossi to step up their attacks, not on me but on all Polish people. They kept using the term "Polack" to describe Poles and stated, falsely, that half of Poland joined the Nazis so they could kill Jews during World War II. The stupidity was astounding—did they not know that World War II started when the Nazis invaded Poland? Four flags of the invading D-Day forces—the United States, Great Britain, Canada, and Poland—fly on the beaches of Normandy. The Polish Air Forces (Polskie Siły Powietrzne) fought in the Battle of Britain and contributed to Allied air operations throughout the war. And during the famous Battle of Monte Cassino in Italy on May 16, 1944, soldiers from the Polish II Corps were part of the final assault on the Nazi positions. The Polish flag was raised over the fortress two days later. Carton and Rossi were obviously unaware of this history of World War II.

When they tried to ridicule me for taking them on, Jim Gearhart, the morning drive-time host, said, "I don't think you've heard the last from Lesniak." That was absolutely true. Along with LGBTQ leader Steven Goldstein, I formed a group called the Coalition Against Bigotry and Hate to notify the show's sponsors of the bigotry being spewed by the so-called Jersey Boys. My objections over the slur on my heritage were joined by members of other ethnic and religious groups and the LGBTQ community. The station did not renew their contract, and their hate was removed from the airwaves. Carton got a high-profile gig at the all-sports station WFAN, but karma caught up with him in 2017 when he was arrested on charges of defrauding investors in a ticket-reselling Ponzi scheme. I'm a forgiving person, but that doesn't stop me from being grateful that he got his comeuppance. And I'm sure I'm not alone. Carton served just over a year in prison and was confined to a halfway house for two more years. I'm sure he won't seek me out for advice, but he would serve himself well if he made amends to the many whom he maligned over his years, given that WFAN gave him a second chance with an afternoon talk show after he did his time in prison and in the halfway house.

Sadly, millions of Americans—people of color, the LGBTQ community, those with disabilities, and others—have experienced far worse bigotry and open displays of hatred. My experience gave me a small insight into their world, and that motivated me to double down on my advocacy for the disadvantaged and the oppressed. But it wasn't just about the name-calling. I also went through a midlife spiritual conversion brought on by another devastating breakup with a girlfriend. My life was thrown into a tailspin, but I emerged from it with a more positive outlook on life and a higher degree of sensitivity and empathy for others. I matured and began to take what life was all about more thoughtfully. I realized that my judgment had been adversely impacted by politics—I was making decisions based mainly on political expediency. Even when I bucked the trend, as I did with my early environmental protection initiatives, I was as much driven by ego as by the cause. I'm not saying I've totally suppressed my ego. The content of this book attests that I haven't, but my life became more balanced and empathetic and I became a fierce advocate for my beliefs, their political impact be damned.

The self-help books I turned to led me to see the world from a different perspective, from a humane perspective, rather than from a purely political and calculating point of view. My favorite was M. Scott Peck's *The Road Less Traveled: A New Psychology of Love, Traditional Values, and Spiritual Growth.* That book and others changed my heart and my political position on one of the divisive issues of our time—the death penalty. As I mentioned previously,

I supported capital punishment earlier in my legislative career. There's no doubt that my position didn't hurt me politically. The early 1980s were a difficult time in many cities, including Elizabeth, and violent crime seemed to be an inevitable and perhaps unsolvable part of modern life. The number of murders statewide skyrocketed from 164 in 1960 to 504 in 1980. Likewise for rapes, from 442 in 1960 to 2,257 two decades later. The total number of violent crimes in New Jersey rose from 6,932 in 1960 to 44,373 in 1980. Yes, the state's population grew from 6 million to 7.3 million—a significant increase— during those twenty years, but that doesn't even begin to explain the disheartening rise in violent crime throughout New Jersey. The public began to demand action, and the death penalty emerged as a political litmus test, even though it actually made little sense. After all, capital punishment has never been proved to be a deterrent to murder, let alone violent crimes in general. But as the debate was framed in the early 1980s, to be against the death penalty was akin to being "soft on crime." And no one wanted that. We all learned from Ed Koch's victory over Mario Cuomo in New York City's mayoral race in 1977 that opponents of the death penalty, like Cuomo, were out of touch with public anger over violent crime. So when the death penalty came up for reauthorization in New Jersey when I was in the Assembly, I voted in favor.

I believed my constituents were in favor of capital punishment, and at the time, so was I. But as I reassessed my life, as I paid attention to my newfound spirituality, I came to the conclusion that capital punishment was barbaric and immoral, just as the Catholic Church was sharpening its own opposition. During his papacy, John Paul II appealed for a consensus to end the death penalty on the grounds that it was "both cruel and unnecessary."

While nobody had been executed in New Jersey since we reinstated the death penalty in 1963, nevertheless the law was on the books and four prisoners were on death row. About twenty years after I voted to reinstate the death penalty, two abolitionists came to visit me in my Senate offices in hopes that I might have a change of heart. They met a different person than the assemblyman who voted to reinstate the death penalty. They had no idea I was already a convert. Celeste Fitzgerald was the director of New Jerseyans for Alternatives to the Death Penalty, and Lorry Post represented a group called Murder Victims' Families for Reconciliation. They concluded I might be the right choice to champion the abolition of the death penalty given my progressive record on other issues and wanted a convert on the death penalty to lead the charge for its abolition. They suspected I had changed my position on the death penalty. They were right.

So we went to work. The campaign put together under the auspices of Fitzgerald's organization was a classic example of combining smart political strategy with shrewd tactics and determination. We were determined, not going to take no for an answer from any legislator without trying all our strategies. The advocates, especially family members of murder victims, brought their sense of righteousness. I brought political know-how, important connections, and an intense sense of purpose guided by my newfound spirituality and my old doggedness to achieve success.

The key strategic decision was to support an alternative to the death penalty—life without parole—instead of just abolishing it. In addition, the advocates proposed the formation of a commission to study the fairness and cost of the death penalty, while calling for an official moratorium on executions. When the necessary legislation stalled because of the proposed moratorium, Fitzgerald's group wisely compromised, agreeing to drop the moratorium. The revised bill overwhelmingly passed both houses. Alas, Governor McGreevey vetoed it, saying that New Jersey already had studied the death penalty to death, the actual words in his veto message. True to form, McGreevey was not willing to take a stand on what he perceived to be an unpopular issue. Even something as simple as studying the fairness of the death penalty—never mind considering its morality—posed political risks that McGreevey was unwilling to take. It should be noted, though, that after McGreevey left office and reflected on his life, he became a fierce advocate for helping former offenders reenter into society. His advocacy has been genuine and effective.

McGreevey's successor, Dick Codey, had supported the moratorium when he was Senate president. We tried again to pass a study commission and a moratorium. This time it passed both houses, and Codey signed it into law. The first step toward abolition was complete. The advocates didn't take for granted that the commission would return a favorable report and that would be sufficient to get legislators' support. They met with every legislator, often with a family member of a murder victim from the legislator's district. Meetings were held in churches, where attendees wrote postcards to be mailed to legislators urging abolition. I would frequently attend these meetings— sometimes there were only ten people, but legislators would receive ten postcards as a result. You'd be surprised how effective ten postcards from a resident of a legislator's district can be.

I testified before the commission on September 13, 2006. Here, in part, is what I said: "In 1982, I voted to reinstate the death penalty. I was wrong. Thank God, no one has been executed to date. And thank God, no innocent person has been executed. As the saying goes, 'there but for the grace of

God. . . .' We now have an opportunity to right that wrong. It is not my intention to debate the moral aspects of the death penalty. I believe it is immoral. Others disagree. That's a debate that should take place in another forum. I'm here to voice my opinion that the death penalty should be replaced by a life sentenced without parole; that the death penalty is not a deterrent to murder; that its cost in tax dollars is wasteful spending; and that there is no way to create a foolproof system to prevent the execution of an innocent person. My heart goes out to every family member devastated by the murder of a loved one. They have every right to be angry and to express that anger. But I'm certain that deep down not one of them would want to act on that anger. . . . I'm not asking that anyone be set free. I'm just asking that, rather than the death penalty, which is irreversible when executed, that we not play God. Let's just instead require that people convicted of murder spend the rest of their lives in prison with no possibility of parole." I also spoke about Byron Halsey, a Plainfield resident who spent nineteen years in prison for the horrific murder and sexual assault of his girlfriend's two children, both under the age of ten, in 1988. One juror held out against the death penalty, thankfully, because it turned out that Halsey didn't commit the crimes. DNA evidence proved that he was innocent and that the murderer was a neighbor who by then was already in prison for other violent crimes. But for one juror, New Jersey might have executed an innocent person and the actual murderer would have never been found.

On January 2, 2007, the study commission released its recommendations. It called for the abolition of the death penalty and its replacement by life without parole in a maximum-security facility. In addition, it recommended that the state fund services and benefits to the families of murder victims from the cost savings it would see by not pursing expensive death penalty cases. The state never did follow up on this latter suggestion. Nobody could honestly say that the commission's decision was inevitable or that it was stacked with death penalty opponents. A majority of its thirteen members were either neutral on the topic or actually opposed to abolition. The advocates wanted it that way, believing the strength of their position would produce a favorable report. The commission's makeup included a state Supreme Court justice, a police chief, two county prosecutors, the state attorney general, a representative from the state bar association, and the sponsor of New Jersey's death penalty, former Senate president John Russo, whose father was murdered in 1970. Russo was the only commissioner to oppose the commission's recommendation to abolish the death penalty and replace it with life without parole. Russo and I were close friends. I once asked him whom else could he trust if he couldn't trust me. "Nobody," he said. I took it as a compliment, though I'm not sure he intended it that way. Russo had no doubts about the injustice of the death penalty. His personal story was tragic and emotional. He and his family, including his father, were spending New Year's Eve in Asbury Park—a family tradition—in 1970 when a stranger, apparently a drug addict, came to the door with a gun and demanded money. Russo's brother tried to shut the door on the stranger, but he opened fire into the house, killing Russo's father as he sat at the dining room table. Russo insisted that his position on capital punishment had nothing to do with his father's death. He said he believed all along that punishment should fit the crime, and that the death penalty was a proper punishment for some murders. I knew Russo was not out for revenge. He had thought long and hard about the issue and concluded that the death penalty was moral and just in some cases. One person close to him vehemently disagreed: His own mother. "I pray you get off of this electric chair thing," his mother once told him. "It gets me so upset to think about it." Russo never let his passion about the death penalty affect our relationship, which remained close throughout. I certainly understood his position.

With the commission's recommendation now on the record, it was time to turn it into a law, working with Celeste and Lorry and their organizations and my legislative colleagues, Senator Shirley Turner, who sponsored the first attempt to form a commission, Senator Nia Gill, Senator Sandra Cunningham, Senator Teresa Ruiz, Senate President Dick Codey, Assembly Speaker Joe Roberts, and Governor Jon Corzine. We were ready to call for a vote. The first vote to abolish the death penalty was in the Senate on December 10, 2007. My floor speech began, "We shouldn't have the death penalty unless we're going to use it. And we shouldn't use it if there is a chance of executing an innocent person. One of our Founding Fathers, Benjamin Franklin, an author of both the Declaration of Independence and our Constitution, believed it was better to set guilty people free than to imprison an innocent person. This legislation not only doesn't set anyone free, it imprisons the guilty for the rest of their lives without parole."

I believed we had the votes needed to pass the bill—twenty-one—but as the balloting began, it became clear it could go either way. We had done so much work, put in so many hours, and now, at the climactic moment in the Senate, it was possible that it was all for naught. The voting scoreboard in the Senate showed the vote stuck on twenty. I needed one more vote for passage; by the same token, opponents needed one more vote to defeat it. My friend, Sharpe James, Newark mayor and state senator, had committed his support but had not yet voted. Sharpe sat next to me in the chamber. I looked at him and shrugged my shoulders, sending a message, "What are you waiting for Sharpe? You committed to vote yes." Sharpe was holding out because his deputy mayor, Senator Ron Rice, was strongly against abolition. Rice, a former police officer and Marine, opposed any legislation he saw as "coddling criminals." He even opposed needle exchange programs that keep drug addicts from getting HIV. Sharpe wanted to avoid a break with Rice on this issue and was holding out to see if I needed his vote, but as the minutes passed I was getting a little nervous. Meanwhile, some other senator—to this day I don't know whom it was because I was so focused on Sharpe's dilemma—cast the twenty-first vote in favor of abolition. That sealed the deal, and Sharpe knew it. "You got your twenty-one votes," he said to me. So he finally cast his vote, or rather he formally abstained from voting in deference to Rice. I have no doubt that if we needed his vote Sharpe would have been with us. After all, he gave me his word, and Sharpe was old school about keeping his commitments.

With the Senate on board, the bill made its way to the Assembly. That chamber's Law and Public Safety Committee conducted a hearing on December 13, 2007, during which sixty-three family members of murder victims submitted a joint statement in favor of abolition. It was powerful testimony: "We are family members and loved ones of murder victims," the statement read. "We desperately miss the parents, children, siblings, and spouses we have lost. We live with the pain and heartbreak of their absence every day and would do anything to have them back. We have been touched by the criminal justice system in ways we never imagined and would never wish on anyone. Our experience compels us to speak out for change. Though we share different perspectives on the death penalty, every one of us agrees that New Jersey's capital punishment system doesn't work and we would be better off without it." In the words of another family member, Vicki Schieber, whose daughter, Shannon, was raped and murdered: "The death penalty is a harmful policy that exacerbates the pain for murdered victims' families." The bill moved forward and headed for a vote in the Assembly. And again, it became clear that the vote was going to be close. Just a few days before the vote, four college-aged young people were murdered execution-style on the grounds of Mount Vernon School in Newark. The killings made national headlines, and the gruesome details led to cries for vengeance. Suddenly, abolishing the death penalty seemed like a bad idea, at least to some legislators. Joe Roberts, the Assembly speaker, supported the bill, but he could not get four holdouts in the Democratic caucus to agree, and without those votes the bill was doomed.

Roberts called me while I was in a caucus of Democrat senators across the hall from the Assembly chamber. He asked me to come onto the Assembly floor in person and take a dramatic look up at the voting board. I understood immediately what message he was looking to send. I was the legislature's most prominent champion of the bill and also had a reputation as someone determined to get his legislation through. I had no problem with that reputation—in fact, I reveled in it. Politics is all about the use (and, as we saw in Washington recently under President Trump, the abuse) of power. I had spent years accumulating power and wasn't afraid to use it on behalf of a cause in which I believed. So I did as Roberts asked. I very conspicuously entered the Assembly chamber and took a good, long look at the board. Within a few minutes, four votes were added to the "Yes" side. The timing wasn't a coincidence. There were four people in the chamber who didn't want to stand in the way of this historic legislation passing the Assembly. And so the bill passed and went to Governor Corzine's desk. He signed it on December 17, 2007, also using the occasion to commute the death sentences of the four New Jersey prisoners on death row.

At the bill-signing ceremony, Corzine said: "For the people of New Jersey, I sign this bill with pride. . . . This is one of those conscience votes that individuals must actually weigh and balance their own sense of morality and I am very grateful to all of you. . . . It should be noted that because of the action of the legislature, this is the first state to legislatively end the death penalty since the U.S. Supreme Court reauthorized capital punishment in 1976." It was a great accomplishment for the state and one that was noted around the world. In Rome, an international lay Catholic group called the Community of Saint'Egidio arranged to light up the famed Coliseum to celebrate our achievement. The community advocates for an end to the death penalty around the world and since 1999 has lit up the Coliseum every time a government has abolished capital punishment or commuted a condemned prisoner's death sentence.

A year later, an anti-capital-punishment group called Focus on the Death Penalty recognized our efforts by presenting Corzine with its annual award. Four others also were honored, including author John Grisham, whose novel *The Chamber* had an anti-death-penalty theme. The organization's founder is actor Mike Farrell, who played B. J. Hunnicutt on the television show *M*A*S*H*. Corzine asked me to go to California to accept the award on his behalf. In an interview before leaving, I told a reporter that I intended to give a book I had just published, *The Road to Abolition: How New Jersey Abolished the Death Penalty*, to the other award recipients. She asked me if I had read any of John Grisham's books. "No," I said. "Do you think he's read any of mine?"

At the award luncheon I sat with Farrell's wife, the lovely Shelley Fabares, who was a teenager on the *Donna Reed Show*. She remains cute as a button, with multicolored streaked hair. When I was growing up every teenager was in love with her.

Farrell was the event's main speaker, and during his talk he said that there were some criminals whose actions are so heinous, so depraved, that they deserve the death penalty. Those words sucked the air out of the room because we all believed that if you were against the death penalty, there could be no exceptions. You either opposed state-sanctioned executions or you didn't. There was one exception that most of us were aware of, and it took place in 1962 when Israel hanged Adolf Eichmann, one of the architects of the Holocaust. Israel did not and does not have a death penalty statute, but in Eichmann's case it decided death by hanging was the only appropriate punishment for the man who helped murder six million Jews. None of us would disagree. But as Farrell talked about those whose crimes were worthy of capital punishment, we all froze, not sure where he was going. And then he laughed and said, "Vice President Dick Cheney, for example." The audience laughed and breathed a collective sigh of relief. Cheney, it bears remembering, was the biggest advocate for the U.S. invasion of Iraq in 2003, one of the worst foreign policy decisions in recent American history—and a decision that cost the lives of hundreds of thousands of innocent Iraqis and nearly five thousand U.S. troops. Farrell then went on to praise New Jersey for abolishing its death penalty. It was a pleasure to hear New Jersey praised as a leader in this human rights issue. And since we repealed capital punishment, several other states have followed suit: New Mexico (2009), Illinois (2011), Connecticut (2012), Maryland (2013), New Hampshire (2019), and Colorado (2020) have replaced the death penalty with life without parole.

In the case of New Mexico, the governor at the time, Bill Richardson, was on the fence about abolition. I was acquainted with Richardson through President Clinton, who had appointed him as U.S. ambassador to the United Nations and as energy secretary. I called the governor, urging him to sign the bill and making the case for abolition. He was cordial enough, even mentioning that Corzine had already called him to make the case, but he was noncommittal. In the end, though, he signed the bill. I believe our support helped him reach that decision.

All these years later, capital punishment was back in the news in 2019 when Trump's attorney general, William Barr, cleared the way for the federal government to resume capital punishment after a lapse of nearly two decades. Sure enough, several people were executed in the final months of the Trump administration. Trump even called for the use of firing squads and bringing back the electric chair. Ugh. Trump was keeping true to form, having called for the death penalty for the infamous "Central Park Five" who were charged with a brutal rape. This was before they were wrongfully convicted, then eventually released. Again true to form, Trump still insists they should have been executed.

The national mood has changed since New Jersey abolished the death penalty, but while the share of Americans supporting the death penalty has risen since 2016, it remains much lower than it was in the 1990s or throughout much of the 2000s. For me, though, it's not about public opinion, not anymore. It's a moral decision, and that's how I approached it. And that's how every developed country in the world, with the exception of Japan, approaches it. Many friends and political acquaintances have said that abolishing the death penalty is my most significant legislative accomplishment. While I'm pleased that they think so, I also achieved several other significant criminal and social justice reforms. For example, New Jersey some years ago imposed mandatory minimum sentences for drug offenses in school zones around the state, but the law was applied mainly for offenses in urban areas, not in suburban communities. That was patently unfair. The law flooded our prisons with people convicted for minor drug infractions. Most were poor people of color, while more affluent people, most of them white, were immune to the law's harsh penalties. It wasn't easy to support eliminating these mandatory minimum sentences for drug offenses in school zones, but I wrote legislation to do so anyway, seeing this as yet another injustice I could help bring to an end. Governor Corzine agreed and signed my legislation. As a result, New Jersey's prison population declined by 20 percent and mass incarceration began to end in the Garden State. America has 5 percent of the world's population but 25 percent of the world's prison population, largely because of mandatory minimum sentences. As Winston Churchill said, "Americans will always do the right thing, only after they have tried everything else."

Near the end of my Senate career I was asked by David Kerr to sponsor the most significant corrections reform proposal in America—Earn Your Way Out. In August 1968, David founded Integrity House, a nonprofit organization devoted to rebuilding the lives of substance users. David saw that hope along with taking responsibility for your life were determining factors in an addict's recovery. So David developed Earn Your Way Out for prisoners, the majority of whom had substance use disorders. I got Earn Your Way Out passed by the legislature, but it was vetoed by Governor Christie. I'm happy to say it was signed by Governor Murphy, thanks to Senator Cunningham's sponsorship after I left the Senate. Earn Your Way Out will change the culture of corrections by giving inmates an opportunity to become better persons when they leave prison than when they entered. Sadly, that hasn't been the case. Prison often hardens inmates, thus the high recidivism rate. Earn Your Way Out requires that a reentry plan be developed when inmates enter prison, not when they leave, as is currently done, and gives time off for participating in the program, which includes education, job training, therapy, and community service. Surprisingly, Earn Your Way Out has strong support from Americans for Prosperity, the conservative organization sponsored by the Koch family, and from Right on Crime at the Texas Public Policy Foundation, a conservative think tank—support I welcomed with open arms.

Another criminal justice initiative I sponsored, reform of solitary confinement, was vetoed by Governor Christie and had to wait for a sympathetic governor, Murphy, to become law. Now there are strict limits on the circumstances when solitary confinement can be imposed and the length of time a prisoner can be confined. Solitary confinement is almost the very definition of cruel punishment, which the U.S. Constitution explicitly prohibits. Its impact is particularly profound on juveniles, whose brains are still developing, and on people with mental health issues, who make up about a third of prisoners in isolation. If prisoners are not mentally ill when entering an isolation unit, by the time they are released, their mental health has been severely compromised. Many prisoners are released directly to the streets after spending years in isolation, a fact that ought to horrify any reasonable person. Bernie Kerik, a former New York police commissioner under Rudy Giuliani, was kept in solitary confinement for sixty days to keep him "safe" from other inmates. He says that he considers solitary confinement to be cruel and unusual punishment and that it's important to consider the long-term effects of how prisoners are treated. Thanks to the work of Senator Nellie Pou and the support of Governor Murphy, solitary confinement as we knew it no longer is used in New Jersey.

Another criminal justice reform measure, expanding eligibility for treatment in place of prison for nonviolent drug offenses, was the result of a frightening personal experience. On Saturday, April 18, 2009, I was awakened at two thirty in the morning by two men, Brian Kinney and Antoine Neal, standing over my bed in Elizabeth. I was home alone. My wife, Salena, had taken our dog Brittany to our house at the Jersey Shore. I stayed back because, ironically, I was scheduled to drive to Pennsylvania the following day to meet with legislators there about abolishing the Keystone State's death penalty. I had produced a pamphlet: "A Blueprint for Ending the Death Penalty. How Pennsylvania Can Follow New Jersey." It asked tough questions about the death penalty, focusing on the possible killing of innocent people to the disproportionate number of poor people and people of color on death row. But I never made it to Pennsylvania. My unwanted visitors saw to that. Kinney and Neal had entered my home by smashing in a basement window. They were looking for money to feed their drug addiction. They obviously had cased our home in the past and were as surprised to see someone inside on a Saturday at two thirty in the morning as I was to see them because we usually went to our Shore home on weekends. Seeing me shook them up. I heard a voice say, "Shoot him!" It was Neal. He was on the verge of panic. Luckily his companion, who was a good deal younger, wasn't ready to do something rash. "Stay cool," Kinney told me as I lay in bed, staring at them in the darkness and trying to figure out what, if anything, I could do. "We're not going to hurt you," Kinney said. "We're good people. We're just in a bad place right now." Those words—we're good people—stayed with me. I can still hear them. Kinney didn't say, "We're not bad people." He said, "We're *good* people. We're just in a bad place right now." That's how they saw themselves. They took my money—luckily I kept my cash in a box in the kitchen, to which I directed them. I kept plenty of cash on hand, a habit from when all the money I had was in my pocket. Neal and Kinney were pleased, didn't harm me, and told me not to make a move. They left my house and, we learned later, went to get high again at a housing development down the street. I stayed in bed, motionless, for about ten minutes after they left. It seemed like an eternity. I thought about my own stupidity during those long minutes. I had an alarm system, but I used it only when we weren't home. I never canceled our newspapers on weekends when we were away, so the pile of blue and yellow wrappers on the front lawn was an invitation to would-be intruders. And we were well aware of the addicts who hung out in the public housing development nearby. Stupid, stupid, stupid.

When I finally got out of bed, I realized that, in addition to my money, they took my phone and my car keys (but not my car). Oh, and they also took a magnum of one of my best wines, Far Niente. I think that's what upset me the most. Without access to a phone or my car, I decided to walk two blocks to the local firehouse to report the crime. Along the way, I was propositioned by a lady of the night working the street. "Want a date?" she asked. I shrugged my shoulders and with gallows humor said, "I don't have any money. I just got robbed." She didn't bat an eye—she just walked away hoping for better luck with the next passer-by. I rang the doorbell to the firehouse, and a fireman came to the door. I explained I needed to report a robbery and the robbers had taken my phone. I was asked my name. I said Senator Lesniak. The firefighter was a young man who didn't recognize me. He called the local police station and said some guy's here saying he's Senator Lesniak and was just robbed. The police came immediately, even waking up Mayor Bollwage to alert him.

The robbery—and the unspoken possibility that it could have been so much worse—was big news statewide. That was bad news for the two perpetrators, Kinney and Neal, who apparently were bragging about their haul. Every confidential informant in the city of Elizabeth was eager to score points with the police by giving them up. The pair were busted a few days after their early morning visit to my house. They agreed to a plea bargain, and I testified on their behalf at their sentencing, not because I'm a superliberal, although I am. I testified because drug addicts need treatment, not a prison sentence so they won't be back terrorizing someone in the future to get money to feed their habits. Unfortunately, Neal had a prior second-degree offense, so he didn't qualify for drug court diversion. I later changed the law to expand qualification for those with prior second-degree offenses.

My empathy for the two men who broke into my home caught the attention of Pam Capaci, who was then the CEO of a Union County–based organization called Prevention Links. It runs programs designed to prevent the abuse of drugs, alcohol, and tobacco and to support those in recovery. Pam asked me to help her start a specialized high school for children with substance use disorders. I thought it was a brilliant idea.

The foundation of recovery from any addiction is to change people, places, and things. That's why children returning to school from rehab for substance use disorder rarely graduate from high school and often wind up in prison, die young, or both. They continue to get peer pressure to use drugs and alcohol. Specialized schools—called recovery high schools—provide the safe environment and support these children need to get an education and stay sober. Recovery high schools throughout the country have a nearly 90 percent graduation rate. It is estimated that one in seven Americans will develop a substance use disorder at some point in their lives. Of those, 90 percent begin using before the age of eighteen. New Jersey youth are disproportionately affected by substance abuse. A 2015 study by Trust for America's Health found that from 2011 to 2013 overdose deaths among twelve- to twenty-five-year-olds in New Jersey numbered 10.7 per 100,000, ranking as the sixth highest rate of overdose deaths in that age group as compared to other states. Youth and young adults under the age of twenty-four composed 20 percent of treatment admissions in New Jersey facilities in 2016. Despite these depressing statistics, the New Jersey education establishment didn't want to relinquish control of their students, saying, "We don't have a drug problem in our schools" or "We can handle this ourselves." No they can't. A cornerstone of recovery is to stay away from the people, places, and things that were part of your addiction. However, the Union County's Superintendent of Schools were all ears and gave their support when Pam and I made a presentation at their monthly meeting.

I secured an arrangement with Kean University president Dawood Farahi to provide the physical space we needed, allowing us to move forward with our other partners, Union County Vo-Tech, thanks to its superintendent Pete Capodice, and Prevention Links, thanks to Pam Capaci and the Union County Board of Freeholders (now called Board of Commissioners), which contributed financial support. We cut the ribbon on the facility at Kean in September 2014 and welcomed our first student the following January. (The student went on to graduate from my alma mater, Rutgers University, after finishing at the recovery high school.) There was a movement to name the new school after me. I declined the honor at first. I never wanted a building, roadway, street, or anything else named after me, but after giving it further thought, I changed my mind. This was a school with a different and necessary mission: it not only provided an education but saved lives. So, with my acceptance, the state's first recovery high school was named the Raymond J. Lesniak Experience, Strength, Hope, Recovery High School. Since its inception, the school has continued to provide services and mentorship to dozens of students who have gone on to attend Rutgers, Montclair State, Rider University, and an array of trade and vocational schools. Many graduates remain in touch with the school's staff and have shared their stories of recovery and hope with new students. It's an inspiring story. In the years since, recovery high schools have opened in Cape May and Monmouth counties. My goal is to have a recovery high school in every region in the state for a very simple reason: every region in the state needs one.

Demands for reform of the criminal justice system, of prisons, and of policing have gone national since the killing of George Floyd while in the custody of Minneapolis police officers in 2020. Video of Floyd's painful death inspired protests not seen since the antiwar demonstrations of the late 1960s and early 1970s. We have seen movements toward change in policing, but that won't be enough to address systematic inequalities in America. To be clear, I am not anti-police. Our law enforcement community protects us every day from criminals, often putting their lives on the line, and they deserve our appreciation, but there is a problem in their ranks. They must be part of the solution. The key, in my opinion, to restoring trust in law enforcement and making Black lives matter is multifold—civilian review boards, transparency, integration of police departments, and training police in methods of de-escalation. What's more, universal use of body cameras will help civilians and police to get at the truth. Resolution of police brutality complaints by civilian review boards must be available for the public to see. Police departments should not be defunded. Indeed, they should receive increased funding to pay for the needed reforms, including enhanced recruitment of minority police officers. America is the greatest country in the world, but it is not without serious flaws. We should acknowledge our flaws and fix them. We've had our collective heads in the sand for too long on many matters, as the social justice awakening of 2020 showed. Just look at how long we denied civil rights to African Americans and the LGBTQ community. Or how many Americans are without health insurance. Thankfully we are moving toward being a more just society under President Biden, after a four-year hiatus under Donald Trump.

Social change comes infrequently in one's lifetime, if at all. If the broad range of social justice reforms being proposed are implemented, we will see profound and long-sought improvements in the inequalities of our society. We should be so fortunate.

Social change also can come from individual examples, as exemplified by Pope Francis, who demonstrates acts of kindness on a daily basis. As a bishop, he would roam the streets of Buenos Aires handing out food to the homeless, and as pope he has invited them to lunch. I'm what is called a "lapsed Catholic," a Catholic in name only. However I have been going to Mass more often, prompted by the advocacy for universal justice by Pope Francis. In a conversation I had not long ago with Rev. George D. Gillen, pastor of St. Genevieve Church in Elizabeth, I mentioned that Pope Francis might bring me back to the church. The pastor whispered in my ear jokingly, "He may bring me back too."

9 · THE FIGHT FOR LGBTQ RIGHTS

It has been a healthy experience for me to think back at my life and career, recount a few stories, and offer a bit of insight through this memoir. But at this point in the story, there's no avoiding sadness, because the issue I want to discuss—equal rights for the LGBTQ community—is entwined with memories of my late wife, Salena. She helped transform me from being a supporter of gay rights to being an advocate for them. It's an important distinction that I saw in Salena's dedication and passionate advocating for marriage equality. Salena died suddenly on July 3, 2019, at the age of forty-three, a victim of arteriosclerosis disease. There were no prior indications of any medical problems. Salena was at our shore house preparing to cook for the many guests we would be entertaining during the July 4th celebrations. She loved to cook and entertain. I had stayed in our Elizabeth home the night before, and as I turned the corner to the shore house the next morning, I saw police cars and an ambulance in our driveway. I went into panic mode, jumped out of the car, and was told there was a young woman dead in the house. I freaked out, screaming and banging my head against the fence. The police chaplain who was there took me to an ambulance, and I was transported to a nearby hospital. I was administered Xanax intravenously. The rest of the day and subsequent days are just one big blur. I'm not alone in experiencing such a tragedy. It's a part of life, as I tell myself. You don't overcome it. You get through it. At Salena's wake, Bill Clinton called to express his sympathy. What a kind and thoughtful person. I hadn't seen him in years. He met Salena several times when we got together at the White House or at fundraisers at our home. I was in a daze throughout the wake and funeral services, but a call from the former president gave me some comfort. U.S. senator Menendez called from South America. At such a terrible moment in my life, I was learning a lesson in humanity and decency. I hadn't previously realized the impact you can have by simply reaching out to those who are grieving. Here were two very busy people—Clinton and Menendez—for whom I could do nothing at this time in their political careers, yet they took the time from far away to reach out and comfort me.

Salena and I lived life to the fullest together for two decades and shared a lifetime's worth of experiences and memories. Salena was a "foodie," an expression she didn't like, but one that's used to describe someone who is a follower of celebrity chefs and constantly watches cooking shows on TV. Every year we went to the South Beach Wine & Food Festival, going to see the top chefs showing off their famous dishes. She reveled in getting her picture taken with Bobby Flay or Guy Savoy. We took bicycle trips through France every year. She would get really pissed when she asked me a question and I answered it in French. Knowing my love of skiing, she took it up. We went to Bruce Springsteen concerts at every opportunity. I laid down one law. Don't expect me to go to a Bon Jovi concert with you. Bad enough I went to Barry Manilow concerts. Salena's greatest joy was preparing for our Operation Santa, when we fulfilled gift wishes of children from disadvantaged families. She would shoo me away any time I tried to help, knowing I would only get in the way. On the political side, with a small group of young activists she formed Dems 2000 to represent the younger generation in the Democratic Party. When I think of her now, as I do every day, I find myself dwelling on the energy she brought not just to our lives together, but also to the causes in which she fiercely believed. The sadness will always be there, but, as I've been told, at some point it is accompanied by gratitude for the years we had together.

Salena's greatest contribution to my public policy beliefs was her fierce advocacy for equality and justice, serving for a time as chair of the New Jersey Civil Rights Commission. Her most passionate concern was LGBTQ rights. When the New Jersey Supreme Court ruled in the case of *Lewis v. Harris* in 2006 that same-sex couples had a constitutional right to the same rights and obligations as heterosexual couples—but stopped short of ruling they had a right to marry—I called the state's foremost crusader for LGBTQ rights, Steven Goldstein, to offer my congratulations. I got an earful in reply. "It's not enough! It's wrong! We deserve the right to marry," screamed Goldstein. When I recounted that conversation with Salena, if you could call it a conversation, I got earful number two. The passion from Steven and Salena was impressive and convincing. That was the moment when I realized I had to do more than simply lend my support to the LGBTQ community. I had to take more of a leadership role to ensure that the state treated our LGBTQ residents as full and equal citizens, entitled to all the rights and privileges enjoyed by heterosexuals, including marriage. I realized that recognition of same-sex marriage was more than simply allowing same-sex couples to marry—much, much more. It was about acceptance. Ultimately, it was about love.

I had seen how disowning or denying your authentic self can hurt—even torture—a person. I saw that in Jim McGreevey, whose Catholic upbringing and stern parents left no room for his authentic gay self. He talked with me about the pain he went through thinking there was something wrong with him, that the feelings he had no control over made him a bad person.

I had seen it in my own family as a young adult. My cousin Eddie was gay. Not that we knew, but we knew. Eddie was with his partner Julio for years, but it was never talked about. We treated Julio as we would any family member. Enough said, even though nothing was said. When Eddie died years ago, we all gathered at the funeral home to offer our final goodbyes before leaving for the funeral Mass. As the funeral home director called us up to the casket, Julio lined up with friends of the family. I took Julio aside and told him that he belonged with us, Eddie's family. Even in these sad circumstances, Julio was afraid to show who he was. That would all change with marriage equality. I've seen the joy and love when someone is free to embrace who they are. I saw it in the eyes of Marsha and Louise Walpin-Shapiro, who were the plaintiffs in the state Supreme Court case mentioned earlier. I came to believe that recognition of same-sex marriage would be uplifting for everyone, and would be an important step toward greater acceptance and a more just society.

I called my colleague from Bergen County, Senator Loretta Weinberg, who was the prime sponsor of a bill that would establish marriage equality in New Jersey. I asked her if she had a prime cosponsor, an important step for any measure if it has a chance of passage. Loretta said she did not. I told her to sign me up. And the journey began. Steven Goldstein organized rallies at the State House that were attended by thousands, for and against. Salena was at every one, proudly wearing a T-shirt from Garden State Equality, the gay rights organization Goldstein founded, for which she was a trustee. I miss her enthusiasm, her commitment to her beliefs, and her love every day. Our strongest opposition, no surprise, came from religious groups, particularly the Catholic Church, Baptists, and Hasidics. At one demonstration a Hasidic boy sneaked away from his group, came up to Goldstein, and bared his soul. "I have attractions to people of the same sex," he said. "I think it's wrong but I don't think it's wrong. I know it will never go away no matter how much I try. It's who I am and I can never say that in my community." Goldstein comforted the young boy and cried. There wasn't much more my friend could do, and he knew it. To counter this faith-based opposition to marriage equality, we produced a letter of support signed by 120 clergy from nineteen faiths and denominations—Christians, Jews, Buddhists, members of the Sankey Tribe of Native Americans, and the Society of Friends, or Quakers, who do not have formal clergy.

As the measure entered the formal legislative process, we convened a hearing of the Senate Judiciary Committee, during which the legendary civil rights leader Julian Bond testified. "Many gays and lesbians worked side by side with me in the civil rights movement, and many do so now," he said. "Am I to now tell them, 'Thanks for risking your life and limb, helping me win my rights, but they're excluded because of a condition of their birth?' They can't share in the victories they helped to win? That having accepted and embraced them as partners in a common struggle, I can now turn my back on them and deny them the rights they helped me win, that I enjoy because of them? Not a chance." We brought in Bond to testify to get the vote of two African American senators who were opposed because of opposition from Baptist churches. Senator Sandra Cunningham, an African American, was a strong supporter, but we needed the other two. We needed every vote possible, but Bond's testimony didn't move them. (Years later, President Barack Obama came out in support of marriage equality, which was helpful in gaining the support of African Americans.) There was a special poignancy in the testimony of sixteen-year-old John Otto, who said: "In New Jersey, I am a second-class citizen, someone who does not have equal rights, someone who it is perfectly okay to treat differently according to the state government. I want the same rights that heterosexual marriage ensures, and I'm asking members of this Senate Committee to stand up and give me that chance." Another teenager, Jessica Petrosky-Cohen, a girl whose parents are gay, reminded us that the public's mood was moving faster than the legislative process. "If you're worried that the people of New Jersey aren't ready to accept us, I'm here to tell you that they have been for a while. So please, I would really like to dance at my parents' wedding."

The committee vote was seven to six, with one Republican, Bill Baroni, voting yes. Baroni is gay, but he had not come out yet when the vote was taken. Two Democrats voted no, Chairman Paul Sarlo and John Girgenti. Obviously it was a close, hard-earned victory, but it was also one that reflected well on the legislative process and on the actions of principled politicians. As the committee chair, Sarlo had the power to block the bill, and perhaps others might have done so. It often happened. But he realized that the public deserved a full debate and a vote on the issue. So he allowed it and was on the losing side. We were grateful that he chose to let the bill be heard despite his opposing views. Girgente was defeated in the next Democratic primary, with his no vote being a key issue against him.

But the closeness of the committee vote, and the fact that two Democrats voted no, told us that we were in for an uphill fight on the Senate floor. We were hoping for a miracle that never came. I basically worked full-time with Salena, Loretta, and Steven during the ensuing weeks to round up as much support as we needed in the Senate. I never do anything halfway, and this certainly was no exception. How to get another yes vote was always on our minds. We had daily conference calls about strategy and how best to make the argument to wavering colleagues. But first Senate president Dick Codey had to post it for a vote, which he did despite significant opposition in the Democratic caucus. I was hoping we'd get support from Senator Sweeney, who had influence in the South Jersey Democratic caucus. Sweeney was noncommittal and ultimately abstained, a position he later said was his biggest regret as a legislator. As the day of the vote approached, we even arranged for a sterilized ambulance to bring Republican senator Diane Allen, a yes vote, to the State House so that she could cast her vote if necessary. Diane was undergoing treatment for cancer, but she also was determined to do what she could to support the cause.

On the morning of the Senate vote, January 7, 2010, I received an email from Jennifer Valez, a former member of my legislative staff: She told me about her brother, "one of the most-loving and generous men I have ever met," who helped raise his three younger siblings. "From the very bottom of my heart," she wrote, "thank you for fighting for his rights." By the time the email arrived, we knew we were fighting a lost cause. We simply didn't have the votes. Nevertheless, we insisted on holding a roll call, even though we knew what would transpire. To his credit, Codey (who would be replaced as president by Steve Sweeney a few days later) agreed to post the vote, which was much more than a gesture in the face of his nemesis, Sweeney. A "progressive" colleague asked me, "Why are you making us vote? You don't have the votes to get it passed." I explained that we couldn't disappoint our supporters by not even having a vote. Weinberg explained further, "We absolutely had to have a vote. A benchmark needed to be set. And history needed a scorecard. We did absolutely everything we could, from field, to messaging, to process." Passions on both sides were on full display during the debate on the Senate floor. Codey, Nia Gill, Teresa Ruiz, and Sandra Cunningham were particularly eloquent, relying on arguments used during the African American crusade for civil rights in the 1960s. Ruiz graciously paid tribute to my efforts to make the legislature more inclusive, saying that the work for equality and justice was far from finished, as the marriage equality effort showed. Cunningham said that as the descendant of enslaved people, she understood the crushing burden of injustice. I broke down in tears during my own floor speech as I made the case for justice for our gay brothers and sisters. "It's not often we have an opportunity to change society and how we treat each other as human beings," I said. "It occurs a few times in our lifetime, if it occurs at all. We have that opportunity today. We can change fear to love, hate to compassion, cruelty to kindness."

Sadly, we didn't change any minds. My Democratic colleague John Girgenti argued that the bill would change "the fundamental definition of marriage in this state. This change strikes at the heart of our society and how we define who we are. Because of these reasons, I will vote no on this bill." I argued that these are the very reasons he should vote yes. Republican senator Sean Kean, no relation to the family of former Governor Kean, shamelessly said, "Friends of mine who are gay own a restaurant and I was very proud to have my reception there and my ceremony there." He then said he would vote no. Some of Senator Kean's best friends are gay, he alluded, as he tried to assuage his conscience and proponents of marriage equality. It didn't work. Kean was defeated in his reelection bid. Republican senator Gerry Cardinale was more direct, "Gays are not normal," he said. But Bill Baroni, the Republican who voted in favor in committee, stood by his convictions despite pressure from his party. During a dramatic speech on the floor, he said: "I am fully understanding that tonight, right now, I will be the first-ever Republican state legislator, on the question of marriage equality, to say the following: I vote yes."

But in the end, we were able to get just thirteen of the chamber's twenty-four Democrats and just Baroni on the Republican side. The miracle didn't come. We were defeated, but not broken. I collaborated with Senator Weinberg on a book, *The Case for Same Sex Marriage*, to send a message we weren't going away. We knew it was only a matter of time before the public, and then other politicians, would see the injustice and join our side. In fact, it already had been happening.

Several years earlier, the Ocean County Board of Freeholders denied pension and health benefits to the domestic partner of a county police officer. The officer, Laurel Hester, had been on the force for twenty-six years and was dying of cancer. She and her partner, Stacie Andree, shared a home in Point Pleasant and had been together for several years. As it became clear that her cancer was terminal, Laurel filed paperwork so that Stacie could receive survivor benefits, including a pension, as would be the case for a married heterosexual couple. Laurel herself appeared before the board in a wheelchair, hooked up to an oxygen tube. She didn't have long to live and she knew it, but she summoned the energy and the will to make the cause for equity and justice for her partner. But the Republican-controlled Board of Freeholders rejected her argument out of hand. One freeholder claimed that granting benefits to Stacie threatened what he called "the sanctity of marriage." That's when activists mobilized, convinced that the public would rally to the cause. And they were right. Steven Goldstein and Garden State Equality held dramatic protests on behalf of the couple, and Laurel delivered a videotaped statement from her sick bed at home, pleading yet again for justice. It was clear to everyone that her sick bed was, in fact, her deathbed. The board relented, and a month later, in early 2006, Laurel Hester died at age forty-nine. And Stacie received the pension benefits she deserved. People in Ocean County and around the state saw in the faces of Laurel and Stacie a moving example of the inhumanity inflicted on gay couples who had to fight for the rights others take for granted. Seeing how public opinion changed so dramatically in their case gave us hope as we continued the fight for marriage equality—and justice. An Academy Award–winning documentary was made of their ordeal and a film, *Freeheld*, debuted at the Toronto Film Festival. Salena and I walked the red carpet with Steven Goldstein, who was portrayed in the film by Steve Carell. It's memories like this that I hold dear to my heart—Salena in her glory expressing great happiness over a cause dear to her heart and, because of Salena and Steven, also dear to mine.

Years later Freeholder John Kelly, who led the charge against Laurel's plea for justice, was nominated by Governor Christie to a plush, high-paying patronage position on the New Jersey Parole Board. Senator Weinberg and I mustered opposition to Kelly and killed his nomination. Sweet.

As the courts began to consider marriage equality as a civil rights issue, New Jersey's *Lewis v. Harris* decision—the victory that wasn't—proved to be a key foreshadowing of what was to come. In 2013, the U.S. Supreme Court ruled that a section of the Defense of Marriage Act (DOMA), which defined marriage as between a man and a woman, was unconstitutional. DOMA was a 1990s piece of legislation that President Clinton signed into law—and yes, I disagreed with my friend on that position, and he has since given his support to marriage equality.

Since DOMA could no longer block spouses in same-sex marriages from receiving federal benefits, viola, suddenly the promise of *Lewis v. Harris* was fulfilled. Our civil unions law was no longer valid under the New Jersey Constitution because it was not marriage and denied civil union couples federal benefits that go to married couples. Steven and Salena and thousands of gay men and women and their straight allies won! But thanks to Governor Christie, the fight for marriage equality wasn't over. State Superior Court judge Mary Jacobson quickly ruled that gay couples could start getting married in New Jersey: "This unequal treatment requires that New Jersey extend civil marriage to same-sex couples to satisfy equal protection guarantees of the New Jersey Constitution as interpreted by the New Jersey Supreme Court in Lewis," Jacobson wrote in a fifty-three-page opinion. Christie appealed the ruling, seeking an injunction against the judge's decision, and ordered municipal clerks not to issue marriage licenses to same-sex couples. And just as quickly the New Jersey Supreme Court denied his request for an injunction. Same-sex marriages could begin on Monday, October 21, 2013.

Immediately after calling Salena with the good news about the court's decision, we started making arrangements for Louise Walpin and Marsha Shapiro to have the state's first same-sex marriage in our home in Elizabeth. But nothing came easy on the road to marriage equality. The town clerk in Monmouth Junction, where Marsha and Louise lived, didn't want to issue a marriage license without the explicit approval of Governor Christie. The clerk, like Christie, was a Republican. I got the municipal attorney to tell the clerk it was okay. The clerk still resisted, saying, "We don't have forms for gay couples." I responded, "I'll bring you a form." The clerk relented and issued the license.

And so, on Sunday night, October 20, Louise, Marsha, Steven Goldstein, Loretta Weinberg, Salena, myself, and about forty other guests—along with television news crews and print reporters—gathered in our living room for the state's first same-sex marriage ceremony. We began the ceremony at about eleven forty-five on Sunday night, knowing that we wanted it finished at seconds after midnight, so that Louise and Marsha would indeed be the first married gay couple in New Jersey history. Loretta Weinberg gave the couple away. Goldstein, who had been such an important part of the journey, said a prayer to begin the ceremony, quoting from the Book of Ruth: "Where you go, I will go, where you lodge, I will lodge, your people shall be my people, and your God, my God. Where you die, I will die and be buried." After they exchanged vows they had written themselves, Louise and Marsha paused as we counted down the seconds to midnight. I told everybody, "Now we have to wait, but it's a short wait considering we have waited for years." Roselle Mayor Jamel Holley administered the marriage vows. Louise and Marsha were declared married under New Jersey law at 12:01:01 AM. In keeping with Jewish tradition, the couple broke a ceremonial glass—just as Jewish couples have done for centuries, only this ceremony was unlike those that came before. Goldstein noted that they not only smashed a glass but also smashed discrimination, now and forever, or so we thought.

The battle for equal protection for gays continues both in America and across the globe, and in memory of my dear Salena, I will continue to advocate for my gay brothers and sisters for their equal protection wherever and however it is denied. It was enormously satisfying to hear Louise telling people that the wedding was even better than she expected. "We are really, really married!" she said. Steven, Loretta, Salena and I were filled with joy. Mission accomplished in New Jersey! But it wasn't until two and a half years later, on June 26, 2015, that the U.S. Supreme Court held in a five-to-four decision that the Fourteenth Amendment requires all states to grant same-sex marriages and recognize same-sex marriages granted in other states. My transformation from supporter to advocate for LGBTQ rights did not end with marriage equality. Salena taught me well. There was and remains more work to be done.

At around the same time as the historic wedding in my living room, I sponsored, along with Assemblyman Tim Eustace, a ban on the cruel and dangerous practice of conversion therapy. Eustace was one of only two openly gay members of the legislature. (Assemblyman Reed Gusciora, from Mercer County, was the first.) Eustace and his late partner, Kevin Williams, gained national attention in the late 1980s when they became New Jersey's first openly gay couple to apply to the state for joint adoption. They faced an uphill battle, but never gave up. Eventually they became the proud parents of three sons, all of whom had contracted HIV. Their one son, Lee, passed away at the age of twelve from HIV complications.

Conversion therapy is the pseudoscientific practice of trying to change an individual's sexual orientation from homosexual or bisexual to heterosexual through the use of psychological or spiritual interventions. There is no reliable evidence that sexual orientation can be changed and medical institutions warn that conversion therapy practices are ineffective and potentially harmful. The American Psychiatric Association (APA) opposes psychiatric treatment "based upon the assumption that homosexuality per se is a mental disorder or based upon the a priori assumption that a patient should change his/her sexual homosexual orientation." The organization has said that it is unethical for psychiatrists to attempt to "change" a patient's sexual orientation. Minors are especially vulnerable to ill effects from conversion therapy, which can lead to depression, anxiety, drug use, homelessness, and suicide.

The bill to ban conversion therapy cleared both houses, and to our pleasant surprise, Governor Christie signed it on August 19, 2013. The next major hurdle in the way of full LGBTQ rights across the country was former president Trump's ban on transgender troops in the military. President Biden quickly reversed it. Still to be achieved is a federal ban on discrimination in education, federal funding, employment, and housing, for which the U.S. Supreme Court laid the groundwork in its decision holding that the Civil Rights Act applies to the LGBTQ community. The Lesniak Institute for American Leadership, as will be outlined later, is advocating for LGBTQ rights in all nations through enactment in Congress of the Globe Act, which would direct the U.S. government to take a lead in promoting LGBTQ rights around the world.

My awakening to this cause and my work on behalf of LGBTQ rights, prompted by my beloved Salena, Steven, and Loretta, has been one of the most gratifying experiences in my life.

10 · ON THE BANKS OF THE OLD RARITAN

My Love Affair with Rutgers University

I don't know why I have a love affair with Rutgers University. Always did, even before they took me back after dropping out twice with mediocre grades. Rutgers showed more faith in me than I gave to myself. I've written about fighting to save the Rutgers name and the fight to keep Rutgers independent from political control, but not about my love affair with Rutgers athletes. In my younger days, I would drive south on Route 1 from Elizabeth toward New Brunswick to a location where I could get clear reception from local radio station WCTC to listen to Rutgers basketball games way back when Phil Sellers was its star player in 1974. That's what you call a real fan. I'm not quite sure what first drew me to Rutgers athletics—it's not as though Rutgers has a storied history like Notre Dame, Michigan, Ohio State, Alabama, and so many others. Then again, that is changing. C. Vivian Stringer has been a legendary women's basketball coach, Greg Schiano and Steve Pikiell brought the football and basketball programs to the next level, and Carli Lloyd put the women's soccer team on the world map. But ultimately, I suppose my keen interest in Rutgers sports has a lot to do with its scrappy, underdog image. Rutgers teams always feel they have to prove themselves, something that resonates with me.

When Rutgers first began thinking about applying for admission to the Big Ten about a decade ago—a decision that had ramifications not only for its sports teams but also for its academic and research programs—I knew immediately that significant facility upgrades would have to be made, or else the school's bid would surely be rejected. Not only did the university need to expand and upgrade its football stadium, it needed to keep its football coach, Greg Schiano, who turned the program into a perennial bowl team. Bob Mulcahy, the university's athletics director, called me one day in a panic. The Board of Governors was waffling on borrowing a hundred million dollars for the stadium expansion and upgrade after a scathing article by the *Star-Ledger* criticizing the school's spending on athletes. Mulcahy asked if I could get Governor Jon Corzine to commit to raising ten million in private funds, which would supplement his plan to raise twenty million in other private funds to reduce the university's financing obligation.

I met with Corzine in the grill room of my golf club, Suburban, and made the pitch. It was easy. As a former chief financial officer and senior partner at Goldman Sachs, Corzine understood the value of the investment to Rutgers and the state. Corzine and I committed to raising the ten million (with Corzine raising more than 90 percent of it), and the Board of Governors went ahead with a hundred-million bond financing. But the ten million we pledged to raise never materialized. Corzine's ethics council issued an opinion, with which I disagreed, that the governor couldn't solicit the private donations. As it turned out, it didn't matter. The board, bolstered by our pledge, supported the financing, Rutgers kept its winning coach for a few additional years, the stadium was expanded, and Rutgers was invited to join the Big Ten. The jump to the Big Ten meant that Rutgers would have to compete with the Michigans, Ohio States, and Penn States of the world—schools that had world-class athletic facilities designed to attract top talent from across the country. Rutgers would have to step up its game to compete with these giants.

As chairman of the Senate Economic Development Committee, I sponsored and got signed into law a twenty-five-million-dollar subsidy to upgrade the university's sports practice facilities, a bipartisan initiative that Governor Christie signed into law. Expanding the football stadium qualified Rutgers to join the Big Ten, but it needed a quality practice facility to attract the best athletes. Basketball coach Steve Pikiell was so proud of the new practice facility he gave me a private tour before the ribbon cutting. It's already paying off big dividends in recruiting for all Rutgers athletic programs. I didn't accomplish this in a cavalier fashion. I never asked anyone, especially my fellow legislators, to do something they were uncomfortable doing. I first commissioned an economic study that showed an investment in Big Ten–quality athletic facilities paid off many times over in attracting contributions from alumni and applications from better students, as well as generating revenue for local businesses and the state. The study done by Econsult Solutions, a

Philadelphia-based economic consulting firm, cost twenty thousand dollars. I solicited ten Rutgers boosters to contribute two thousand each. Super Rutgers fan Jeff Towers immediately stepped up and said, "Whatever you're short, I'll make up the difference," which he did. Later his wife, Amy, who graduated from another Big Ten school, Wisconsin, was appointed to the Rutgers Board of Governors. A wise choice by Governor Murphy. Membership in the Big Ten Conference also includes the Big Ten Academic Alliance (BTAA), which is made up of fourteen top-tier research universities that together conduct $10.5 billion in government-funded and private research annually. Rutgers University belonged in the BTAA, but first it had to get invited to the Big Ten Athletic Conference. Rutgers had brought in a new president, Bob Barchi, in 2012 to complete the difficult task of merging the school with the University of Medicine and Dentistry, a medical school in Essex County plagued by corruption. Barchi handled the merger well and deserves full credit for that achievement. But he was less interested in the success of the school's athletic programs—it simply wasn't a priority. That had to change. It did, with my less-than-subtle urging. The economic study I commissioned got his attention, as did a letter I sent to him, which I leaked to the press. The letter prompted a headline in the *Star-Ledger*, New Jersey's most widely read newspaper: "Lesniak to Barchi: We're in the Big Ten. Act like it!" Barchi shared the letter with the chair of the Rutgers Board of Governors, Greg Brown, and asked him what it meant. Brown replied, "We're in the Big Ten. Act like it!" Barchi got the message and developed a long-term plan to make Rutgers athletics competitive in the Big Ten. The school even lured back Schiano, the architect of its breakout successes, who had left Rutgers for the NFL. I'm convinced that great things are ahead not only for the football team but for the entire athletic program—and the university's reputation as a world-class center of academic research. You can bet on it. Literally—except not on Rutgers, until we amend our state Constitution again to allow betting on New Jersey college sports teams. (More on that later.)

11 · SPORTS BETTING

A Good Bet

My dad loved to bet on the horses. It was one of the few things we did together. My dad, mom, and I would often spend a Saturday afternoon basking in the summer sun and betting on the horses at Monmouth Park, one of the state's great assets.

From time to time I would place a bet for my dad with the local bookie who worked out of the corner grocery store. This shouldn't be shocking knowing the neighborhood where I grew up.

And I wasn't the only one who did. That's how it was back in the days before some states like New York and New Jersey adopted off-track betting. Unlike European countries, where the neighborhood bookie worked out in the open and was just another local business person, our bookie operated in the semi-shadows. Everyone knew what was going on and that it was illegal, but it was more or less accepted, like making and selling booze during Prohibition.

So horse racing was very much a fondly remembered part of my childhood. And when I was elected to the New Jersey legislature, I also came to appreciate the importance of horse racing to New Jersey's economy. It wasn't just the racing itself but the breeders scattered around the Garden State. Most people don't know that New Jersey has more acres of horse farms than any other state in the country, including Kentucky. The horse farms employ thousands of workers and provide the nation's most densely populated state with much-needed open space. But the industry began to fall on hard times. Our racetracks, Monmouth Park and the Meadowlands, were in danger of closing unless new revenue could be generated. It wasn't just New Jersey. Horse racing once upon a time was among the nation's biggest spectator sports. But by the beginning of the twenty-first century, it wasn't hard to get a seat in the grandstand. And with the decline in attendance came a decline in purses, the amount of money at stake in each race. And declining purses meant a decline in the quality of horses entered to race, which contributed to the decline in attendance. Every race can't have a Secretariat running. Just like in human sports, racing fans want to see the best athletes competing. As a person with such warm memories of the track, I was sad to see the industry's decline. As an elected official who understood the importance of racing to the state's economy, I was determined to do what I could to revive what was once called the "sport of kings." The demise of the industry meant that thousands of working people, the folks who worked in the stables or behind the concession stands or at the breeding farms, would no longer be able to earn a living at it.

I came up with a novel thought: legalizing sports betting to attract younger fans to our racetracks the same way snowboarding revived the ski industry. I was an avid skier, although my bilateral knee replacements have since curtailed my downhill skiing, and saw a dying alpine ski industry revived by Gen X snowboarders. In addition to the potential for crossover betting and attracting younger fans, the added revenue from sports betting would improve racing's bottom line and support increased purses to help the tracks adapt to twenty-first-century fans who flock to the racetracks when big purses attract the best horses.

At the time, it was almost universally believed I had zero chance of overturning a decades-old act of Congress and overcoming opposition from the powerful sports leagues led by the superpowerful NFL. The United States, unlike so many other countries around the world, outlawed sports betting outside of the historical anomalies of Las Vegas and the state of Nevada, and three states, Delaware, Montana and Oregon, which were allowed limited forms of sports betting. The ban was advanced years ago by the professional sports leagues, which initially believed it would protect the integrity of the sport. As time would go on, it became an archaic remnant, not unlike the blue laws still in force in Bergen County, New Jersey, where stores remain closed on Sunday. I decided to do something about it. Why shouldn't sports fans be able to put down a wager on their favorite teams? They do it all over the world legally and every day in America through bookies and on offshore internet sites. Why not legalize it in the United States?

The tracks would not be the only beneficiary, as I saw it. The state's casinos in Atlantic City also were suffering, thanks to the failure of everybody concerned to develop a more diverse economy, one that would have lifted up residents and led to a more prosperous and more equitable city. That was the idea when Governor Byrne signed legislation legalizing casino betting back in the 1970s. But it just didn't happen, and by the late twentieth century, those glittering casino hotels along the boardwalk belied the decay in nearby neighborhoods. One particular casino owner managed to go bankrupt several times. You know his name—the forty-fifth president of the United States.

The failures of the city's casino economy were plain to see, and plenty of visitors took notice. All that glitter along the boardwalk was just for show—the poor of Atlantic City were still poor, all these years after the casinos were well established. Drug addiction was all too commonplace, as was street crime. Few visitors dared to venture much beyond Pacific Avenue, which is adjacent to the boardwalk, and most simply stayed inside the casinos. Government bore some responsibility for these conditions, but the casino operators themselves were at fault as well. They did little to turn Atlantic City into a destination beyond gaming, and then as neighboring states began to legalize casinos they made investments in new markets in Pennsylvania, Delaware, New York—in other words, to competitors of Atlantic City. Five casinos closed their doors within months of each other in late 2013 and early 2014. Fifteen thousand jobs disappeared. It was a disaster. Something had to be done, and as chairman of the Senate's Economic Growth Committee, I recognized that it was not sufficient to simply apply a few Band-Aids to the wounds; Atlantic City required drastic and vital surgery. And that meant taking on the professional sports leagues, the NCAA, and the Justice Department to overturn the federal legislation and the exceptionally American tradition of pretending that sports betting wasn't a part of daily life for millions of us. Indeed, when it came to football at both the college and professional levels, sports talk shows on radio and television often paid more attention to the "spread" than the actual score of the game.

It was a big bet on my part. There was nothing safe about it. I was criticized by Governor Christie and legal "experts" for wasting my efforts on an impossible task. But I believed I was right even if the odds were against me. As is so often the case in politics, I also had a personal as well as an ideological reason to get involved in this seemingly quixotic crusade. A former Assembly colleague and law partner of mine, Rudy Garcia, was one of more than fifty people arrested in 2007 in a sting targeting illegal sports betting operations in New Jersey. The charges were dropped a year later when it became clear that Rudy wasn't part of the gambling ring. He was just one of the thousands of New Jersey residents who liked to wager a few dollars from time to time on sports. Rudy placed bets for himself and a few friends with a bookie in Monmouth County, and that was against the law. Meanwhile, a New Jersey resident vacationing in Las Vegas could make bets on the games, and it was all perfectly legal. The obstacle was federal legislation called the Professional and Amateur Sports Protection Act (PASPA), which President George H. W. Bush signed in 1992. The bill, sponsored by New Jersey senator Bill Bradley, basically prohibited most states from legalizing sports betting but did not extend the prohibition to places like Nevada, where sports betting was an added attraction for its casinos. That was the flaw in the federal ban, which I uncovered. Congress could have made sports betting a crime, but that would have had to include Las Vegas. As any first-year law student knows, the due process part of the Fifth Amendment to the Constitution wouldn't allow that, so Congress came up with an ingenious way to get around the Fifth Amendment, and prohibited states other than Nevada and a couple of other states that had limited forms of sports betting from "authorizing" sports betting. Congress got away with that for twenty years until I challenged it using states' rights contained in the Tenth Amendment to overturn it, but more about that later.

I had no doubt about Bradley's sincerity in championing the legislation. As the greatest college basketball player in New Jersey history (in my view) and a Hall of Famer as a New York Knick, Bradley knew more about sports than most other lawmakers. He believed sports betting threatened the integrity of the games, and to be sure, he had some history on his side. Many sports fans are at least vaguely familiar with the infamous Black Sox scandal in 1919, when gambler Arnold Rothstein fixed the World Series by paying off Chicago players to throw the series to the Cincinnati Reds. That prompted the sad story of a young boy saying to Shoeless Joe Jackson, one of the Black Sox conspirators and the team's best player, "Say it ain't so, Joe." It *was* so. Lesser known but just as relevant was the point-shaving scandal in college basketball in 1951, when players from seven teams took money from gamblers to manipulate the scores of their games.

Bradley, a Princeton grad and a Rhodes scholar, knew this history cold. And let's not forget that baseball in the early 1990s was dealing with another gambling scandal—one of the sport's greatest players, Pete Rose, was banned from the game for life in 1989 for gambling on games while serving as manager of the Reds. To this day Rose, one of the game's best hitters, is barred from the sport's Hall of Fame, along with Shoeless Joe, and is basically persona non grata because of his involvement with gamblers. No sport can survive if its fans have reason to believe that what they're seeing on the field is tainted, that outcomes are being manipulated, and that the games themselves are corrupt. And in the eyes of most sports leagues, gambling is the ultimate corruption, a sin for which there is no chance of redemption. Baseball's Hall of Fame includes some outright racists like Ty Cobb and some owners who actively participated in keeping African Americans out of the major leagues until 1947. But neither Rose nor Jackson will likely ever enter the hall because of their association with gamblers.

Major League Baseball and other sports leagues were vocal supporters of Bradley's bill. The loudest voice, however, belonged to the National Football League, and I understood—to a point—why they were concerned. No league attracts as much attention from gamblers as the NFL. Even casual fans probably know whether or not their home team is favored in any given week, and it's impossible to discuss an upcoming game without mentioning the point spread. These are all overt acknowledgments of the underground economy that exists in the NFL's shadow, which the FBI estimates is in the hundreds of billions of dollars a year. While bookies are happy to take your money if you're looking to bet on baseball, basketball, or hockey, it's the NFL that keeps bookies in business. It's clear that no sport is as vulnerable to a Black Sox–type scandal as the NFL, but it's hard to uncover fixing schemes if gambling is in the hands of organized crime and offshore sports betting websites. The professional sports leagues, along with the NCAA, were adamant in their support of Bradley's legislation. In their view, it was the best and only way to ensure that gambling interests didn't corrupt outcomes. They failed to appreciate the corrosive effect of our schizophrenic attitude toward betting—while we are law-abiding people, we look the other way as billions of dollars are funneled into an underground economy that is based on an overt violation of the law. And, of course, there are always going to be people willing to respond to public demand for a product, whether it's booze in the 1920s or a sports bet in later years. Smart public policy should recognize this and figure out how to best regulate behavior that may not be to everybody's liking but is simply inevitable.

What the sports industry leaders also failed to appreciate is how their greatest fear—an organized attempt to undermine the integrity of their game—could be detected and foiled in real time if betting were legal and regulated, rather than existing in the Wild West. I sought to set the record straight.

My first gambit was to write to New Jersey's congressional delegation, Republicans and Democrats alike, asking members to get behind legislation to repeal PASPA. I got crickets. No one wanted to take on the NFL, the other professional sports leagues, and the NCAA. That was frustrating, but I wasn't about to give up. I thought I'd expand my horizons and make the case to elected officials from across the country. After all, I thought, New Jersey wasn't the only state with a stake in this issue. Every state—with the obvious exception of Nevada—had a reason to support legalization of sports betting. So I approached the National Conference of State Legislators, an organization devoted to protecting states' rights. But that devotion didn't include bumping heads with the big-time sports leagues. The organization rejected my request that its members ask Congress to repeal its ban on sports betting. While it seemed as though I was getting nowhere, people in the sports world were well aware of what I was doing and how my argument was a threat to the status quo. In a snit, the NCAA actually canceled its tournaments in New Jersey because of my effort to legalize sports gambling. I said that under that standard the only state eligible for a tournament would be Utah because Mormon residents there presumably wanted nothing to do with gambling. (Ironically, as it turned out, they did.)

Having failed to get Congress to repeal PASPA, I put on my legal hat and concluded that the law violated the Tenth Amendment, which guarantees states' rights. Can you imagine a liberal like me using states' rights—which was the mantra of segregationists for decades—as the foundation of my legal challenge to PASPA? Unlikely, yes. But I saw it as the foundation of my court case. Although virtually no legal "expert" believed I had a chance, the president of Monmouth Racetrack, Dennis Drazin, and Joe Brennan, the president of an internet company, IMEGA, agreed to join my lawsuit in federal district court. I persuaded Governor Jon Corzine to add the state of New Jersey as a plaintiff, but as the case was unfolding, Corzine lost reelection in 2009 and was replaced by Chris Christie, who followed the advice of Atlantic City's casinos—which were headquartered in Nevada—and didn't support my effort. That was a fatal decision for our cause. Federal district court judge Garett Brown held that only the state can assert a state's rights claim and dismissed our lawsuit. Christie's chief counsel, Jeff Chiesa, had written to the court, "After careful consideration, Governor Christie has decided not to participate in this action . . . the Governor has determined that the State's limited resources would be better utilized by focusing on other, more immediate issues facing the citizens of New Jersey."

I suppose that was to be expected. Christie's transition team had advised him not to "waste money" pursuing sports betting "until federal laws change." I'm not sure how much "careful consideration" he gave my case. I'm guessing not much. More likely, he was influenced by the Nevada based casinos' opposition and had his vision of running for president in one of the earlier Republican primaries in Nevada.

My lawsuit had another flaw, according to Judge Brown: New Jersey's Constitution did not allow sports betting, the judge said, so it really didn't matter if my argument about the Tenth Amendment was sound. No problem. During the 2011 legislative session, I led an effort to get my fellow lawmakers to approve a ballot referendum designed to amend the state Constitution to allow sports betting. I suppose I should be grateful to the judge for pointing me in this direction because by taking my case to my colleagues and then directly to the voters, Governor Christie was cut out of the process. I just needed to round up two-thirds of both chambers to get the referendum on the ballot. Getting two-thirds of the Senate and Assembly to agree on anything isn't easy. But I was confident my argument would win over colleagues on both sides of the aisle. During the Senate debate on the referendum, Senator Dick Codey, a Seton Hall fan and coach of a youth basketball team that won the fourteen-and-under Boys AAU National Championship, raised a concern about promoting betting on amateur athletic events. Codey was close with Bill Bradley, who by then was no longer a member of the U.S. Senate, so I had little doubt that Codey's concerns were a reflection of Bradley's views. Codey's words carried some weight, in part because of his intense interest in the issue and in part because he had been governor and had built up some good will after he filled in after Jim McGreevey's resignation. I sensed that some of my colleagues shared Codey's views. If this were a normal piece of legislation requiring a simple majority, I wouldn't have been overly concerned. But I needed two-thirds, and in the Senate that meant twenty-seven out of forty votes. A compromise seemed in order: I included in the referendum's language a prohibition against betting on any New Jersey–based amateur teams or any amateur sports event played in New Jersey. So if you wanted to bet on my alma mater, Rutgers, to win the Big Ten championship or the NCAA Basketball Tournament in March, you'd have to go somewhere else. It was a small price to pay to get legal sports betting enacted into law. And voters had their say: the referendum passed by a two-to-one margin. *Un morceau de gâteau.* Piece of cake.

Or maybe not. It turned out there were still a few extra layers needed to bake this particular piece of cake. Two weeks after the election, I introduced a bill that would authorize sports betting at New Jersey's racetracks and casinos. It passed the Senate 35–2 and the Assembly 72–0, and Christie signed it into law. It was clear that my colleagues and the governor took notice of the margin by which the sports betting referendum passed. New Jerseyans, it was clear, supported sports betting and had been willing to change the state's basic set of laws—its Constitution—to make it happen. As the state was laying the groundwork to begin taking sports bets, the NFL, NBA, NCAA, Major League Baseball, and the feds filed suit in federal court to stop New Jersey from taking bets on sports. Dennis Drazin of Monmouth Racetrack was raring and prepared to go, but the sports leagues obtained an injunction to stop the process while the courts considered the legality of my legislation in light of PASPA, the federal ban on sports betting. In February 2013, federal district court judge Michael Shipp ruled that PASPA did not, in fact, violate the Tenth Amendment, as I had argued. The judge ruled that the law "neither compels nor commandeers New Jersey to take any action." We appealed to a panel of Third Circuit judges, including Donald Trump's sister, Maryanne Trump Barry, but in a two-to-one decision (with Judge Trump Barry in the majority), the judges upheld PASPA. We appealed to the U.S. Supreme Court but were turned down.

It seemed like a lost cause, except for a bit of silver lining in the Third Circuit's dissenting opinion from Judge Julio Fuentes, who argued that if New Jersey repealed its laws banning sports betting, that would not violate PASPA, since the federal law simply banned states from "authorizing" sports betting. I immediately seized on that opening as it was alerted to me by the attorney for Monmouth Racetrack, former Seton Hall Law School dean Ron Riccio. I went back to the legislature with a bill to repeal the ban on sports betting at the state's racetracks and casinos. The bill passed quickly and easily, but Christie vetoed it. "While I do not agree with the Circuit Court's conclusion, I do believe that the rule of law is sacrosanct, binding on all Americans," he wrote in his veto message. "That duty adheres with special solemnity to those elected officials privileged to swear an oath to uphold the laws of our Nation. . . . I cannot sign this bill, which was introduced on the same day the Supreme Court declined to hear our appeal, and then rushed to final passage just three days later. Ignoring federal law, rather than working to reform federal standards, is counter to our democratic traditions and inconsistent with the Constitutional values I have sworn to defend and protect." Christie's words would come back to haunt us later in both the district court and the Third Circuit Court of Appeals, where the judges would quote from the governor's statement in ruling against us.

More immediately, though, Christie's veto did him no favors with legislators, including his fellow Republicans. Christie was at the height of his popularity at the time, still basking in the glow of his smashing reelection in 2013 and the high marks he had gotten in the aftermath of Superstorm Sandy. Bridgegate and BeachChairGate would later change that dynamic. Christie's fellow Republicans had always been fearful of challenging him, especially after his reelection. But on this issue, GOP lawmakers were willing to take him on because they understood the economic impact that sports betting could have on their districts. The district of my Republican friend, Senator Joe Kyrillos, included Monmouth Park, whose CEO, Dennis Drazin, was a big supporter of our efforts. Other Republican lawmakers represented large swaths of the state's horse country, especially in Somerset and Hunterdon counties. Survival of the racetrack and breeding industry was of utmost importance to them. Kyrillos confronted Christie with the prospect of a veto override. That's serious political hardball because governors never want to be overridden (and rarely are). They're fearful that once legislators get a taste of overriding one veto, they will enjoy it and come back to override again and again. So Christie agreed to sign a new bill with a few nonsubstantive tweaks so he could save face. Score one for Senator Joe Kyrillos for preserving the survival of my sports betting efforts.

This time Christie signed the bill as promised and then retained Ted Olson, a renowned and experienced litigator, to represent the state against a legal challenge from the U.S. Justice Department and the sports leagues. Olson had represented George W. Bush in his recount victory before the Supreme Court in 2000 and then went on to serve several years as the nation's solicitor general. He surprised many of his conservative allies by not only supporting marriage equality but leading the legal charge against a ban on gay marriage in California in 2010. Christie made a good choice in getting Olson to defend the state from the onslaught that was about to come. And the onslaught came. We again suffered two defeats in the courts as the sports leagues, the NCAA, and the Justice Department continued to fight us, recognizing in my legislation a genuine threat to the comfortable status quo they preferred. At the district and circuit court levels, the judges ruled that PASPA was constitutional, and therefore New Jersey's law legalizing sports betting was null and void. We decided to gamble everything on one last bet: we appealed the case to the U.S. Supreme Court. There was no guarantee that the Court would hear our case. The justices hear only about 3 percent of appeals, and the solicitor general, whose opinion carried significant weight, advised the justices to dismiss our petition. But on June 17, 2017, the Court announced that it would hear arguments in the case. That was a thrilling moment because once the Court took our appeal despite the solicitor general's recommendation, I was absolutely convinced we would win. Oral arguments took place on Monday, December 4, 2017. Twenty states had joined the case on our side, having awoken to the chance to get revenue from sports betting that they rejected years ago when I testified in that regard before the National Conference of State Legislators. A handful had already passed bills that would allow them to get into the betting game as soon as possible if the Court ruled in our favor.

Olson focused his argument on my contention that the federal ban on sports betting violated the Tenth Amendment. I could tell by the line of questions from some of the justices, including Chief Justice John Roberts, that the Court seemed inclined to agree with us. I followed the arguments with Governor Christie in the courtroom in Washington. Strangely, Christie had to be sworn in on motion to sit in the lawyers section. Even though he was a U.S. attorney, he was never admitted to practice before the U.S. Supreme Court. I snickered along with a few others in the attorney section. When oral arguments were over and we left the building, I gave Christie a huge hug despite his earlier opposition. It wasn't as significant as the famous Christie-Obama hug when the president came to inspect damage after Hurricane Sandy, but it conveyed our mutual happiness and confidence that we had the winning argument.

As is generally the case with the Court, several months passed between the arguments and the announcement of a decision. It needn't be said that we were on the edge of our seats through the winter and spring of 2018, waiting to hear what the justices decided. We found out on May 14, a week after my seventy-second birthday. I was in the locker room at Suburban Golf Club near my home in Elizabeth, getting ready for a round. My cell phone rang (they're allowed in the locker room). It was Dennis Drazin, the president of Monmouth Park and my partner in this long and tortuous journey. He had two words to share with me: "We won!" I didn't have to ask, "Won what?" That's how I found out that the Court agreed with us. In a 7–2 decision, the Court found that PASPA was unconstitutional because of its intrusion on powers reserved for the states. Samuel Alito, a native of Trenton, wrote the majority's decision, which focused on the heart of my contention that PASPA violated the Tenth Amendment. Congress, Alito wrote, had attempted to "issue direct orders to state legislatures." And that simply was unconstitutional, as I said all along. So much for my quiet day on the links. I gave up on the idea of playing golf that day and began making calls to people who had supported us all along, first to Resorts Casino owner Morris Bailey, who like me was also a fan of horse racing, and then to my Assembly partner Ralph Caputo, Senate president Steve Sweeney, and Senator Joe Kyrillos. Of course I called my dear wife, Salena, who said, "I knew you would win." And she did. That's why I miss her so dearly. She had so much faith and confidence in me.

As an elected official with a deep love for my native state, I was very satisfied with a result that I knew would help revive an important part of our economy and create thousands of jobs. As a lawyer, I was proud that the highest court in the land basically said, "You know, Lesniak, you were right about that constitutional argument you made." Not bad for a two-time college dropout from Rutgers University and a graduate of St. John's Law School. It became real on June 14, 2018, when I joined Governor Phil Murphy at Monmouth Park to place the state's first legal sports bets. Murphy exercised the prerogative of his office, placing the first bet—he put down twenty dollars on Germany to win soccer's World Cup, which started that day in Russia. Murphy, of course, had been U.S. ambassador to Germany during the Obama administration. So while Murphy placed the first bet, I placed the first winning wager. I bet on France to win the Cup. It was a bit of a sentimental choice for me, given what a Francophile I am. Turned out it was a pretty smart bet as well. France emerged victorious. In the following weeks, as this new world of sports betting took hold, New Jersey's casinos came to life quickly, exceeding Nevada's sports betting numbers. Three casinos reopened, ten thousand jobs were restored, and our racetracks were saved from closure.

Many of my friends believe that bringing legal sports betting to America is my greatest achievement. I'm not sure about that. One thing is certain, at least at this juncture—the world has not come to an end just because you can now put down a few dollars on your favorite team or golfer or tennis player. The integrity of sports has not been damaged. As a sports fan, that means a lot to me. Yes, I saw sports betting as an economic development tool that could help New Jersey's struggling casinos and racetracks, but I also understood that we needed to make sure that we never have another Black Sox or point-shaving scandal again. Legalizing, regulating, and monitoring sports betting would make that task easier. It would also strip away some of the hypocrisy that was hiding in plain sight, especially with the NFL playing games in Wembley Stadium in London, where fans were placing bets from their seats. The National Hockey League, National Football League and the Women's National Basketball Association all have franchises in Las Vegas. We all know big-time football and basketball are a huge business, and part of that business has involved the black market of sports betting. Thanks to my impossible dream that came to fruition, betting is now in the open and therefore is much more transparent. Three New Jersey casinos have reopened and our racetracks are thriving, fulfilling my dream.

12 · A WAKEUP CALL AND A NEAR LOSS

When the late, great speaker of the House, Tip O'Neill, famously said that all politics is local, he spoke for generations of elected officials like myself whose political careers depended on attending to the needs and views of our constituents. I did that very well, but I didn't pay attention to a growing power base that almost defeated me.

The year was 2011, and I was coming off several big legislative and political achievements that made a difference in the lives of people all across the state, including, of course, people in my district and my hometown of Elizabeth. I was fortunate to have great advocacy partners in abolishing capital punishment in the state, Celeste Fitzgerald, Coalition for Alternatives to the Death Penalty, Lorry Post, Murder Victims' Families for Reconciliation, Governor Corzine, and Assembly speaker Joe Roberts, and won global recognition for that achievement. Environmental legislation I championed for years had great support from Governor Tom Kean, Senator Dan Dalton, and my other colleagues in the legislature and made a tangible difference in every corner of the state. I was nearing victory in my campaign for marriage equality thanks to Senator Loretta Weinberg and Garden State Equality and its legions of gay supporters and straight allies, the number one straight ally being my wife, Salena.

What's more, my connections to national politics were never stronger, thanks to my work on behalf of Bill Clinton years earlier. I had helped elect presidents and governors, earning a reputation as a prolific fundraiser. And that meant when I made calls on behalf of a cause I believed in or for a constituent who needed assistance, to those I had helped in elections or to former staff members (since I, unlike Donald Trump, hired the best people, and they became established in senior positions in Republican and Democratic administrations), my calls were returned quickly. Through it all, my constituent service remained second to none. I insisted on that. My staff members were a presence throughout the district, as they always were, and were available to meet with constituents who walked into my storefront office in downtown Union Township.

I regularly won reelection in a cakewalk, which I took as validation of everything I was doing, whether in the district or in Trenton or in Washington. I saw no reason to think that 2011 would be any different from past elections, when I was either unopposed or won with about 80 percent of the vote. I was slow to realize that there was a Republican-leaning group of Democrats that had taken control of the Elizabeth Board of Education and had set its sights on me. They were determined to take me down in that year's Democratic primary—and I was late in realizing just how well organized they were. The board has a budget twice the size of the city's and thousands of employees under its control. It had named a school in the city after Ronald Reagan (a revealing choice for such a Democratic city) and actively supported Chris Christie's 2009 campaign for governor. Politics, not education, was their primary purpose. And their goal was much more than taking me out. They had set their sights on taking over the Union County Democratic organization, and with me out of the way they would have a clear path, having made inroads in the municipalities of Linden, Hillside, and Roselle, and had an ally waiting in the wings in Union Township. Can you imagine the havoc that would have occurred if a Republican-aligned group took over our county party? You might think it odd that members of a Board of Education were so involved in partisan electoral politics. You wouldn't be wrong—it *was* odd. And it was absolutely corrupt. Board members intimidated teachers, custodial and cafeteria workers, security guards, bus drivers, you name it. If you worked for the board, you had to work for and contribute to their candidates.

The board got behind Jerome Dunn, who was an assistant school superintendent in the city. He had no political experience. He simply was a pawn in the Board of Education's larger game of getting more control over local politics. My campaign was hampered by bilateral knee replacements I had a few months before the primary, the results of too much treacherous downhill skiing and from previous sports injuries. I had the operation before I became aware of the political threat against me. The most powerful campaigning tool in a local election is door-to-door campaigning, and that tool was unavailable to me. So I went about exposing their corruption and using my legal skills to make them comply with election laws. A *Star-Ledger* investigative reporter, Ted Sherman, wrote about the board's widespread political shakedowns in an article: "Patti Gallante, a teacher now retired from the Elizabeth public school system, said only one thing about her job ever scared her: the school board. Through e-mails and political mailings to her home, Gallante said she would constantly get solicitations from members of the city's board of education asking for money. There were dinners, cocktail events, testimonials and tables of tickets to be bought and sold. It was a nonstop stream of beseechings. . . . Teachers and other employees, who kick in tens of thousands of dollars in donations, say they feel pressured by supervisors and board members to buy tickets to fundraisers. They say they are reminded that attending campaign events is in their best career interest." I sued their campaign for multiple violations of election laws. They thought they were above the law. They weren't. I was able to tie up their campaign, and their money, for weeks, which I believe made the difference in the outcome. Still, Jerome Dunn had an army of conscripts who feared for their jobs if they didn't turn out for rallies or put up lawn signs or somehow contribute to the effort to beat me. They were going to come out to vote. I knew that. I had to make sure that my voters knew the stakes and understood that this primary would be like few others I had faced in more than three decades as a legislator.

On Election Night, I stuck to my usual routine, dining with friends at Benito's restaurant at the Five Points in Union Township. The food was terrific as always, but pretty early on I had a sinking pain in my stomach. The other side was coming out in big numbers, and the early returns showed me behind. That hadn't happened since my ill-fated run for mayor of Elizabeth. But our planning and our sense of urgency began to pay off as the night progressed. The tide turned eventually, and when all 16,959 ballots were counted, I prevailed by about 800 votes. The sinking pain in my stomach miraculously disappeared. It was a gratifying victory for several reasons. First of all, I had beaten a group that used the resources of the city's Board of Education for political advantage. Second, my voters responded when they understood I was in trouble. They weren't used to that, but once they realized the stakes, they turned out. Very gratifying.

I was up for reelection again two years later because of New Jersey's unique political calendar—state Senate terms are two years followed by two four-year terms, then back to two years, and so on to account for census-driven redistricting. The Board of Ed faction apparently interpreted their narrow loss in 2011 as a moral victory, concluding that I would be vulnerable in 2013. Big mistake. They gave me and my supporters no credit for learning from the close call and recommitting to Tip O'Neill's rule about local politics. I reconnected with the district, redoubled our outreach, and worked hard to make sure voters knew I had my finger on the district's pulse.

One of the most-fulfilling connections I fostered was with the growing Haitian community in Elizabeth. In the aftermath of the catastrophic earthquake of 2010, I started a relief organization, NJ4Haiti, led by my chief of staff Hiver Ambroise and Elizabeth Haitian leader Stanley Neron, who was elected to the Elizabeth Board of Education a few years later. Hiver was born in Haiti, as were Stanley's parents. I hosted a delegation from Haiti—Céméphise Gilles Sénatrice de la République d'Haiti and Lietenant Alex Gelluss Pierre consulate General of Haiti New York attaché security—at my home and noted that this tragedy would take a decade or more to overcome. We solicited contributions of water, medical supplies, and food shipped every month for years thanks to the efforts of Hiver and Stanley and the warehouse space donated by Dave Gibbons of Elberon Development Company. And I got an opportunity to use my French when speaking to the delegation from Haiti. Unfortunately, tragedy struck again in late summer of 2021 when Haiti was again hit by another earthquake and, on top of it, a hurricane. NJ4Haiti sprung into action again, gathering needed supplies and shipping them to the devastated island.

There's no doubt that my French was helpful in dealing with the tragedy in Haiti. But, my campaign consultant, Scott Snyder, said to me, "Senator, you speak French, but your district's 50 percent Hispanic!" So I went about learning to speak Spanish. It will never be as good as the French I learned more than twenty years prior, but I am able to engage in casual conversation, which was helpful when speaking to my Hispanic constituents. Indeed, Elizabeth hosts a Colombian Festival drawing forty thousand Colombian Americans along Morris Avenue every year. I recently had the honor of introducing Íngrid Betancourt (another Torricelli girlfriend—remember Bianca Jagger?), who, as a candidate for Colombia's president, was kidnapped and held captive by the Revolutionary Armed Forces of Colombia for six and a half years. She's a national hero.

After introducing her to speak, she said to me in a laugh, "You introduced me in Spanish, French, and English!" What happened was when I was lost speaking in Spanish, my default was to go into French, then when I realized I was speaking in French, I switched to English, before going back to Spanish. The crowd loved it and gave her an overwhelming welcome.

In any case, as I was reconnecting with my constituents, I continued to expose the Elizabeth Board of Education's corruption. Two whistleblowers came forward—two female employees, Carmen Southward and Sue Mettlen, who simply couldn't stand by and watch children used as pawns for the board's political wannabes. Their male colleagues were either too timid or too cynical to come forward. Carmen and Sue exposed board members and their supporters getting free lunch for their children even though they exceeded the income cap as well as supervisors hawking fundraiser tickets on school grounds, another violation of state law. If you were a school employee you had to contribute and volunteer for their campaigns or suffer whatever punishment they could mete out. My opponent was different in 2013, and so was the result. This time I won by 4,500 votes out of about 14,000 cast. Winning by 4,500 rather than 800 made my meal at Benito's taste better, even though it was the same meal I ordered two years prior. A landslide will do that. Now it was my turn.

In the years immediately following my resounding reelection, I supported several well-qualified candidates for the Elizabeth Board of Education and, with the help of Mayor Chris Bollwage and other local political leaders, eventually replaced every one of their members. I exposed additional examples of corruption and intimidation by the board—for example, the board's ringleader, Raphael Fajardo, put his sister in a made-up position as a truant officer for pre-K students, even though there is no attendance requirement for students that young! The State Department of Education refused to pay to fund the position, but that wasn't a problem for them. The board simply funded it through local property taxes. An outrage on so many levels. The board also sued one of our campaign workers, Antonio Rivera, for allegedly distributing flyers defaming the school board as racist. They received bad advice from their board attorney at McCarter English, a very reputable law firm, who filed the lawsuit on the taxpayers' dime. In this case six hundred thousand dimes. Public entities cannot be defamed. My juices flow when I can use my legal skills to fight political opposition. I had the complaint dismissed and the court awarded sixty thousand dollars in counsel fees to be reimbursed to the Board of Education by board chairman Raphael Fajardo and Superintendent Pablo Muñoz, who were the plaintiffs. The McCarter English law firm coughed up the sixty thousand for its bad advice. In addition to being a tenacious politician, I was, and still am, a tenacious litigator.

The biggest winner in this conflict was not me. It was the hardworking families and the children of my home city of Elizabeth. They deserved a Board of Education whose members were more interested in improving reading and math scores and having knowledge of civics and the history of America and the world than in playing politics. I was more than happy to help bring about that result—thanks to a wakeup call and a near loss.

13 · ANIMAL WELFARE

I first became aware of animal welfare issues when my canine companion of nineteen years, Brittany, got sick and died. I picked Brittany—or, I should say, she picked me—at the West Orange Animal Shelter. I showed up at the shelter looking to adopt a companion, and went through the usual process of looking over the dogs and picking out a few to walk before returning them to their cages. But one puppy wouldn't go back to her cage. She came running back to me after I finished our walk. What could I do? As I said, I didn't choose Brittany. Brittany chose me. She was a Brittany-Spaniel mix, so her name suggested itself. Not original, but cute. I enjoyed every moment of our nearly two decades of companionship. I have fond memories of her running to greet me whenever I walked through the door from the garage into the kitchen. But as she got older, she started having trouble walking. I took her to one vet who advised me to put her down because she wouldn't have a very good quality of life. That didn't satisfy me, so I took her to another vet and got the same answer. I tried Monmouth County's renowned Red Bank Animal Hospital, where after a few days in the hospital she looked me lovingly in my eyes and died.

At the hospital, my wife Salena pointed out a flyer on a billboard about an organization called Save US Pets, which raises funds for animals needing lifesaving treatment that their families couldn't afford. Salena and I hosted a fundraiser for the group, and pretty soon word got around in the animal welfare community that I could be a voice and an advocate on their behalf. I accepted the challenge with pleasure.

It took me a while to get over losing Brittany, and despite Salena's pleas, I originally refused to get another dog. But finally I relented. Salena adopted Penny from Rescuzilla in the Bronx. She was found starving behind a dumpster. Salena named her Penny after a character in our favorite show, *Big Bang*

Theory. She saw herself as Penny and me as Sheldon. I'm not insulting like Sheldon, but as Salena would say, I am a lot like him. I can't disagree. I had no intention of adopting a second dog until I went to St. Hubert's, the renowned rescue organization in Madison, for a meeting with Wayne Percelle, CEO of the Humane Society of the United States, which was giving me its Legislator of the Year Award. After the meeting, Heather Cammisa, the CEO of St. Hubert's, took me on a tour of the dogs and cats they rescued and asked that I take a photo holding a recently rescued puppy who was found along with her mom and four siblings. Two of the siblings had frozen to death. The photo shoot was a setup. They placed tiny Sammy in my two hands. They knew I wouldn't walk out without adopting her. Salena named her Samantha because she liked the name. We call her Sammy. Salena would call her Samantha to scold her.

Championing animal welfare in New Jersey was easy. We have a multitude of animal welfare organizations with huge membership and dedicated leaders, including the Humane Society of the United States, the Sierra Club, the Animal Protection League of New Jersey, the League of Humane Voters of New Jersey, New Jersey Voters for Animals, the Animal Legal Defense Fund, the Center for Biological Diversity, South Jersey Regional Animal Shelter, Friends of Animals United New Jersey, People for Animals, Inc., Jersey Shore Wildlife Rescue, the Humane Rescue Alliance/St. Hubert's, the Humane Society Wildlife Land Trust, and the Monmouth County SPCA, to name a few. That's some list!

With support like that, my goal of seeing New Jersey become known as The Humane State is within reach. Indeed, we're well on the way.

It was shortly after the Save US Pets fundraiser that two internationally recognized tiger lovers, Bill and Kizmin Nimmo, paid me a visit to ask that I sponsor legislation to combat the trade in tiger parts, which are used as analgesics in Eastern cultures. The worldwide black market in tiger parts was ravenous and ruthless, and as a result tigers were being hunted to the point of extinction and imported into the United States and other countries for their parts. The Nimmos were asking that New Jersey do its part to ensure these magnificent animals were not exploited in our state. You might not think the issue had anything to do with New Jersey, but the Nimmos knew otherwise. They were involved in efforts to save tigers that were in a sanctuary in South Jersey. When the sanctuary closed, the Nimmos rescued its seven tigers and relocated three of them to a sanctuary in Florida and four to a sanctuary in North Carolina. They formed a rescue organization called Tigers in America that has gone on to rescue three hundred more tigers across this country.

I agreed to help the Nimmos and their organization, but first asked them how they managed to find me—they aren't from New Jersey, despite their presence in the state caring for the tigers in the South Jersey sanctuary, and their activism takes them around the globe. It turned out that Bill Nimmo asked a friend who lived in New Jersey a simple question: "Who would you recommend to see if you want to get something done in government?" The friend replied, "See Senator Ray Lesniak." That was encouraging to hear because that's exactly how I see myself. It's wonderful to have great ideas about public policy or constituent service, but if you can't convert your words into actions, then they are just words. That's not what I do. I agreed to sponsor legislation to tag and trace the tigers in New Jersey—there were about a dozen of them at the time, housed by public and private owners—to prevent them from being sold for slaughter, with their bones used for dubious medicine or their coats for rugs. The bill easily passed both houses, but it was vetoed by Governor Christie. Despite that disappointment, I remain close to Bill and Kiz and continue to provide guidance for their tiger protection efforts, which included my sponsorship of a ban of imports into New Jersey of "trophies" of endangered species.

Next on my agenda was a ban on the use of gestation crates, the horrible practice of keeping pregnant sows confined in cages where they can't even stand up and turn around. Since female pigs are pregnant 70 percent of their lives, this produced a near lifetime of confinement. So I sponsored legislation banning the use of gestation crates. It passed both houses, but Christie vetoed it. The bill came to Christie's desk while he was running for the Republican Party's presidential nomination in 2016. The first contest of the nomination season took place at the caucuses in Iowa, the top pork-producing state in the nation. Christie clearly calculated that vetoing my bill would win him votes in the highly visible first test for presidential aspirants. The ban on gestation crates fell by the wayside because of Christie's ambitions. He wound up getting only 1.7 percent of the caucus votes, despite his kowtowing to the pork industry. A gratifying result, but of no help to the suffering pigs.

Christie wasn't all bad on animal welfare, at least when his presidential fortunes didn't get in the way. He signed my legislation banning transactions in ivory and rhino horns, with New Jersey the first of only four states—New York, Washington, and Vermont are the others—to adopt such a law. Many species of elephants and rhinos are on the verge of extinction as a result of poaching, often by terrorists who raise funds to support their killing through the sale of elephant tusks and rhino horns. The United States is the second largest importer of ivory tusks and rhino horns, after China. Federal laws prohibiting their importation have so many exemptions as to render them useless. Some hundred thousand African elephants are slaughtered every year. Five of the world's most unstable countries—South Sudan, the Central African Republic, the Democratic Republic of the Congo, Sudan, and Chad—provide a home to people who travel to neighboring countries to kill elephants.

Year after year, the path to many of the biggest, most horrific elephant killings traces back to Sudan, which has no elephants left but gives comfort to poachers funding the ruthless terrorist group al-Shabaab. Boko Haram, a jihadist organization responsible for horrific attacks in northeastern Nigeria, is also funded by poaching. In my pitch to Christie to get him to sign my legislation, I emphasized that the bill would help cut off funding to these terrorist groups. That resonated with him.

Christie also signed my ban on imports and transportation through New Jersey of trophies of endangered species. This legislation was prompted by the cruel killing of Cecil, a magnificent male lion who was shot with a bow and arrow in 2015 in Zimbabwe and was found three hundred yards away, suffering along the way until he died. Cecil became an international story of the cruelty of trophy hunting. I find it disgusting that people will kill a defenseless animal simply so they can display their manhood—or, in a few cases, their womanhood—on a wall or under their feet. My legislation banning transactions in ivory, which included rhino horns, and banning imports into New Jersey of trophies were victories for the planet's most endangered species.

Unfortunately, I couldn't keep the momentum going under Christie when I again tried to get New Jersey to do its part on behalf of elephants and wild animals in circuses. My bill was named after an animal named Nosey, a thirty-six-year-old African elephant who was part of a small circus traveling across the country. In late 2017, Nosey was seized from her owner, Hugo Liebel, who operates the Great American Family Circus in Lawrence County, Alabama, because of allegations of animal cruelty. Nosey was found chained and swaying back and forth in her own waste, suffering from urinary tract and skin infections, intestinal parasites, painful osteoarthritis, dehydration, and malnutrition. A court ruled against her owner, and she now lives at an elephant sanctuary in Tennessee and will never again endure violent blows from sharp bullhooks or be forced to give rides to humans despite crippling injuries. Nosey had an "inadequate food supply" and showed "signs of stress," an animal control officer said in court records. The national People for the Ethical Treatment of Animals organization said the elephant was tightly chained and obviously in distress. Nosey's plight became the symbol of the cruelty of taking animals out of the wild and brutalizing their lives for our entertainment.

I wrote legislation to ban elephants and other wild animals from circuses in New Jersey, which would have done our small part in the larger effort to free elephants from the brutality they endure in captivity. Christie vetoed the bill on his way out the door in 2018, but Senator Nilsa Cruz Perez and Assemblymen Raj Mukherji, Jamel Holley, and Andrew Zwicker picked up the mantle in the next legislative session. It passed both houses nearly unanimously in 2018.

To help persuade new Governor Phil Murphy to sign the bill, we held a vigil in Margate near Atlantic City at the base of the iconic statue of Lucy the Elephant. Not long afterward, I was speaking to a class of students at High Technology High School in Monmouth County accompanied by Brian Hackett, New Jersey state director of the Humane Society of the United States, when my cell phone went off. That was a little embarrassing. I quickly reached into my jacket pocket to turn off the phone but then saw the call was from Governor Murphy. I excused myself, took the call, and learned from the governor that he was going to sign the bill while speaking to me on the phone. With Murphy's permission, I put him on speakerphone so the students could hear the good news directly from the governor. "This law would not have been possible without the years of hard work and advocacy by Senator Ray Lesniak, whose legacy on issues of animal rights is second to none," he said. "These animals belong in their natural habitats or in wildlife sanctuaries, not in performances where their safety and others are at risk." It was all serendipity. And the students loved it.

Another disappointment of mine that the legislature later remedied was my attempt to ban the cruel practice of shark finning. Sharks, as dangerous as they appear to be, are an endangered species because of the popularity of shark fin soup. Commercial fishermen will cut off a shark's fins and dump it back in the water, where it bleeds to death. New Jersey was the only state in the Northeast that allowed shark finning. On two occasions I was able to get a ban on the practice through the Senate but was stymied in the Assembly by opposition from the commercial fishing industry. Eventually, thanks to the leadership of Senator Troy Singleton, Governor Murphy signed a ban on shark finning.

We've won significant victories to protect animals from cruelty and extinction, but there is much more to do in New Jersey. For example, instead of using nonlethal means to contain our black bear population, New Jersey has often used an annual bear hunt where even cubs are allowed to be slaughtered. Bear hunts do not reduce human-bear conflict and are no more than trophy hunts, spilling blood of innocent creatures for pleasure. Hunting creates an increase in opportunity for animal-human interactions. The widely used practice of baiting acclimates bears to human food, and they can smell unsecure garbage from miles away. With more effective trash management and bear-smart policies, not more killing, it is possible to live in harmony and coexist peacefully with bears. Thankfully, Murphy has declared a ban on bear hunting while he is governor, and his administration has asked me to recommend a comprehensive nonlethal bear management program.

New Jersey also allows puppies from loosely regulated "puppy mills" to be sold in retail stores and over the internet. A puppy mill is an inhumane high-volume dog breeding facility that churns out puppies for profit, ignoring the needs of the pups and their mothers. Dogs from puppy mills are often sick and unsocialized. Puppy mills commonly sell through online classified ads, flea markets, and pet stores. In fact, the majority of puppies sold in pet stores and online are from puppy mills. Responsible breeders will be happy to meet you in person and show you where the puppy was born and raised—and where their mom lives too. In the mills, mother dogs spend their entire lives in cramped cages with little to no personal attention. When the mother and father dogs can no longer breed, they are abandoned or killed. Due to poor sanitation, overbreeding, and a lack of preventive veterinary care, the puppies from puppy mills frequently suffer from a variety of health issues, creating heartbreaking challenges for families who should be enjoying the delights of adopting a new family member. Many dogs and cats bought from puppy mills wind up on the streets and ultimately are killed or euthanized.

Camden County freeholder Jeffery Nash Jr. and his wife Krista are prominent advocates for animal welfare and got Camden County to ban the sale of dogs and cats from mills. I tried to do the same at the state level, writing legislation that sought to regulate pet dealers—anyone who sells more than ten dogs and/or cats. The Humane Society of the United States says there are about ten thousand puppy mills in the country producing some 2.4 million puppies each year. Internet sales have fueled the business, which is largely unregulated. The bill passed the legislature, but again Christie vetoed it, leading the Assembly sponsor, Dan Benson of Mercer County, to say: "This bill had one simple intention: to stop pet shops and consumers from buying from pet dealers who have had multiple USDA violations." Sadly, puppy mills still exist throughout America.

On April 4, 2019, the Lesniak Institute for American Leadership, one of my post-Senate pursuits, hosted Chelsea Clinton at Kean University. She spoke about her new book for children, *Don't Let Them Disappear*, about rhinos, tigers, whales, pandas, and other animals that may indeed disappear unless people—and young people in particular—take action. I know an up-and-coming politician when I see one, and Chelsea fits the description. She was four months pregnant at the time, but she spent an hour signing every one of the three hundred books and taking pictures with the children who came to see her—and that was after discussing animal extinction with me onstage for half an hour and taking questions from the children for another half an hour. The message she left with the children was inspiring—actually, she left all of us, adults included, with a feeling of hope and a sense of mission. It was a privilege to help prompt the discussion and give her a platform for her campaign to save animals from extinction.

I continue my advocacy to save elephants from extinction at every opportunity. On February 7, 2020, I gave the keynote speech at a protest outside the embassy of Botswana in Washington to protest that nation's issuance of permits to kill elephants. The speech was aimed at Botswana president Mokgweetsi Masisi, but I also made note of the role that the United States plays in importing ivory and rhino horns, asking that Congress follow New Jersey's lead in banning transactions in them. "All killing for vanity items is contrary to God's will," I said. "It brings out the worst in human beings. Simply put, it is cruel and inhumane."

I'm often asked why I'm so concerned with animal cruelty when we have so many more important problems facing us. My response is that ending cruelty in all aspects of society is important. How we treat other creatures on Earth and how we treat the planet reflects how we treat our fellow human beings. I'm not a vegan. I eat meat and fish. I'm not against hunting for food. I believe in the food chain followed by all species, human and animal. But I also believe we should be humane with our treatment of animals, whether they are raised for food or as our pets or are in the wild. Mahatma Gandhi once said, "The greatness of a nation can be judged by the way its animals are treated." Gladiators once killed fellow human beings for entertainment. Slavery was once accepted as part of society. Human beings have been and continue to be killed because of the color of their skin, their heritage, their religion, or their sexuality. Animals are killed every day around the world for trophies to hang on walls. As a society, we need to speak out and take action against all evils. As Pope Francis said, "Our indifference or cruelty towards fellow creatures of this world sooner or later affects the treatment we mete out to other human beings. We have only one heart, and the same wretchedness which leads us to mistreat an animal will not be long in showing itself in our relationships with other people. Every act of cruelty towards any creature is contrary to human dignity." I try to live by those words every day.

14 · TAX INCENTIVES

Some issues inspire people to take to the streets. Some issues lend themselves to soaring rhetoric. Some issues are made for television talk shows. Tax policy isn't one of them—unless you have one of the more than hundred thousand permanent jobs and building trades jobs created or retained by New Jersey's tax incentives, or unless you're the New Jersey treasurer and are pleased with revenue from our tax incentives to the tune of more than thirteen billion dollars over the years. I'm not talking about broad tax policy, the kind you hear about in presidential elections when Republicans promise prosperity for all if we cut taxes for wealthy people or when Democrats promise to raise taxes on the wealthy. I'm referring to a very specific subset of tax policy—the proper use of tax incentives to encourage economic growth at the state and local levels.

I'm well aware that tax incentives aren't the most exciting topic in the world, nor are they supported by many of my progressive friends, some of whom oppose any tax incentives to attract investment and jobs. But I'm a policy wonk—younger folks would call me a nerd—so arguments over tax incentives get me going. Maybe that's because my support for tax incentives doesn't exactly align with the standard definition of progressive economic policy. I especially enjoy policy debates when I'm the contrarian.

I'm as progressive as they come, as my record shows, but on the subject of corporate tax incentives, I'm a heretic. I've been around for a while, so I understand how the world of economics works, plus my undergraduate degree at Rutgers, after switching from liberal arts to engineering to chemistry, ultimately was economics. We are a capitalist society with free markets, although that's another subject entirely. (I would say that our markets are not free, that exterior costs to society are not reflected in the cost of a product, which distorts the supply and demand curves—yikes, there I go off on my nerd impulses.)

Our capitalism created a vast middle class and the richest country in the history of the world. Business owners from large to small exist to make a profit, create jobs, and contribute to the general prosperity.

In a country like ours where tax policy varies by locality and businesses are increasingly mobile, we in New Jersey have to remember that we're competing with forty-nine other states and also across the globe. I wish that wasn't so. But wishing is no substitute for policy, as Donald Trump demonstrated during the coronavirus pandemic. New Jersey has high taxes and is an expensive place to do business. That's inarguable. It doesn't mean that New Jersey is a bad place to do business or to live. Obviously I think it's a great place to live—I've never lived anywhere else—and a great place to work. But we can't ignore the fact that business owners large and small have to factor in their cost of doing business when they consider setting up shop in New Jersey or possibly relocating elsewhere. As they say in *The Godfather*, or as Dr. Fauci responded to President Trump calling him an idiot, "It's not personal. It's business."

So, in my view, New Jersey has no option but to award tax incentives to create and keep jobs here and to attract investment. After all, we are at or next to the bottom of every study assessing the business-friendly nature of all the states. Admittedly, the process can be unseemly, leading to criticism from people on the left who mistakenly see incentive programs as giveaways. And sometimes people and companies seeking incentives do the process no favors.

For example, a couple of years ago the world's richest person, Jeff Bezos, basically ran an auction to get tax incentives for Amazon's second headquarters, known as HQ2. More than two hundred fifty local governments flooded Amazon's offices with proposals, all of which involved some form of tax incentives. New Jersey offered Bezos a package worth seven billion dollars in an attempt to attract fifty thousand high-paying jobs and boost economic development in Newark, the state's largest city. But Amazon decided to divide up the new headquarters, settling on New York City (which offered more than two billion dollars), northern Virginia, and Nashville. And I should note that the city's Democratic mayor, Bill de Blasio, was overjoyed with Amazon's decision to locate in New York—and de Blasio considers himself one of the nation's foremost progressives.

All of these incentive packages were designed to woo a company that paid federal income taxes in 2020 for the first time in four years, a lot like Donald Trump. And, in a final irony, a group of local progressive Democrats and grassroots organizations in New York rose up against the city's offer, leading Amazon to walk away from the deal. De Blasio and New York governor Andrew Cuomo were furious with the opposition, and for good reason. Amazon would have brought thousands of good-paying jobs to the Long Island City section of Queens, an old industrial waterfront neighborhood that is being transformed for the economy of the twenty-first century.

I certainly align myself with progressives on tax reform, and I sponsored legislation that would recoup taxes that shield companies in tax havens abroad by requiring combined tax returns. The practice is too detailed to describe here, even if I thought I was able to. But there are seven states, Massachusetts, Michigan, New York, Texas, Vermont, West Virginia, and now New Jersey, that require it. While I was in the Senate my combined tax returns legislation didn't move due to stiff opposition from Governor Christie and the business community. It has moved since and was signed into law by Governor Murphy.

I'm in accord with my progressive friends on federal tax policy. Broad taxes need to be cleaned up so the Donald Trumps of America—and he's hardly the only one—pay their fair share, along with corporations. I'm not referring just to increasing tax rates on high-income earners. I'm referring to loopholes and giveaways that need to be reformed, but don't hold your breath waiting. For example, the main offices of the National Football League were classified as a "trade association" for decades and so had tax-exempt status under federal law. That wasn't a particularly good look for one of the world's richest sports organizations, so it recently gave up its tax exemption. But bear in mind, it did so voluntarily, not because Congress took action. That tells you something.

Regardless of tax policies in Washington, D.C., New Jersey has no choice but to recognize the obvious: the cost of doing business in the Garden State is high, and it has to tailor its economic development policies to compete with other states and foreign countries in order to attract and retain investment and jobs. As chairman of the Senate Economic Growth Committee, I am the proud father of New Jersey's tax incentive programs, which began with targeted legislation that transformed an abandoned and contaminated garbage dump site in Elizabeth into the Jersey Gardens Mall, one of the most successful in the country and one that has generated thousands of jobs and millions of dollars in revenue, benefitting the city of Elizabeth and the state as a whole. It has more visitors from out of state than any other location in New Jersey. Early on in his tenure—and early into my post-Senate life—Murphy went on a tirade about New Jersey's tax incentive policies, asserting incorrectly that they cost the state eleven billion dollars. In fact, they generate billions that would have gone to other states, along with the jobs that went with them.

Underlying Murphy's tirade was his feud with South Jersey political boss George Norcross, who adroitly used tax incentives to bring economic vitality to Camden, the poorest city in America of its size, and in the process benefited his business interests. Norcross is a controversial figure in New Jersey politics in part because his private interests often intersect with public policies he supports. But it's important to bear in mind that his support for tax incentives in Camden was designed not to line his pockets but to help lure investment back to that beleaguered city. There are numerous examples around the state of economic development projects that simply wouldn't have happened without smart, targeted tax incentive programs. For example, without incentives, Revel, the casino development in Atlantic City, would be a half-built, abandoned white elephant, casting a dark and depressing shadow over the city's future. Instead, after a few bumps in the road, hundreds of building trades workers were put to work completing the building and hundreds of permanent employees who would otherwise have been unemployed got jobs. All thanks to tax incentives that did not cost taxpayers a dime. And the site itself, now operating as the Ocean Resort Casino, has been revived thanks in a significant part to our successful effort to legalize sports betting.

Meanwhile, about 120 miles north of Atlantic City, hundreds of workers file into Panasonic North America's headquarters in Newark every day, thanks to the state's tax incentive programs. Those offices, and those jobs, would be in Atlanta, not in a beautiful building on Raymond Boulevard in the city's central ward, if New Jersey hadn't come up with a smart package that provided all parties with a win-win solution. And Panasonic's presence in downtown Newark, not far from the city's Penn Station commuter hub, has helped support countless other jobs in the area and given a needed boost to the city's image. The Panasonic deal has been an enormous plus for Newark, but one that would have gone missing if the state hadn't made it easier for the company to do business in the Garden State by offering tax incentives.

Not far from that location, a five-block collection of old rundown buildings near Halsey Street has been transformed into Teachers Village, a new and vibrant neighborhood consisting of 204 moderately priced apartments. That project also benefited from my tax incentive legislation, and it has not only helped transform the city's image but also led to further improvements and the creation of new businesses, from restaurants to cultural amenities.

It's important to restate the obvious: New Jersey's tax incentive program brings in private dollars that might have gone elsewhere. For example,

Goldman Sachs invested a hundred million in the Teachers Village project. It's fair to say that money would not have come to Newark without the incentives the state offered. Something else to keep in mind: as we were reminded when New Jersey was bidding for Amazon's new headquarters, our competition includes one of the most desirable pieces of geography in the world, New York City. Yes, the city also has high taxes and also is an expensive place to do business. But people want to live and work there because of the convenience, the infrastructure, and the simple appeal of being able to say that you've made it in New York City. It's hard to quantify in terms of policy, but there's no question it's a factor in decision making. The pandemic changed that dynamic, but you can't count out New York City for long. So it's notable when a business chooses to cross the Hudson River and come to New Jersey.

That's what happened in 2018 when Mesorah Publications Inc., the largest Jewish publishing company in the world, moved its operations and one hundred employees with an average yearly wage of fifty thousand dollars plus health benefits from Brooklyn to Rahway, New Jersey. Tax incentive legislation was able to make such an impact on the company's bottom line that it gave up its New York address—no small thing. Mesorah president Gedaliah Zlotowitz said at the time: "We are grateful that, because of the Grow NJ program, we had the opportunity to move our business to Rahway. We are looking forward to having a positive impact on the local economy and to bring manufacturing jobs to New Jersey."

There are many more examples of the benefits flowing from the state's tax incentive program, but unfortunately Governor Murphy didn't acknowledge any of them when he attacked the incentives. A task force he assembled to study the issue also chose to remain mute on the subject, instead focusing exclusively on abuse of the process while ignoring its significant benefits of job creation and retention and increased revenue flowing into the treasury. You'd have thought that the governor would at least have acknowledged that his former employer, Goldman Sachs, received a $167 million tax credit to move offices from New York City to Jersey City—a move that further strengthened the incredible revival of a city that could have been left for dead a generation ago, although much still remains to be done to revive and rehabilitate all sections of the city, not just the Gold Coast.

There are examples of what happens in the real world when tax incentives are allowed to expire because of politics. New Jersey had a robust and effective program of tax incentives for motion picture and television productions in New Jersey. The program was due to expire during the Christie administration, and we in the legislature put together new legislation to keep the industry in the state. It ought to have been a no-brainer, until, that is, opponents emerged on the right and the left.

Conservatives opposed tax credits going to rich Hollywood moguls who support Democrats. Liberals opposed tax credits because they flowed to corporations. Christie wound up vetoing the incentives. The result was predictable: the industry shut down in New Jersey and moved back across the Hudson to New York City. These tax incentives had real-life benefits at the micro level. Companies that benefited from the program employed technicians and set construction workers and offered valuable internships to students from the New Jersey Institute of Technology and Montclair State University.

Generally speaking, tax incentives have come under intense criticism from all sides—some fair, some unfair, some based on a thoughtful analysis of the program, some based on politics. Debating the merits of these programs based on facts and figures is fair enough. But bringing politics into the discussion helps nobody. That's how New York lost the Amazon deal (and fifty thousand jobs).

And in New Jersey, we've seen what happens when politics, rather than economics, drives the debate. South Jersey Chamber of Commerce senior vice president Christina Renna said a couple of years ago that two companies planning to move to Camden decided against it, with one citing the "political climate" that seemed hostile to tax incentive programs. So let me set the record straight—most tax incentives don't cost the state treasury one dime. Quite the opposite: they increase revenue. If a company does not locate in the state or leaves because the costs of doing business are lower elsewhere, we lose 100 percent of its taxes. A tax incentive that brings in or keeps jobs from leaving our state generates 80 percent of those taxes. And 80 percent of X is more than 100 percent of zero. Simple math. The $11 billion of tax incentives that Phil Murphy said has been squandered will instead produce $13.75 billion more for the state treasury than if there were no tax incentives.

As with all government programs, tax incentives should be periodically reviewed to determine their effectiveness. I recognized that when I sponsored the Economic Opportunity Act, which directed the New Jersey Economic Development Agency to retain a premier, nonprofit, nonpartisan entity to review and analyze economic incentive laws. That provision resulted in a series of recommendations from the Bloustein School of Planning and Public Policy at Rutgers University. The Bloustein study suggested that changes should be made in our tax incentives because the economy in both the state and the nation as a whole had improved since the incentives were first implemented.

At the time, the study noted, aggressive measures were necessary for economic growth and job creation and retention. That was then. Things were different when the study was released, or at least they were before the COVID-19 pandemic led to dramatic reversals in 2020, making tax incentives important again for New Jersey's economic development. While tax incentives often are associated with job creation and retention, that's not the only purpose of these programs. Tax incentives can be used to provide affordable housing for New Jersey's low-income residents. They are also needed to attract supermarkets into low-income areas where residents are forced to pay higher prices for less healthy foods than are available in the large supermarkets.

As Governor Murphy himself has stated, New Jersey cannot disarm itself in the battle to attract and keep jobs. I would add that New Jersey cannot abandon the poorest areas of our state, which continue to need robust tax incentives to grow and prosper. South Jersey, particularly the city of Camden, had lagged behind North Jersey in economic development and job creation. That's why I agreed to amendments to the Economic Opportunity Act that enhanced incentives for businesses to locate in the four cities that have the lowest median family incomes—Camden, Trenton, Passaic, and Paterson—and in the South Jersey counties of Atlantic, Burlington, Camden, Cape May, Cumberland, Gloucester, Ocean, and Salem.

So I'd say this to progressives who oppose tax incentives: Yes, I'm progressive, too. But that does not preclude me from supporting tax incentives that are necessary for New Jersey to attract investment and create and retain jobs in a state where the cost of doing business is high and to revitalize our poorest cities. Rather than simply oppose tax incentives on ideological grounds, progressives should help shape these programs to achieve the goals they support.

That's why I pushed for a missing element to our tax incentives: programs to encourage affordable housing, which in turn can create a more balanced redevelopment and a more comprehensive urban development strategy. We need to transform the state's urban centers into vibrant communities, where now the local businesses are shuttered by six o'clock each evening during the week and closed on the weekends. Our cities have to be more than just urban office parks. They need to be a place to call home. Likewise for food deserts where low-income families need supermarkets in order to be able to buy affordable, fresh, and healthy foods. The people who run the state's cities understand this. Trenton mayor Reed Gusciora noted, "Affordable housing tax credits are a great incentive to build quality, affordable housing in cities like Trenton. As we foster economic development in the Capital City, we need to make sure affordable housing is available for all our residents." Plainfield mayor Adrian Mapp paid tribute to the proposal by saying, "We are building 'livability' in Plainfield. Our intent is for all residents to improve their quality of life as they grow in place. The affordable housing tax credits proposed by Senator Raymond Lesniak in 2016 provide the opportunity to incentivize investors to provide quality housing that is affordable for everyone. As an elected leader I view it as not just a duty, but an obligation."

As I mentioned, tax incentives are not the most sexy topic to discuss, but without them New Jersey would be left in the dust by neighboring states when it comes to job creation and business investment. Without tax incentives, we will continue to suffer a dearth of affordable housing for our low- and moderate-income families and continue to have food deserts in low-income neighborhoods. You can take a breath now—I've gotten my nerdiest side out of the way in discussing tax incentives. Yes, the topic isn't sexy. It's just important. And Murphy wound up agreeing with me about the importance of tax incentives, annoying his progressive supporters by signing the biggest tax incentive yet—a fourteen-billion-dollar program I helped design as special counsel to the Senate, appointed by Senate president Sweeney. Businesses are again flowing into, not out of, New Jersey. I applaud Governor Murphy's about-face. It takes a strong person to recognize a need and change positions on an issue. Governor Murphy showed he was not stuck in his ways, the mark of a strong leader.

15 · GUBERNATORIAL CAMPAIGN

Not the Last Hurrah

As I approached my fortieth anniversary in the state legislature, I had some hard thinking to do. I was up for reelection in 2017, and based on my previous resounding reelection, I wasn't particularly concerned. All signs pointed to another relatively easy reelection, although I certainly wasn't going to take it for granted. A lot had changed since 2013, that comeback win. Chris Christie was about to leave office after having squandered all the political capital he gained in the aftermath of Superstorm Sandy. By the time he gave up his presidential campaign in 2016 after poor performances in the early primary states, his approval rating was heading toward the high teens. The New Jersey electorate had soured on Christie because of the drip, drip of scandal from the infamous Bridgegate affair, in which several close aides ordered the closure of lanes leading to the George Washington Bridge. The ensuing traffic nightmare paralyzed Fort Lee, which was the exact outcome Christie's aides wanted. They wanted to punish the town's Democratic mayor for not endorsing Christie's reelection, which Christie won with 60 percent of the vote. Talk about overkill!

Christie also fell out of favor because he spent so much time out of state running for the Republican presidential nomination. Then the floor fell out when an intrepid *Star-Ledger* photographer snapped images of the governor and his family sunning themselves at the empty Island Beach State Park that had been closed during July 4th weekend because of a state government shutdown. New Jersey had had enough of him. He left office with an approval rating of 15 percent, the lowest of any other New Jersey governor upon leaving office. Ironically, term limits—New Jersey governors are limited to two terms—were the best thing to happen to Chris Christie because they allowed him to leave office without confronting his low approval rating by seeking reelection.

On the national front, Donald Trump was in the White House, and that's something I still have trouble believing. His total disregard for the truth, his lack of decency, his attacks on our allies while cozying up to the autocrats of Russia, North Korea, and China and other despots gave me grave concern about the future of America. His embrace of white supremacy, his demeaning and demonizing of minorities, and his anti-LGBTQ policies disgusted me. Last, his desperate attempt to overthrow Joe Biden's victory was nothing less than despicable. It led to a violent insurrection against Congress during which five people died—a police officer who was beaten, a rioter who was shot, another rioter who died of natural causes and two police officers who committed suicide. I thank America for voting him out of office and electing Biden. Trump was against everything I fought for while I was in the state legislature.

I took some time to think about where we were heading as a state and as a nation, and what role might be best for me in the later years of my career. And so I decided to run for governor in 2017. It was no small decision, obviously—you don't run for governor just for the fun of it. But more to the point, running for governor meant that I would give up my seat in the Senate. A legislative career that began with my election in 1977 would come to an end in January 2018. So be it, I decided. This was something I had to do.

I was far from the only person interested in making the race. With Christie term-limited, there was a slew of potential candidates from both parties, but New Jersey is a true blue state, and after eight years of Chris Christie we were not about to elect another Republican governor. Most of the local pundits were more or less ready to hand the office to my colleague Steve Sweeney, the Senate president, who clearly had been preparing for years to make a run for it. The assumption was that New Jerseyans would revert back to choosing a Democrat for governor, and Sweeney was thought to be the strongest Democrat in the field. He would have the South Jersey organization behind him and a record of eight years as the Senate president, which gave him statewide name identification and policy-making creds. Jersey City mayor Steve Fulop had been gearing up for a governor's race seemingly from the moment he took over the state's second largest city in 2013. He was a young man with an impressive backstory, having quit his job at Goldman Sachs after 9/11 to join the Marine Corps. He served a tour in Iraq not long after the U.S. invasion in 2003. He was not as well known as Sweeney but had support in voter-rich

North Jersey and its political leaders who wanted a greater "seat at the table" for the region. Fulop was considered to be a strong candidate for those looking for an alternative to Sweeney. And then there was somebody very few knew. Phil Murphy had been U.S. ambassador to Germany during Barack Obama's first term, and while that job obviously was an impressive and important position, it didn't exactly come with much political clout. Murphy also was a relative newcomer to the state, moving to New Jersey from his native Massachusetts in the late 1990s. Suffice it to say, a lot of people were saying, "Phil who?" when Murphy jumped into the race. But I knew. Murphy had made many contacts with heavy hitters throughout the country as finance chair of the Democratic National Committee. As Phil would often say, "I have a Rolodex second to none." Of course no one uses a Rolodex anymore, but everyone knew what he meant. What Murphy lacked in political experience and Jersey authenticity he more than made up for with money. It was clear from the moment he entered the race he would spend whatever it took, not unlike Jon Corzine back in the day. There were a handful of hopefuls on the Republican side as well, although the clear favorite was Christie's lieutenant governor, Kim Guadagno.

The campaign was setting up to be a fight in both parties, with the national press on hand to take note of what New Jerseyans were thinking in the first full year of the Trump era. While New Jersey is hardly a swing state these days, it has been something of a bellwether given that the governor's race always follows a presidential election. Christie's victory over Corzine in 2009 foreshadowed the Republican takeover of the House in 2010. Tom Kean's win over Jim Florio in 1981, while minuscule, hinted at the coming Republican dominance of the 1980s. And Brendan Byrne's rout of Charles Sandman in 1973, at the height of Watergate, presaged the Democratic landslides of 1974. The campaign was shaping up to be important, exciting, and well-covered. I was certain that I made the right decision to give up the Senate for a chance to lead the state I loved. Upon reflection, I should not have been so certain.

I made more mistakes during my gubernatorial campaign than I made in my entire political career. No wonder I did so poorly. It was as though I learned nothing from my forty years of success in politics. Perhaps the first and fatal mistake was running in the first place. Indeed, an early supporter of Fulop, powerful Bergen County chairman Lou Stellato, kept urging me to run for Senate president instead. But I never was a good hand holder, and that's part of the job description for a Senate president. I've always been the type who upsets apple carts, not a good trait for a job in which you're supposed to arrange the apples on the cart in order to get things done. What's more, I was frustrated in the Senate. Despite my record of significant legislative achievements, I wanted to do more. We in New Jersey have given significant powers to our governors, who don't have to compete with any rival statewide office-holders. My frustration over this imbalance of power would be brought home when I challenged the state Department of Environmental Protection's give-away settlement with ExxonMobil. The Appellate Division held and the State Supreme Court affirmed that no one could challenge the settlement despite its unfairness. A regular citizen or a state senator was out of luck. Very frustrating.

Another mistake was not recognizing the immense power that Murphy's unlimited money brought to the table to capture the coveted Democratic Party "line"—or actually thinking I could overcome the line statewide. You'd have thought I would be aware of what money can do for a campaign, having helped Corzine beat Jim Florio in the 2000 Democratic Senate primary campaign using his immense money to get support. Maybe I was just too accustomed to beating the odds, something I had been doing all my life. I also was thrown off initially by the big reaction I received from emails to the LGBTQ community, animal lovers, environmentalists, Rutgers sports fans and alumni, and others. I crafted a campaign based on coming in second in every county while the other contenders—Murphy, Sweeney, and Fulop—divided up the county Democratic organization lines. I could not compete with Murphy's money and Sweeney's and Fulop's political power for organizational support. In essence, I was letting the others battle each other for first place while I slipped into second everywhere and quietly accumulated the most total votes. But that strategy—and the entire campaign—was thrown for a loop in late September 2016, when Murphy's campaign convinced Fulop to drop out of the race. The Murphy people threatened Fulop with a huge TV buy that would focus on the mayor's Christie-like decision to order a "safety check" designed to tie up trucks for hours outside the Holland Tunnel. The mayor was feuding with the Port Authority, which operates the tunnel, and the city's police chief alleged that Fulop devised the "safety check" as a way of gaining leverage in his battle with the authority. While the plan ultimately was canceled, it didn't show Fulop in a very good light.

There's also an amusing backstory to Fulop's dropping out, as there usually is in New Jersey politics. As he was confronted with what Murphy's campaign threatened to throw at him, Fulop at first refused to back out and endorse

Murphy. But later in the day he called in his close supporter, Jim McGreevey, to tell him what had transpired and that he had reconsidered and would meet with Murphy the following day to tell him he would drop out and endorse him. Wait a minute—McGreevey was supporting Fulop? Didn't I twice save his gubernatorial campaigns and later his future when the most powerful politicians were gunning for him and threatening his livelihood? I did, but Fulop had given McGreevey a six-figure job and maneuvered to get him life-time health benefits through a two-month position with the Hudson County government. Only in New Jersey. McGreevey turned his back on me in the governor's race and chose to support Fulop instead. In politics, personal loyalty often loses out to a "what have you done for me lately" mentality, and that certainly was the case here. I understood why McGreevey was supporting his most recent benefactor, but what hurt were comments he made that diminished my campaign. He told people I wasn't a serious candidate and that I was simply angling for some other position. That hurt. In any event, Fulop met with Murphy the next day to tell him he was dropping out of the race and supporting him. But Fulop was hit with a surprise—Murphy told him that McGreevey had already called him to say that he had spoken with Fulop and convinced him to drop out. Fulop was not happy. It wasn't long before he and McGreevey were trading charges and countercharges in the media. McGreevey's gamesmanship didn't cause the breakup, but it certainly didn't help. McGreevey was intent on scoring points with the likely next governor, and it didn't sit well with Fulop.

Fulop's decision changed the dynamics of the race. With Fulop's endorsement, Murphy now had organizational support in Hudson County and a trophy endorsement in addition to all his money. I called Sweeney, my colleague, caucus leader, and rival for the nomination, a few days after Fulop's announcement to see if he planned to stay in the race. There was a sense that Murphy was gaining momentum, and I wondered if Sweeney might have been having second thoughts. It was one thing for me to sacrifice my seat. It was another thing for Sweeney, who was, after all, Senate president, to sacrifice his. But Sweeney had a quick and decisive answer for me when I asked him if he was in for the long haul. "Absolutely."

"Absolutely" lasted twenty-four hours. I can't say I blamed him for dropping out. He had a lot to lose—the Senate president is the second most powerful position in government. But his departure made all of my plans and strategy instantly irrelevant. I was counting on the other three—Murphy, Fulop, and Sweeney—to split organizational support among them, leaving me as (hopefully) everybody's second choice. I'd be the obvious alternative. But that plan was now officially dead and buried. And I didn't have a Plan B.

I knew things were not shaping up as I had hoped, so I had to come to terms with the thought that maybe this wasn't a very good idea after all. My friend and longtime ally, Elizabeth mayor Chris Bollwage, made it clear he didn't want me to give up my seat (and power) in the Senate. Chris wanted only the best for me, but he also knew that I was good for Elizabeth. He had a convincing argument. So the week after Sweeney's shocking decision, I announced that I too would drop out and resume my reelection campaign for Senate. I wasn't happy about it—I hated the idea of giving up, because that doesn't come naturally to me. But it just seemed to make sense. "I wasn't in this for my personal ambitions," I told the *Star-Ledger*. "I was in this to advance my agenda for the things I've been fighting for my entire career. Rather than take the chance of giving that up, I'm gonna stay in the Senate and I'm gonna fight harder than ever."

That's what I said, and that's what I believed at the moment, but I was not as content as I claimed to be. A couple of evenings later, I had dinner with Bollwage and my friend and law partner Paul Weiner. We spent a lot of time talking over the governor's race and my decision to switch gears and run for Senate again. Bollwage left on the early side, as I concluded not to run for governor, happy as can be and with good reason. He and I were a good team for Elizabeth. We had been in the trenches together and emerged victorious. As a friend and an ally, he wanted me back in the Senate, fighting on the same side for the same goals. With Chris gone, I felt more comfortable telling Weiner how I really felt. "I know the odds are against me but I just feel I need to make this race," I told Paul. "I just can't live with myself if I don't run." Paul looked me in the eye and said, "Then run." That's what I needed to hear. Suddenly it was all clear to me: It didn't matter what others thought or what my chances were. I had to get back into the race. I called Chris and told him the good/bad news. Suffice it to say, he wasn't happy, and I understand why. But I was content.

Getting back in the race was as easy as issuing another press release. Without much in the way of campaign funds, I had only one campaign consultant on my payroll, Sean Caddle of Arkady Consultants. Sean was the architect of my resounding Senate campaign rebound in 2013. No doubt I saw him as a miracle worker, but there really are no miracles in politics. I should have known better. While it was easy to get back into the race, it was clear that dropping out in the first place was yet another mistake. My potential financial supporters turned me down when I solicited them, saying they committed to Murphy after I left the campaign. They saw Murphy as the winner and didn't want to offend him by contributing to me. That's how politics works. It's not that these supporters changed their opinion of me. They just didn't want to be on a losing team. Loyalty goes only so far.

So without two of the frontrunners, Sweeney and Fulop, the Democratic primary narrowed to Murphy with his thirty-five-million-dollar war chest, myself, and two other candidates, Assemblyman John Wisnewski, with his financial and voter base of Bernie Sanders supporters (Wisnewski was Sanders's New Jersey campaign manager for his presidential bid), and a former assistant treasury secretary during the Obama years, Jim Johnson, who had a financial base from his national law firm.

I couldn't raise the two million dollars needed to receive four million in state matching funds. Over and over again I heard people tell me: "I committed to Murphy after you dropped out" or "Ray, you can't win against Murphy's money." I loaned my campaign the half million necessary to qualify for the debates—that's half a million I'll never see again. I did well in the debates, or so I was told. But then I made another mistake. I focused on my long list of achievements rather than, as Bill Clinton advised me, the future. In any event, I had no money to get on TV while my three opponents flooded the airwaves with the state's matching funds or, in Murphy's case, with his own money. If you're not on TV, you're not in the race, even though your name is somewhere on the ballot. I believe if I had had a war chest of six million—the two million needed to qualify for the four million in matching public funds—it would have made the race interesting. But I didn't and finished a distant fourth. Perhaps if Ma Green and my mom were still around I would have fared better.

Murphy won the primary easily, overpowering his opposition with the money he spent lining up support from political leaders, his TV advertising, and his progressive message. One saving grace about the influence of money in a political campaign is no matter how much you spend, if your message doesn't resonate, you won't win. Murphy went on to win the general election over Christie's overmatched lieutenant governor, Kim Guadagno. But just because a Democrat was back in the governor's office didn't mean that the governor's priorities automatically became law. Murphy spent a good portion of his first term fighting with the legislature. Subsequently, after prolonged bickering, Murphy and Sweeney worked together for the good of the people of the state of New Jersey.

I wasn't happy about how it all turned out and certainly was sad to know my political career was over. I cried for a day but got over it quickly and began thinking about my policy-making future. You don't just turn off a spigot running full blast for forty years. I still had a passion for public policy and more than a handful of causes I wanted to push. I wasn't about to live in the past, telling glory-days stories to old friends over a glass or two of wine. I'm too restless for that, and besides, I believed (and still believe) I have something to contribute.

EPILOGUE

After forty years in the state legislature and having had the good fortune of turning my life around after an inauspicious beginning, I found myself without a platform to express my views and, more importantly, to make an impact on public policy. I was determined that my gubernatorial loss would not be a last hurrah.

I had a close relationship with the president of Kean University, Dr. Dawood Farahi, who was at my side in France when I won the Memorial de Caen Human Rights Competition. Dawood suggested I establish a public policy institute at the school that would help inspire students to pursue public service, participate actively in civic society, and learn from those of us who have been in the trenches. Farahi, who transformed the university from a local college in Union Township to a world-class facility with campuses in Ocean County and Wenzhou, China, immediately saw the possibilities for his students. He not only encouraged me to start an institute but wanted it named in my honor. That's how Kean University's Lesniak Institute for American Leadership was founded in 2018. Its stated mission: teach the next generation of leaders how to follow their passions with action and advocate for the issues that shaped my political career—environmental protection, social and criminal justice, and animal welfare.

The institute quickly went to work, under the direction of a recent Kean University graduate, Sarah Mack, advocating for public policy initiatives that were left undone when I lost my platform in the Senate. It held several well-attended forums and rallies—drawing in sizable audiences that watched on social media—on issues like a ban on wild animals performing in circuses (Nosey's Law) and discussions of the most significant criminal justice reform that will change the culture of corrections, Earn Your Way Out, and limitations on the use of solitary confinement. Bills related to these issues that I sponsored while in office but were vetoed by Governor Christie passed both houses and were signed into law by Governor Murphy. The Lesniak Institute has become a place where civic-minded people can come together and have a civil discussion, something that seems to be all too rare these days. It's also a place where students gather (in person before the pandemic, virtually during it) and talk about the issues they are facing in life, matters that are only a distant memory for me. It's been another good wake-up call and immensely satisfying.

Among its many other activities, the Lesniak Institute, its interns, and its volunteers have visited and given toys to hospitalized children and gifts to their parents, in partnership with an organization established in 1963 by Rabbi J. J. Hecht in New York named Toys for Hospitalized Children. The founder's grandson, also Rabbi J. J. Hecht, is now in charge. The group was formed when the elder Rabbi Hecht, while he was visiting a patient, observed nuns giving out toys to only the Catholic children and decided to form an organization to issue toys to all hospitalized children, regardless of their religion. Seeing the smiles of these children when we give them a gift, some of whom are profoundly sick, is one of the most rewarding experiences of my life. The Lesniak Institute also held a contest for students, with scholarships for finalists, to design the Humane State license plate and write essays on the theme that New Jersey is a humane state and hosted a forum to discuss gun control, including a presentation by a SWAT team member. The forum also had a student who was a member of the NRA. It was a lively, civil, student discussion. We also held forums on bigotry and hatred, the problem of dirty trucks on our roadways, and the need for continued criminal justice reform. The Lesniak Institute hosted the aforementioned book signing with Chelsea Clinton and held a forum focusing on the Black Lives Matter movement and its search for racial justice—the institute intends to be at the forefront of public policy discussions in New Jersey. The Lesniak Institute also carried on Operation Santa, which Salena and I had been hosting for nineteen years. It holds a Christmas party for foster children and their families. The children share with us their Christmas wishes, and we solicit donors to fulfill them (within reason of course, no horses or wide-screen TVs). Santa gives them their gifts at a party with food and a DJ that we host at Kean University. Because of the pandemic we couldn't host the party in 2020, so I delivered the gifts with dinner to fifty households, dressed up as Santa of course. I never had more fun or experienced more gratitude for having that joyful experience. Operation Santa was Salena's favorite. She went all-in. I was fondly thinking of her when I delivered the gifts.

So while I'm retired from the state Senate, I'm not retired from continuing to follow my passions. Those who know of me would never believe I had an inferiority complex and low self-esteem, but I did. So you can imagine how I felt when Senator Sandra Cunningham, introducing me at an event in Jersey City, described me as the most prolific legislator in the history of New Jersey. I have to keep achieving because accomplishments serve to give my life value and bring me joy. It is my goal that they also bring joy, hope, and opportunity to others.

The successful Broadway show *If/Then* tracks two paths that a life could take based on what fork in the road the character takes. I've had dozens of forks in my road of life. Sometimes the direction was in my control. Other times the choices were made for me.

What if I didn't tank the entrance exam to Don Bosco High School? I'm not saying I would have become a priest, but who knows whether I would have been the legislator Senator Cunningham described?

What if my mother allowed me to play football instead of practicing the accordion? That's not to say I would have been a football star, but I certainly wouldn't have been able to afford Rutgers or St. John's Law.

What if my dad didn't shoo me away when I tried to help him tear apart his car engine? Perhaps I would have followed most of my classmates' footsteps, gotten a job out of high school, and, as my dad would say, worked for a living rather than being a lawyer and legislator.

What if I took that Wall Street job with a white-shoe law firm and didn't have the opportunity to protect poor folks from cuts in vital health services and to advance women's right to choose all medical procedures over their bodies?

And what if I wasn't fortunate enough to be assigned to Special Services in the Army to play football and baseball instead of going to the jungles of Vietnam?

There have been many more what-ifs in my life that turned out okay, even if I didn't know it at the time. The bottom line is I've been able to enjoy the abundances of life God wants us to enjoy. They often are staring us right in the face without us knowing it.

I am grateful for my twenty years with Salena. I miss her so much. As in every intimate relationship, we had more than a few bumps in the road, but we always came back to embracing our love for each other. Salena was one tough cookie, with strong opinions that I needed to hear and she wasn't hesitant to express. We loved each other so much. In sharing my grief over Salena's death with others who have endured the loss of a loved one, I've been told that it gets better, that the sadness that comes up from a memory of her becomes gratitude for having her in my life for twenty years. They speak from experience. I'm having a difficult time believing it, but who am I to doubt it?

Hopefully this book will be instructive in some fashion and will encourage and help readers make the world a better place for all its inhabitants, including those who don't look or talk like us, or who walk on all fours. And hopefully the final chapter is yet to be written.

ACKNOWLEDGMENTS

This memoir came about as a result of the biggest tragedy in my life, the sudden death of my beloved Salena, who died of a heart attack with no symptoms in 2019 at the young age of forty-three. Salena was my guiding light, calling me out when I was being full of myself. "Oh, my God, I'm thirty seconds into a story and you've already turned it around to being about you," she'd often say, pointing to my narcissistic side. Or, "Don't give me that, 'Jane, you ignorant slut look,'" referring to my Sheldon from *Big Bang Theory* side. But Salena was a very caring person and my biggest cheerleader, an inspiration for my social justice causes, changing me from being a supporter of marriage equality to an advocate for it. Salena was so happy we got married after being together for twenty years. I miss her deeply. I was disappointed when I lost the 2017 race for governor, but as things turned out, I wouldn't want to be governor without Salena at my side. This memoir is dedicated to her.

Grieving Salena's death and being confined at home because of the pandemic left me with long, lonely days with only my sadness to keep me company, unable to share my feelings in person with my friends. But writing this book gave me relief. It has been therapeutic, helping me to be proud of what I achieved in life and to be grateful for being able to enjoy the abundances of life God wants us all to enjoy.

Thanks to President Clinton, who wrote the foreword and who had the thoughtfulness and compassion to call me during Salena's wake. We hadn't seen each other for years. What a wonderful person.

Thanks to President Joe Biden, whose recovery from multiple tragedies in his life gives me hope. Thanks to Shane Derris, a former chief of staff of my Senate office, who inspired me to write this book when he interviewed me about how to succeed in politics. I have often been asked about writing a book about my long history in politics, so I sat down and began to write, not just about my political experiences but also about my life experiences. I have a multitude of friends to thank for helping me get through life and to succeed in politics. Thanks to my friend of more than forty years, Sue Scarola, who suggested I write my memoirs during the COVID-19 shutdown. Several years ago, Sue alerted me to the annual human rights contest sponsored by Le Musee de Caen in Normandy, France, and I'm honored to say I won it.

With great gratitude I thank my parents, John and Stephanie Lesniak. My dad, for his hard work that enabled my mom, my sister Marge, and me to have a nice home and family life and for demonstrating to me how to stand up to discrimination, and to my mom for her hard work raising Marge and me and for urging me to get involved in and helping me to succeed in politics. My mom also urged me to play the accordion, which helped me earn the tuition for my undergraduate and law degrees. Thanks to our neighbors Bridget and Tom Vaughn for befriending my mom and me. Tom was my alternate father when my dad wasn't there for me. I owe great thanks to the great Union County power broker "Ma" Green, who was most responsible for my political success, along with my mom, and to Linden Democratic chairman John Zaleski, who exercised his political influence to help me win my first election to the New Jersey state Assembly, and to Adam Levin and Dave Johnson, who helped me withstand a challenge to my reelection by powerful Elizabeth mayor Tom Dunn. Thanks to Sheriff Ralph Froehlich, who did the unprecedented and broke with the Union County Democratic Committee to support my reelection to the state Assembly, and thanks to my running mates, Linden mayor and senator John Gregorio and Assemblyman Tom Deverin, for their support of this ambitious and aggressive young man. Thanks to Union County Democratic chair Chris Dietz, who helped me get my first job out of law school, for giving me an opportunity to fulfill my desire to advocate for social justice. Thanks to Bruce LaCarubba, director of the State Office of Legal Services, who took a chance and hired me, and to my partner at Legal Services, Phyliss Warren, who fought alongside me for justice for poor folks. Phyliss also introduced me to an album by Biff Rose, *Children of Light*, which formed my outlook on life. I strive to be a Child of the Light every day. Are you a Child of the Light?

Thanks to Governor Jim Florio for naming me New Jersey Democratic Party chairman, which enabled me to be closely involved in Bill Clinton's 1992 presidential campaign. Thanks to Governor Tom Kean for our partnership in advancing the most significant environmental protection laws in the country. Thanks to United Nations Assembly ambassador Al DeCotis for encouraging and helping me get involved in the Clinton presidential campaign. Thanks to Sean Caddle, the campaign consultant, for my election turnaround from near defeat to a huge victory. Thanks to my first political consultant, Hank Sheinkopf, who guided my first election to the New Jersey State Senate and, more important, for introducing me to Rabbi J. J. Hecht, director of Toys for Hospitalized Children, which, in partnership with the Lesniak Institute for American Leadership, does God's work bringing toys to children in hospitals and gifts for their families. Thanks to Elizabeth mayor Chris Bollwage for being my political partner and friend for four decades. Thanks to NJ Advance Media investigative reporter Ted Sherman and two courageous Elizabeth Board of Education employees, Carmen Southward and Sue Mettlen, who helped me topple the corrupt political machine that controlled the Elizabeth Board of Education.

Thanks to Pam Capaci of Hope Sheds Light and Prevention Links for getting me involved in and naming the Raymond J. Lesniak Experience, Strength, Hope Recovery High School. Thanks to Kean University president Dawood Farahi, who recommended that I form the Lesniak Institute for American Leadership at Kean when I left the New Jersey Senate, and to Sarah Mack for her great work as the institute's executive director. Thanks to Garden State Equality founder and New Jersey's foremost LGBTQ advocate Steven Goldstein and marriage equality sponsor Senator Loretta Weinberg for taking me on the journey toward civil rights for our LGBTQ brothers and sisters. Thanks to Louise Walpin and Marsha Shapiro for giving Salena and me the honor of hosting New Jersey's first same-sex marriage, and thanks to Assemblyman Jamel Holley for officiating the marriage and to Goldstein for saying a marriage prayer. Goldstein gets another thanks—that's three!—for joining me in forming the Coalition Against Hate and Bigotry, which drove the Jersey Boys, Craig Carton and Ray Rossi, off the air on 101.5 FM. Thanks to Celeste Fitzgerald for tabbing me to lead the fight to abolish New Jersey's death penalty and to Governor Jon Corzine, Assembly speaker Joe Roberts, Senator Shirley Turner for their support of that effort. I had many colleagues, Democrats and Republicans, who helped advance my legislative initiatives. I thank them all, with an added thanks to Senator Sandra Cunningham for her kind introduction of me at an event she hosted in Jersey City.

Thanks to my chief of staff, Hiver Ambroise, Elizabeth Board of Education member Stanley Neron, Congressman Donald Payne, and Dave Gibbons of Elberon Development Group for making our Haiti earthquake relief effort, NJ4Haiti, a success. Thanks to Monmouth Racetrack president Dennis Drazin, internet gambling guru Joe Brennan, Seton Hall Law School dean emeritus Ron Riccio, Senate president Steve Sweeney, Lieutenant Governor Sheila Oliver, and Assemblymen John Burzichelli and Ralph Caputo for their support of my successful challenge to overturn the federal ban on sports betting. Thanks to former Morris County prosecutor Mike Murphy for the tidbit about Richard Nixon and his stepdad, Governor Richard Hughes.

Thanks to Ashley Prout McAvey, Vermont for Wildlife, for her jacket quote. Jen Samuel, Elephants DC, and Adrienne Possenti, Robin Chandler

Vitulle and Michelle Weirich of Free All Captive Elephants for helping me save elephants and rhinos from extinction, to Brian Hackett, New Jersey state director of the Humane Society of the United States, Kathleen Schatzmann, Animal Legal Defense Fund, Bill and Kizmin Nimmo of Tigers in America, and the numerous advocates and organizations in New Jersey who give a voice to voiceless animals who are our domestic pets or who exist in the wild as God wanted them to exist.

Thanks to my group therapy friends and my therapists, who must remain anonymous, who helped me get through life. Thanks to my daily Zoom partners who filled up my life during the COVID-19 shutdown, Saul Leighton, Sue Scarola, Tanis Deitch, Richard Faherty, Marilynn Lomazow, Suzanne Devanney, Ed and Pam Palmieri, Elizabeth Legiec, Steve Lomazow, Suze Bienaimee, Joe Ascione and Dave Snyder. Thanks also to Richard for his helpful comments about my writing and to Marilynn Lomazow for formatting the book's pictures. Thanks to my law firm partner Paul Weiner for allowing me to focus on public policy and politics while he managed the law firm.

Thanks to my rescued pitties, Penny and Sammy, for their company and comfort, and also to my rescued spaniel, Brittany, for being my best friend for nineteen years until her passing. I believe when choosing a dog or cat to be your companion, you should "Adopt Not Shop."

And many thanks to my editor at Rutgers University Press, Peter Mickulas, who did wonders with this manuscript, and to copy editors Joseph Dahm and Michelle Witkowski. Thanks also to the marketing, sales, and publicity departments at Rutgers University Press for their diligence and ingenuity.

Many others helped me through life or to write this memoir. I apologize for not acknowledging them. I thank you all with great gratitude.

INDEX

Note: page numbers in italics refer to figures.